Key Geography Found

David Waugh
Former Head of Geography
Trinity School
Carlisle

Tony Bushell
Head of Geography
West Gate Community College
Newcastle upon Tyne

Stanley Thornes (Publishers) Ltd

The previous page shows St Paul's Cathedral and the City of London.

First edition published in 1991 and reprinted sixteen times
Second edition published in 1996 by:
Stanley Thornes (Publishers) Ltd
Ellenborough House
Wellington Street
CHELTENHAM GL50 1YW

96 97 98 99 00 / 10 9 8 7 6 5 4 3 2

British Library Cataloguing in Publication data

Waugh, David
Key geography foundations: Pupils' book
– (Key geography)
I. Title   II. Bushell, Tony   III. Series
910

First edition   ISBN 0-7487-1100-7
Second edition   ISBN 0-7487-2584-9

Printed and bound in China

Acknowledgements

Second edition designed and reset by Hilary Norman
Illustrations by Tim Smith, Kathy Baxendale, Nick Hawken, John Yorke
Cartoons by Mike Gordon
Edited by Katherine James
Photo research by Julia Hanson

The authors and publishers are grateful to the following for permission to reproduce photographs and other material in this book:

Aerofilms Ltd (pp. 11, 34 bottom, 45 top, 47 top, 76 bottom left, 78 all, 83 middle, 96 bottom right); ASDA (p. 58 bottom right); Australian Overseas Information Service (p. 65 left); S D Burt (p. 16 right); Celtic Picture Agency (p. 79 top); Channel Tunnel Group Ltd. (pp.74, 75); David Davis/Collections (p. 61); Gena Davis/Collections (p. 83 top); Dundee University Satellite Receiving Station (pp. 24, 26); Chris Fairclough Colour Library (pp.52 left, 58 bottom left, 77 top right); Ffotograff/Patricia Aithie (pp. 47, 81 top, 83); Forestry Commission (p. 96 top left); Sally and Richard Greenhill (pp. 70, 76 top right); Jason Hawkes/Julian Cotton Photo Library (p. 54 bottom); Hutchinson Library (pp. 30, 41 left and right, 45 bottom, 53 left); Katherine James (pp. 114, 115); Janomot Newsweekly (p. 32); Mary Jefferies (p. 16 left); Andrew Lambert (pp. 96 centre top and bottom); Landscape Only (p. 10); Adrian Meredith Photography (p. 68 middle); National Express (p. 68 right); Network/Charles Sturrock (p. 58 top left); Panos Pictures (pp. 28, 32 top and bottom); Science Photo Library/NASA (p. 42 bottom); Spectrum Colour Library (p. 1); Liz Staves/Collections (p. 25); Tower Hamlets Local History Library (p. 54, left and right); Tropix (p. 58 top right); Wales Tourist Board (p. 77 bottom right); Dr A C Waltham (pp. 47 right, 79 bottom, 105 top left); Simon Warner (pp. 44 top and bottom, 53 right, 34 top, 77 left, 96 top right, 107); Ken Woodley (p. 16 centre right).

All other photographs supplied by the authors.

Blockbusters name and grid reproduced by kind permission of Central Independent Television plc in association with Mark Goodson Productions and Talbot Television Ltd (pp. 5, 90, 91). The map extracts on pp. 97, 106 and 109 are reproduced from the 1994 Ordnance Survey 1:50 000 map of Cambridge (Landranger 154) with the permission of the Controller of Her Majesty's Stationery Office © Crown Copyright.

Every effort has been made to contact copyright holders and we apologise if any have been overlooked.

Contents

What is physical geography?

This is the study of the natural features of the earth. Some of these are shown in diagram **A**.

A

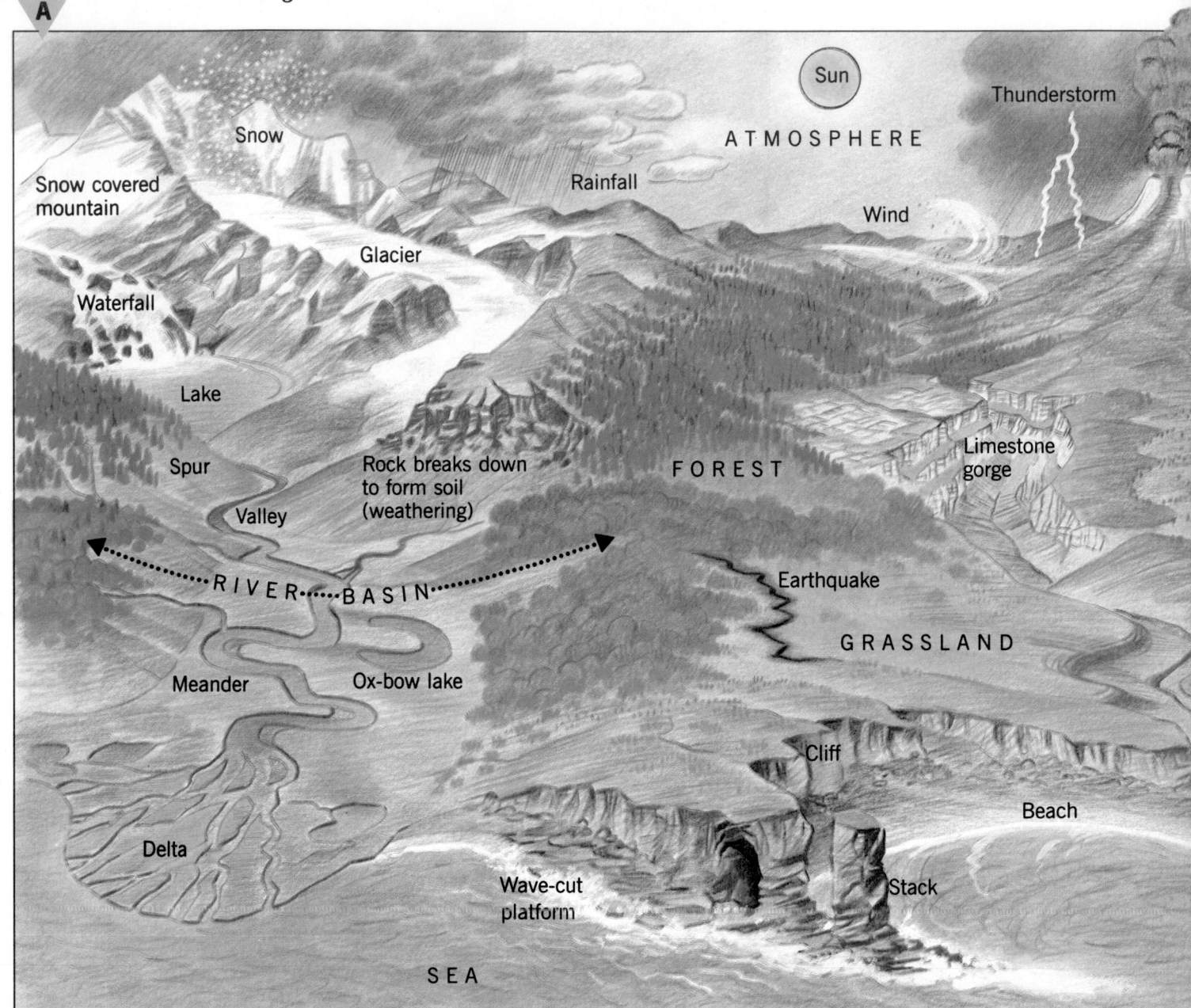

The **atmosphere** is the air around the earth. Changes in its **temperature**, moisture (**rainfall**) and pressure give us **climate**. Climate changes between seasons and from year to year. Different parts of the world have different climates.

Rain mostly collects in **rivers**. The area drained by a river is its **river basin**.

Rivers carry water and other materials to the **sea**. The materials carried (**transported**) by a river can produce **landforms**. This happens when a river wears away land (**erosion**) in one part of its basin and later drops the carried material (**deposition**) elsewhere.

Landforms can also be formed by **volcanoes**, the **sea** and by ice.

The atmosphere and the earth's surface do not stay the same. Usually any change is very slow. When sudden physical changes happen they may create severe **hazards** such as **storms, floods, drought, volcanic eruptions** and **earthquakes**.

The earth's surface is made up of many different kinds of **rock**. Where these rocks break up into smaller pieces (**weathering**) they form **soil**. Each kind of rock will give its own type of soil.

Living plants (**vegetation**) cover most of the earth's land surface. The climate and the soils of an area allow certain types of plant to grow there. Different types of vegetation (**forest, grassland** and **desert**) provide homes (**habitat**) for animals and birds.

Activity

Make the *Blockbusters Gold Run* by solving the following clues to get a linking route across the puzzle. The letters in each shape are the start of words written in **bold** on these two pages.

Start at the left hand side and make your way across the puzzle. When you solve a clue, write down the answer and, if you have a copy of the puzzle, shade in the shape.

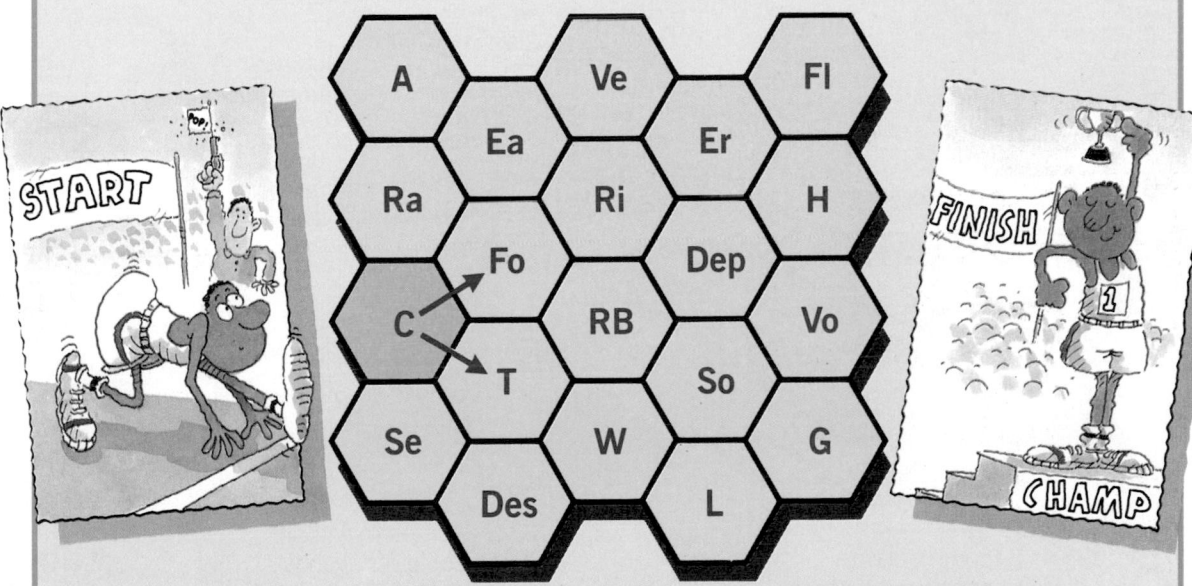

A the air around us
C temperature, moisture and pressure gives us this
Se rivers flow into this
Fo an area covered with trees
Des an area with very few plants
Ri rain collects in these
W how rocks break into smaller pieces
Dep when material is dropped by rivers
L formed by rivers, volcanoes, ice and the sea

H a place where animals and birds live
G a type of vegetation between forest and desert
Fl a physical hazard
Ra the moisture in the air
Ea a physical hazard
T the sun causes this to rise
Ve live plants
RB an area drained by a river
Er the wearing away of the land
So small pieces of rock
Vo a landform and a hazard

What is human geography?

This is the study of where and how people live.

TV mast
Communications

Aeroplane
Communications

Mining and quarrying
Economic activity

Large city
Settlement

Motorway
Communications

Farming
Economic activity

SHOP N SAVE

Shopping centre
Economic activity

Vehicles moving people and goods
Trade

Population geography looks at the spread (distribution) of people over the earth's surface. It tries to explain why some parts of the world have many people living there while other parts have very few. It studies areas where the numbers of people living there are growing rapidly, and looks at the problems that come from this growth. It suggests reasons why people move from one area or country to another (**migration**).

It looks at how such movements lead to people having different customs, religious beliefs and ways of living.

Settlement geography is about where people live. It looks at why settlements grow up in a particular place, and why some remain small in size (villages) while others may grow into very large **urban** centres (cities). It describes problems that go with living in very small places as well as those of very large ones. It looks at how land is used in cities and how this use can change over time.

Communications describes the methods of transport by which people may move about – to work, to school, to the shops and for recreation and holidays. It also includes the movement of goods (**trade**) and information, such as conversations on the telephone and programmes on the television.

Economic geography (economic activity) looks at how people try to earn a living. It is about industry, about jobs and about wealth. It is usually divided into three types. These include farming (a **primary** activity); making things in a factory (a **secondary** activity); or looking after people (a **tertiary** activity or service). It looks at why some activities are only found in certain places and why some parts of the world are richer and more developed than others.

People are very concerned with their **quality of life**. This might be how happy or content they are; the amount of money they have; or how much they like living and working in a particular area. The quality of life may differ greatly both within a country and between countries.

Industry
Economic activity

Small village
Settlement

Activity

On a copy of the *Kriss Kross Puzzle*, solve the puzzle by fitting 11 words and phrases into their correct position in the diagram. The 11 words and phrases are those written in **bold** on these two pages. One has been done to help you get started.

QUALITYOFLIFE

MIGRATION

What is environmental geography?

The **environment** is the combination of the **physical** (natural) environment of climate, landforms, soils and vegetation, and the **human** environment which includes settlements and economic activities. It is the study of the surroundings in which people, plants and animals live.

A

Clean river

Port

Fishing

Sheltered bay protects ships from storms

Areas of scenic value attract tourists

Headlands for walks

Holiday resort with large hotels and amenities

Pier

The environment includes natural **resources** such as coal and iron ore, soils, forests and water. These are used to meet human needs. Some of these resources are **renewable**. This means that they can be used over and over again, such as rainfall. Others are **non-renewable** and can only be used once, such as coal. Sometimes people use these resources to their advantage. For example they use water for drinking purposes, iron ore in industry, and landforms such as islands or lakes for leisure. People often misuse these resources by using them up (minerals), by destroying them (soils, forests) or polluting them (rivers, seas and the air).

Different environments have different qualities and different uses. Each needs to be **protected** and carefully **managed**, like National Parks and the reserves of oil. Many environments have been damaged in the past. Those which have, such as mining areas, rivers and the older parts of some cities, need to be improved.

There is now a growing concern over the **quality of the environment** and how it may be **conserved** while at the same time being made as useful as possible.

B

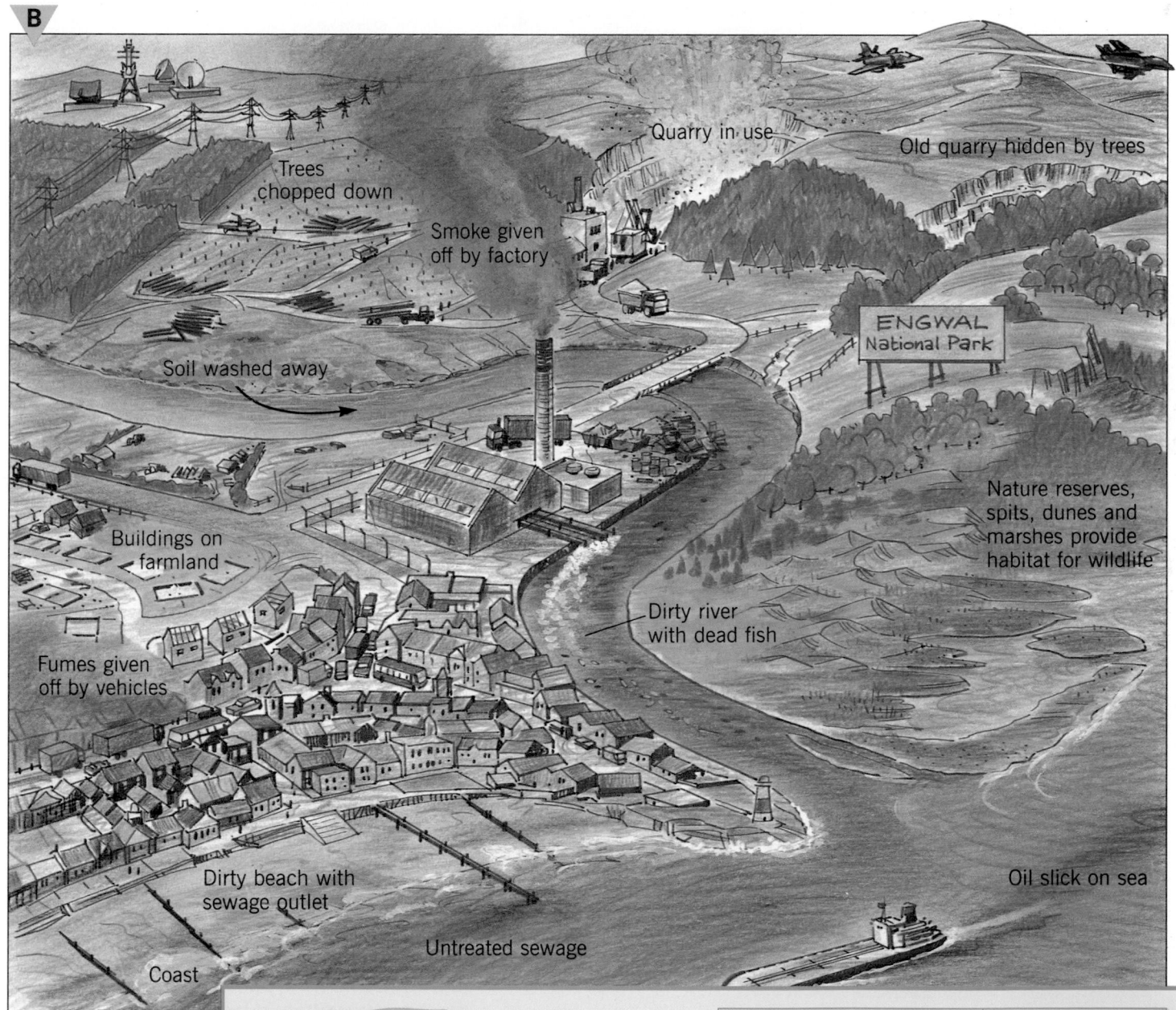

Quarry in use

Old quarry hidden by trees

Trees chopped down

Smoke given off by factory

ENGWAL National Park

Soil washed away

Nature reserves, spits, dunes and marshes provide habitat for wildlife

Buildings on farmland

Dirty river with dead fish

Fumes given off by vehicles

Dirty beach with sewage outlet

Oil slick on sea

Untreated sewage

Coast

Activities

Physical (natural) environment	Human environment
River	Town

1 a) Make a copy of the table on the right.
   b) List the features shown in the drawing **A** in the two columns. Two of these features have already been named for you.

2 In what ways has the area shown in drawing **B** been
   a) polluted or destroyed
   b) protected?

9

How do we study geography?

Geographers need to know about **places**. They should be able to describe where a place is found (located), why it is there (site) and what it might be like to live or work there. Places can include physical features like rivers, mountains and deserts. Places can also be made by humans, e.g. houses, cities, and roads.

Places can vary in **size**. Just as the classroom is a place in a school, so is the school a place in a town, the town a place in a country, and the country a place in the world.

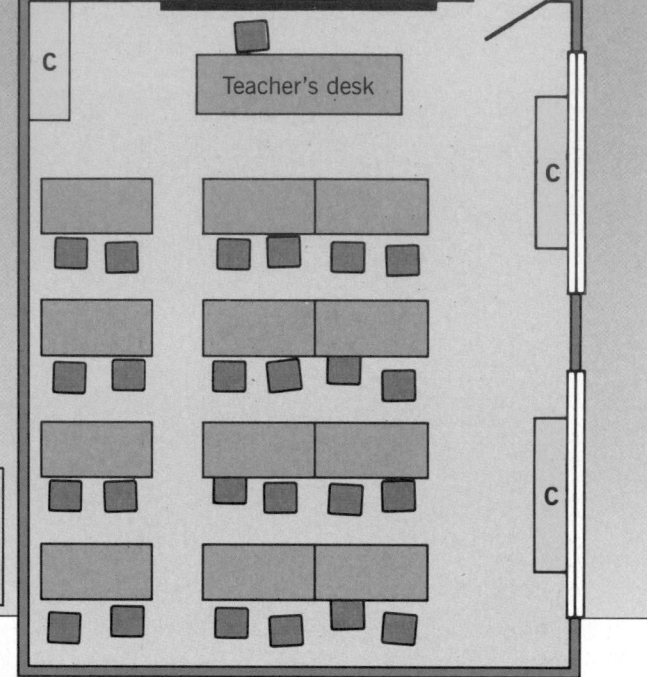

A

Diagram **A** is a plan of a classroom. A classroom is a **place** in a school. If the classroom is neat and tidy (like your bedroom at home!) everything will have its own place. The teacher will have a desk, atlases will be kept on a shelf or in a cupboard, and chalk in a box.

Teacher's desk

Key
Chair •—▸ Door ▬▬▬ Chalkboard
Desk ▭ Window C Cupboard

B

In the distance are some low **hills** which are partly covered in **trees**. There is a **village** in the centre of the photo, with a **church** and several **buildings**. The church has a **tower**. A small **road** passes through the village. In front of the village is a **river** which is crossed by a **bridge**. The land around the village consists of **fields** in which **grass** appears to be growing. The fields are separated by **stone walls** and a few **deciduous trees**. The photo was taken on a **sunny** day in **summer** in the **country**.

How do we describe what a place looks like?

Although no two places in the world are exactly the same, they may have similarities. We have to learn how to describe one place so that we can compare it with a second place. We can show how they are similar to or different from each other.

The best way is to use a photo, possibly from a book or a magazine. When writing a description it is important to pick out **key words**. Key words are the important ones to learn and to remember. In the description below photo **B**, the key words have been written in **bold** type so that they are easier to pick out.

We can also describe a place by drawing a labelled (annotated) fieldsketch. Sketch **C** on page 11 is drawn from photo **B**. The labels on the fieldsketch are very similar to the key words in the written description.

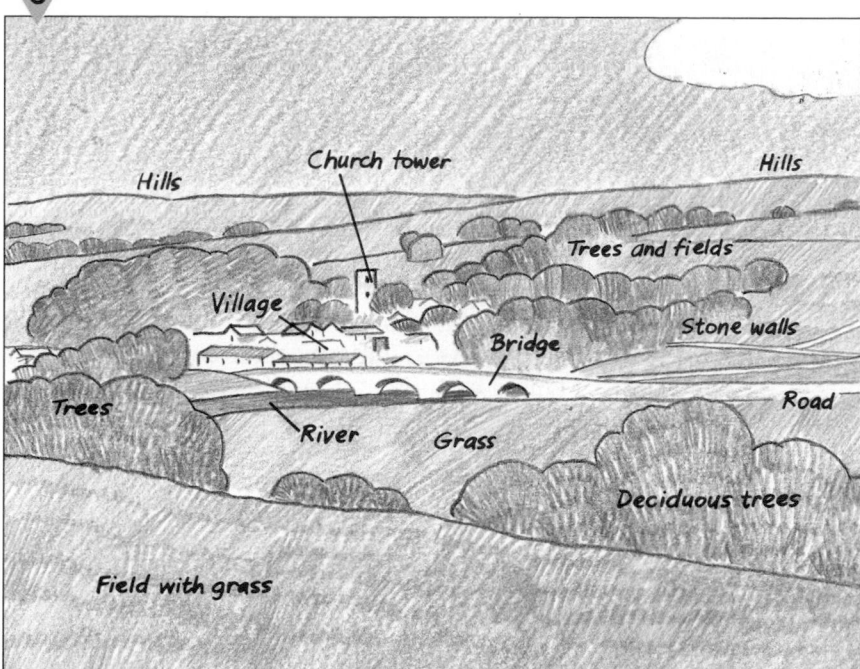

C

D

Activities

1 Photo **D** was taken in central London. The key words have been missed out of this description and are listed at the end.

Copy out the description in **E**, putting the key words in the correct places.

2 a) Make a copy of the tables below.
b) Complete the table for photo **B** by adding the key words from fieldsketch **C**.
c) Complete the table for photo **D** by using the key words listed in question 1.

E

In the distance is a _____ with a _____ and several _____ . Next to the river there is a _____ . In the centre of the photo there are several _____ _____ which appear to be _____ . There are _____ full of _____ . The photo was taken on a _____ day in a big _____ .

bridge   castle   city   offices

roads   ships   sunny   river

tall buildings   traffic

Photo B	
Physical features	*Human features*

Photo D	
Physical features	*Human features*

3 a) Which photo has more physical features than human features? Why?
b) Which photo has more human features than physical features? Why?

4 Which of the two places shown in photos **B** and **D** would you rather visit or live in? Try to give reasons for your answers.

E X T R A

Using photo **D** of London, find out the name of the river, the bridge, the castle and the tallest building.

Summary
Geographers study places where people live and those they avoid. Places can be described from photos or by drawing a labelled sketch and underlining key words.

How do we find out where places are?

People often need to know where places are. They need to know this if, for example, they are going shopping or on holiday. Many people, like lorry drivers and ambulance drivers, need to know where places are to do their job. With television we are always hearing about different places on the 'News' and in other programmes. Geographers use maps to find (locate) places. Although the most accurate map is the **globe**, the easiest for us to use is an **atlas**.

A globe shows the actual shape of the earth. To help us to find places, imaginary lines called latitude and longitude are drawn onto the globe. Look at diagram **A**.

A

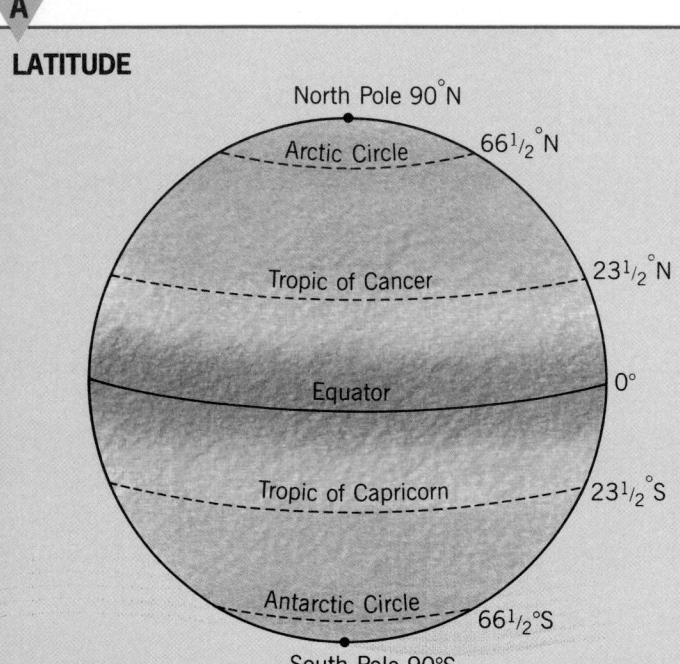

LATITUDE

North Pole 90°N
Arctic Circle — 66½°N
Tropic of Cancer — 23½°N
Equator — 0°
Tropic of Capricorn — 23½°S
Antarctic Circle — 66½°S
South Pole 90°S

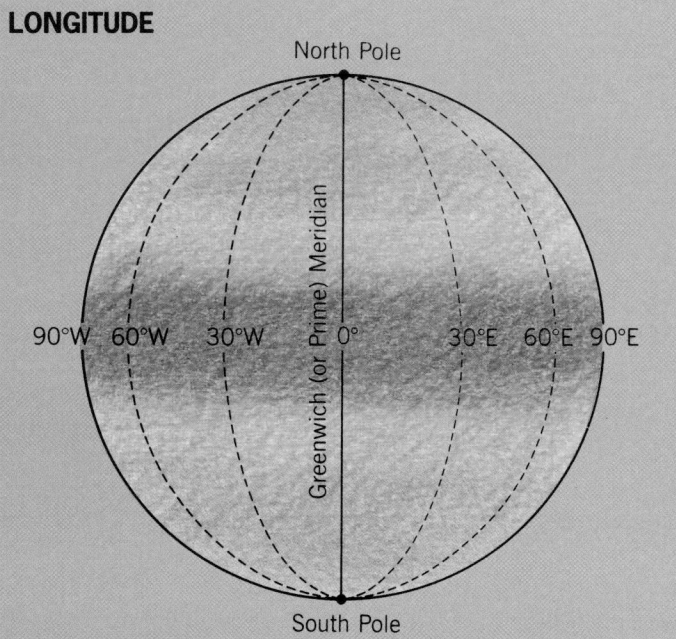

LONGITUDE

North Pole
Greenwich (or Prime) Meridian
90°W 60°W 30°W 0° 30°E 60°E 90°E
South Pole

The Equator, which goes around the centre of the earth, is the main line of latitude. Other lines of latitude are drawn at equal distances (parallel) to the Equator. Lines of latitude therefore go from side to side (horizontally) across the globe. They tell you how far north or south a place is from the Equator. They are measured in degrees. Degrees are given the symbol °. The latitude of the Tropic of Cancer is written as 23½° N.

Lines of longitude are drawn from the North to the South Pole. The most important line or prime meridian is also called the Greenwich Meridian. This is because it passes through Greenwich in London. Lines of longitude tell you how far east or west a place is from Greenwich. If you travel east until you reach 180°E, and a friend travels west until he or she reaches 180°W, you will both end up in the same place. Longitude 180°E is the same as longitude 180°W. This is known as the **International Date Line**.

Activity

In an atlas the ball-shaped globe has to be shown on a flat surface. Is this possible? Try this yourself by peeling an orange in one piece and trying to lay the peel flat onto a piece of paper. What happens to the peel when you do this? How many different shapes can you make with it?

It is impossible to draw the earth accurately onto a piece of paper. Parts of it will always either have the wrong shape or be the wrong size. Two ways of drawing the globe as a flat map (projecting it) are shown in diagrams **B** and **C**.

1 In diagram **B** the continents are the correct **shape**. However, those countries near to the poles have been stretched and so their size appears larger.

2 In diagram **C** the **size** of the countries has been projected correctly. This time their shape has changed (become distorted).

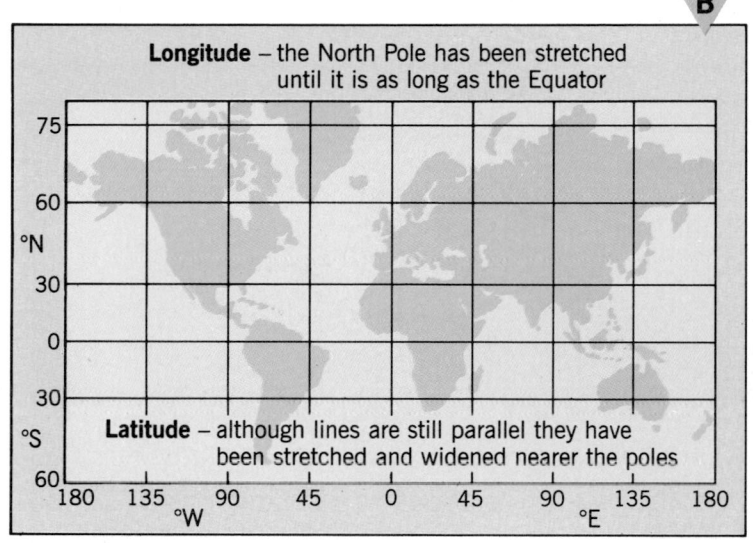

B Longitude – the North Pole has been stretched until it is as long as the Equator

Latitude – although lines are still parallel they have been stretched and widened nearer the poles

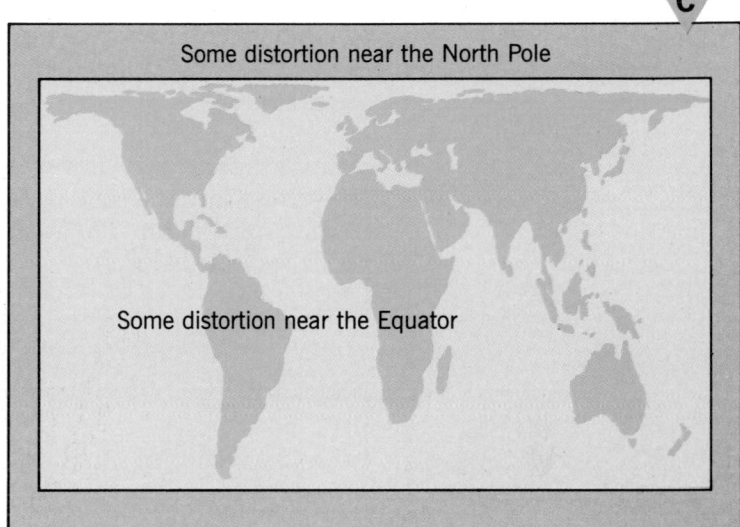

C Some distortion near the North Pole

Some distortion near the Equator

Using an atlas

The contents page at the beginning of an atlas tells you on which page each map can be found. But, as each map will have many places on it, an individual place may still be hard to find. This is made easier by using the index which is at the back of the atlas.

An index lists places in alphabetical order. If two places have the same name they are listed alphabetically according to the country in which they are found (located). Diagram **D** shows part of an index from an atlas.

D

Place	Country	Page	Latitude	Longitude
Lagos	Nigeria	34	6°N	3°E
Leningrad	USSR	28	60°N	30°E
Lima	Peru	48	12°S	77°W
Liverpool	UK	18	53°N	3°W
London	Canada	44	43°N	81°W
London	UK	18	52°N	0°
Los Angeles	USA	46	34°N	118°W

Lagos, for example, is found 6 degrees north of the Equator and 3 degrees east of the Greenwich Meridian.

Activity

- Use the contents page and the rest of an atlas to find an example of each of the following types of map:

  relief   population   types of pollution

  climate   conservation   soils   land use

  vegetation   political (countries)   transport

  water supply   geology (rocks)   hazards

- Which of these maps show physical geography?
- Which show human geography?
- Which show environmental geography?

Write your answers as a table.

✔ Remember

If you draw a map, it must have:

✔ a title
✔ a north point (compass direction)
✔ a scale
✔ a key.

Summary

People need to know where places are for shopping, work and holidays. Places are shown on maps which are to be found on a globe or in an atlas. To find a place in an atlas you may have to use the index. The index tells you the page, country, latitude and longitude of a place.

Why do we use graphs in geography?

We often use a lot of **data** (information) in geography. Data are facts and figures. We can find data either by collecting information from fieldwork (**primary** data) or by looking it up in books (**secondary** data). Data can be recorded and shown quickly and clearly by drawing either tables or **graphs**. In Maths you will probably have learnt how to draw several types of graph.

Activity

Diagram **A** shows four types of graph which you may have already used in school. Match each graph with the terms on the labels in the next column:

scattergraph

pie chart

line graph

bar graph

A

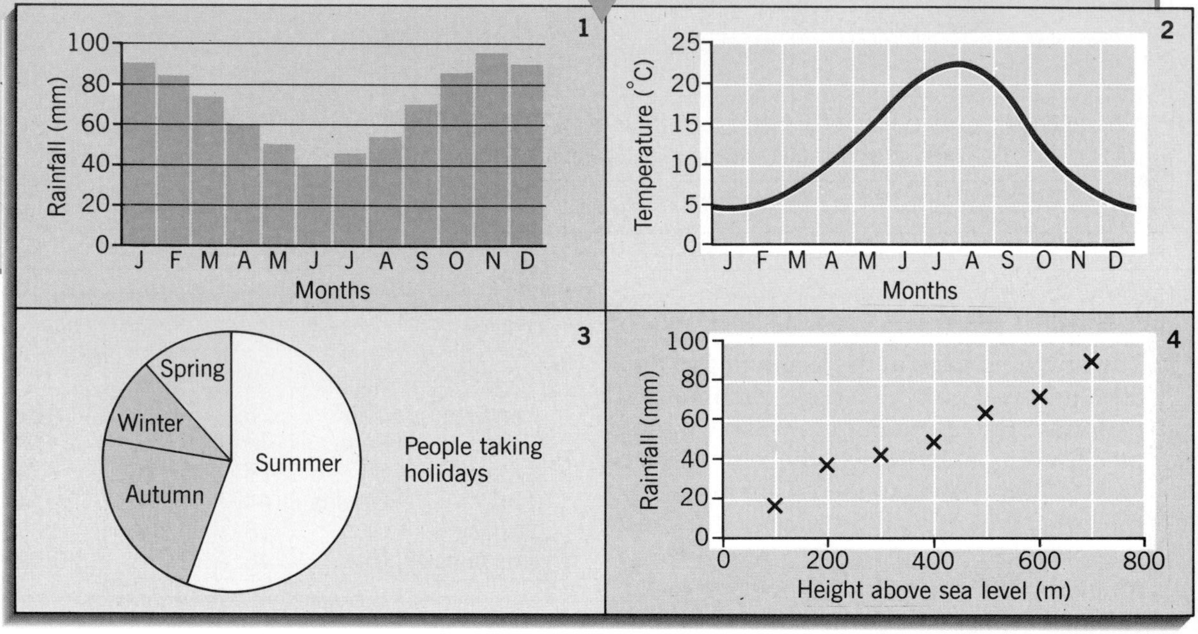

1
100
80
60
40
20
0
Rainfall (mm)
J F M A M J J A S O N D
Months
2
25
20
15
10
5
0
Temperature (°C)
J F M A M J J A S O N D
Months
3
Spring
Winter
Summer
Autumn
People taking holidays
4
100
80
60
40
20
0
Rainfall (mm)
0 200 400 600 800
Height above sea level (m)

What do graphs show?

In geography we are interested in the **shape** of the graph. We try to describe (**interpret**) and give **reasons** for its shape.

Some graphs can help us to **predict** what might happen in the future.

B

Trends show general direction

This graph shows a steady, steep rise (increase). As students get older they grow taller.

1.7
1.6
1.5
1.4
1.3
1.2
1.1
Height of students (m)
6 8 10 12 14
Age of students (years)

This graph shows a steady, slow fall (decrease). There are fewer people aged 70 than there are aged 40.

24
18
12
6
0
People in UK (millions)
40 50 60 70
Age of people (years)

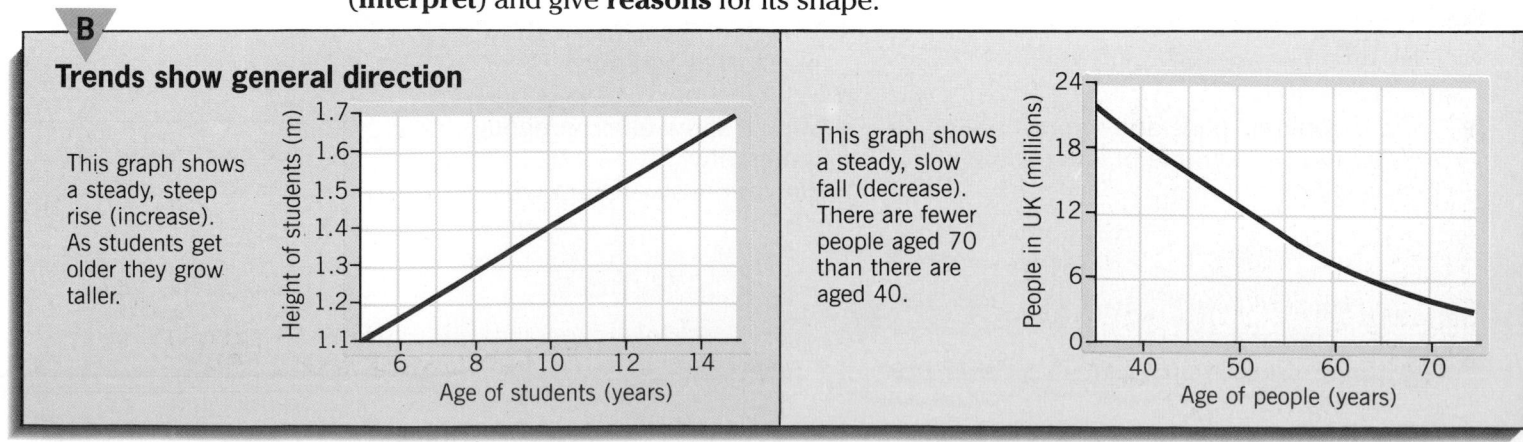

C Changes over a period of time

This graph shows that the population of the world grew very slowly between 1700 and 1900, but then increased rapidly between 1900 and 2000.

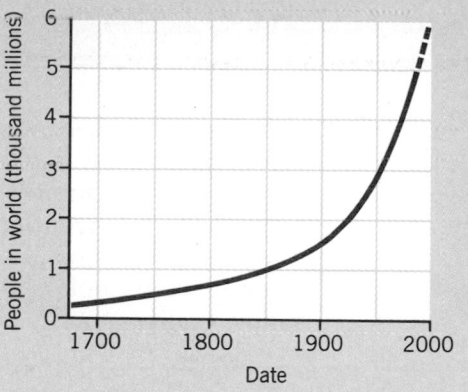

This graph shows that most cars are on the road between 0800 and 1000 hours, and between 1600 and 1800 hours. The high points on the graph are called **peaks**. There are fewer cars in the middle of the day and at night. The low points are called **troughs**.

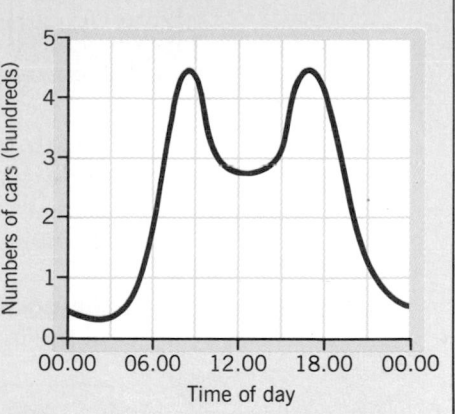

D Comparisons

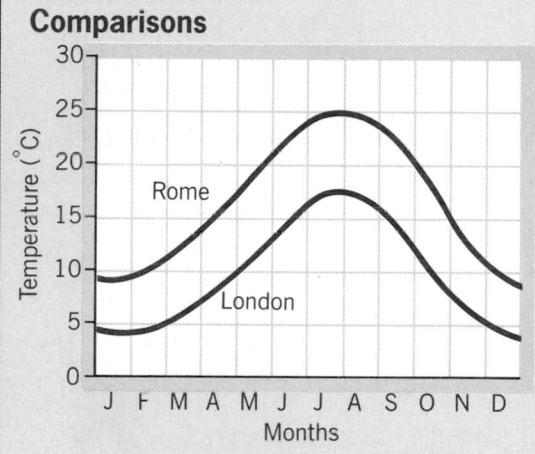

This graph compares the temperatures of London and Rome. It shows that Rome has a warmer winter and a hotter summer than London.

E Relationships

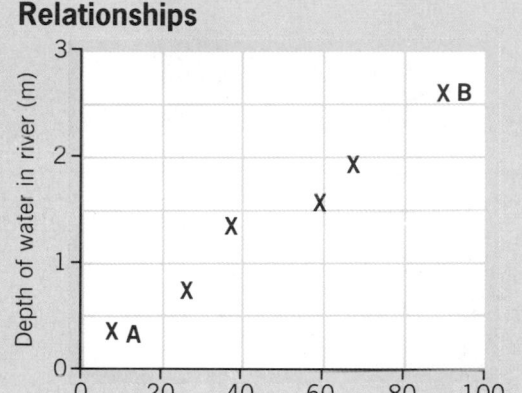

Point **A** on this graph shows that if there is only a little rainfall, then the amount of water in the river is small. However, if there has been a lot of rain (point **B**) then the amount of water in the river will also have increased. This shows that there is a relationship or link between rainfall and the amount of water in a river.

✔ Remember

When you draw a graph, it should have:

- ✔ a title to say what it is showing
- ✔ labels along the bottom and up the side to explain what it is showing
- ✔ figures that are plotted very accurately.

Summary

Graphs are a method of presenting and interpreting geographical data. Four types of graph are the bar graph, line graph, pie chart and scattergraph.

How might you observe and record the weather?

Weather can be described as the condition of the air around us over a short period of time. It is about being hot or cold, wet or dry, windy or calm, cloudy or sunny.

Meteorology is a study of the weather. One of the important tasks of meteorologists is to measure and record all the features of the weather every day. Many expensive and complicated instruments are needed to record weather accurately but you can get a good picture of what conditions are like by **observing** (looking around) and using simple equipment.

A

Temperature
This is a measure of how hot or cold it is. You can do this by looking at the clothes that people are wearing. Thermometers are used to measure temperature accurately.

| Very cold | Cold | Mild | Warm | Hot |

B

Precipitation
Water in the air falls to the ground in one of several forms. Four of these are rain, snow, sleet and hail.

0°C / 0°C — Below 0°C / Above 0°C

C

Wind speed
This tells us how strong the wind is. We can get a good idea of this by looking at smoke and the trees. The Beaufort scale is used to measure wind strength.

0 Calm	2 Light breeze	4 Moderate breeze	6 Strong breeze	8 Fresh gale
Smoke rises vertically	Wind felt on face; leaves rustle	Dust and paper lifted; small branches move	Large branches in motion	Twigs break off trees

D

Cloud type
Cloud comes in many shapes, sizes and heights. Cumulonimbus, cumulus, stratus and cirrus are the most common types.

 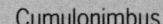    

| Cumulonimbus | Cumulus | Stratus | Cirrus |

E

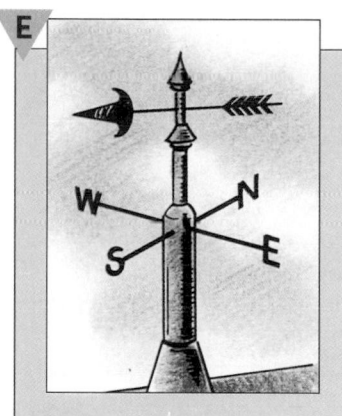

Wind direction
This is the direction **from** which the wind blows. It is measured by a wind vane.

F

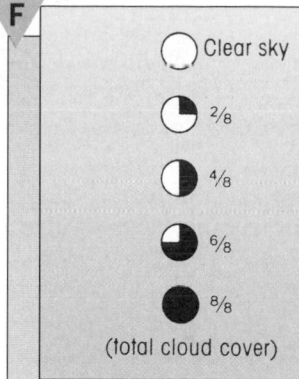

○ Clear sky

◔ 2/8

◑ 4/8

◕ 6/8

● 8/8

(total cloud cover)

Cloud cover
This is the amount of the sky covered by cloud. It is measured in eighths.

G

Visibility
This is the distance that can be seen. It is measured in metres.

H

General weather
This describes the weather in words. Words like rain, snow, showers, fog, mist, thunder, cloudy, fair or sunny are used. Light or heavy can be added to precipitation.

Activities

1 What is weather?

2 **a)** Make a copy of the star diagram **I** on the right.
b) Write the name of the weather feature next to each sketch.

3 Describe how each of the following is measured:

temperature   *wind strength*   *wind direction*   *cloud cover*

I

Weather features to be observed and recorded

4 Make sketches of the four cloud types in **D**. Under each sketch write a cloud description from the following list.
● Low grey shapeless cloud that forms in layers.
● High clouds that are wispy, light and featherlike.
● Dome shaped clouds with dark flat bases.
● Huge, towering clouds that often give showers.

5 Look at the table **J** below which shows what the weather was like on a summer day in Wales.
a) Copy out the table headings.
b) Make your own recording of today's weather. Use the information on these two pages to help you.

E X T R A S

1 Keep a record of the weather for a week. Do this at the same time each day. Record your readings in a table.

2 See if you can spot any link between the wind direction and other features of the weather.

J

Day	Temperature	Precipitation	Wind speed	Wind direction	Cloud amount	Cloud type	Weather
Sunday July 15	Warm	Rain showers	Force 2	Westerly	4/8	Cumulus	Mainly sunny with some rain
Monday July 16							

Summary

Weather is the day to day condition of the atmosphere. A simple record of the weather may be made by careful observation of what is going on around us.

How can local features affect temperature and wind?

On a fine summer's day are some of the classrooms in your school hotter than others? When the sun shines or a cold wind blows, is one side of your classroom warmer or colder than the other? On a hot sunny day can you notice a difference in temperature between a dark, tarmac playground and a grassy area like the school field? Are there some sheltered places around your school where you can get out of the wind?

Look at cartoon **A** which shows how different the conditions can be on two sides of a hedge.

Each particular place or site tends to develop its own special climate conditions. When the climate in a small area is different to the general surroundings it is called a **microclimate**. Some of the causes of microclimates are given below.

A

B

Shelter

Trees, hedges, walls, buildings and even hills can provide shelter from the wind. Wind speed may be reduced and its direction changed. Places sheltered from cold winds will be warmer.

Physical features

Trees provide shade and shelter and are usually cooler than surrounding areas. Water areas such as lakes and seas have a cooling effect and may also produce light winds. Hill tops are usually cool and windy.

Surface

The colour of the ground surface affects warming. Dark surfaces such as tarmac and soil will become warmer than light surfaces such as grass.

Buildings

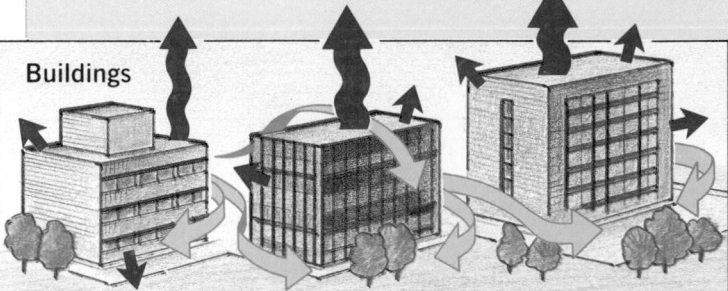

Buildings give off heat that has been stored from the sun during the day or which leaks from their heating systems. Temperatures near buildings may be 2°C or 3°C higher.

Buildings break up the wind and can reduce wind speeds by up to a third. Sometimes the wind can increase speed as it rushes round buildings.

Aspect

The direction in which a place is facing is called its aspect. Places facing the sun will be warmer than those in shadow.

In Britain the sun rises in the east and moves through the south before it sets in the west. South facing places get most of the sun and are usually the warmest.

Sun at midday

Cool around edge of lake

Main wind direction

Cool in trees with less wind

Cool and windy in shade and facing wind

Cooler classrooms due to shade and effect of wind

Grassy play area sheltered from wind

Hotter classrooms on sunny side of school

Play area warmed by dark tarmac surface

Some warmth from building

C A school's microclimate

Activities

1 Describe a place at your school which is
   a) often sunny
   b) usually in the shade
   c) sheltered on a windy day.

2 Copy and complete diagram **D** by filling in the bubbles with the following words or statements.
   ● Climate conditions of a small area
   ● Physical features
   ● Dark surfaces warm up most
   ● Reduces the effect of wind
   ● Buildings
   ● Aspect

D Local weather conditions

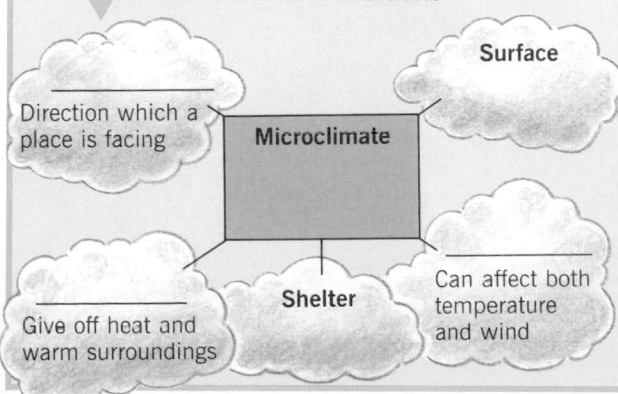

Direction which a place is facing

Surface

Microclimate

Shelter

Give off heat and warm surroundings

Can affect both temperature and wind

3 From photo **C** give **eight** features of the school's microclimate. List your answers under the headings:

Aspect   Shelter   Others

EXTRA

Microclimate Enquiry

1 **Aim** – to find out what effect aspect has on temperature

2 **Equipment** – thermometer

3 **Method:**
   a) Take several temperature readings on the north and south facing sides of the school. Make a note of the weather each time (e.g. sunny, cloudy, windy).
   b) Make a copy of the table below and display your results.
   c) Describe your findings.
   d) Suggest reasons for your findings.

Time	North facing	South facing	Weather conditions
Average			

Summary

Site conditions such as aspect, shelter, physical features and other factors can influence temperature, local wind speed and direction.

19

What is Britain's weather?

Weather is what happens in the atmosphere day by day but **climate** is different. It is the weather taken on average over many years. Climate is about warm dry summers, cool wet winters or, as at the North and South Poles, being cold all year. In Britain the weather is always a popular topic of conversation, probably because it is always changing or it's never quite what we want it to be. Changes also occur in the climate. It can change from time to time (seasonal) or it may be different from place to place.

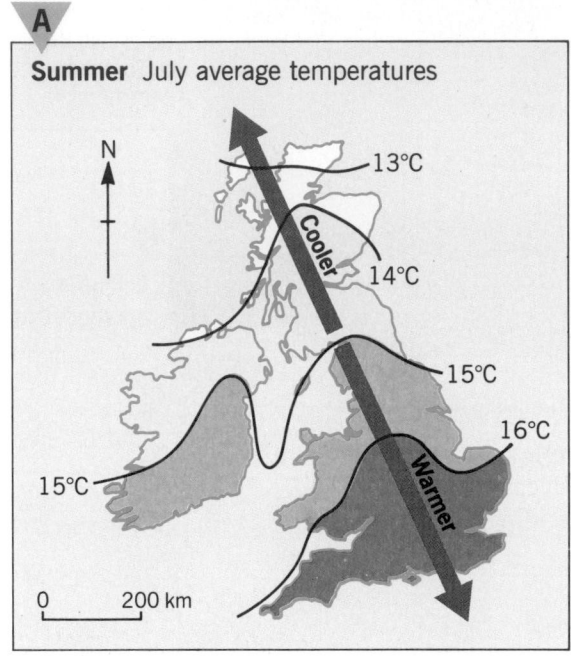

A

Summer July average temperatures

N

13°C
Cooler
14°C
15°C
16°C
15°C
Warmer

0   200 km

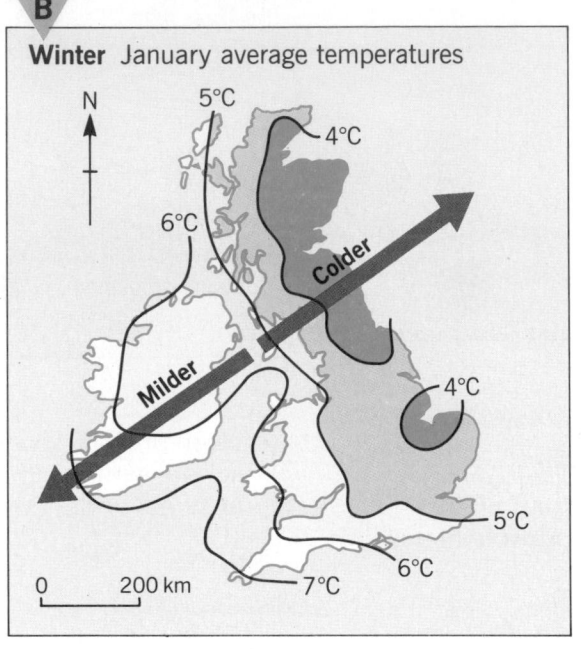

B

Winter January average temperatures

N

5°C
4°C
6°C
Colder
Milder
4°C
5°C
6°C
7°C

0   200 km

The average monthly temperatures for summer and winter are shown on maps **A** and **B**.

If you look closely you should see three main differences.

1 As expected, temperatures are higher in the summer than in winter.
2 Temperatures at any one time are not the same all over Britain.
3 The pattern of temperature is different in the two seasons.

Map **C** shows three important reasons for these variations in weather and climate. Another two are:

1 **Wind direction** – where the air has come from. A north wind will be cold, a west wind will be moist.

2 **Distance from the sea** – the sea keeps coastal places warm in winter but may cool them in summer. Places far inland will have warmer summers and cooler winters.

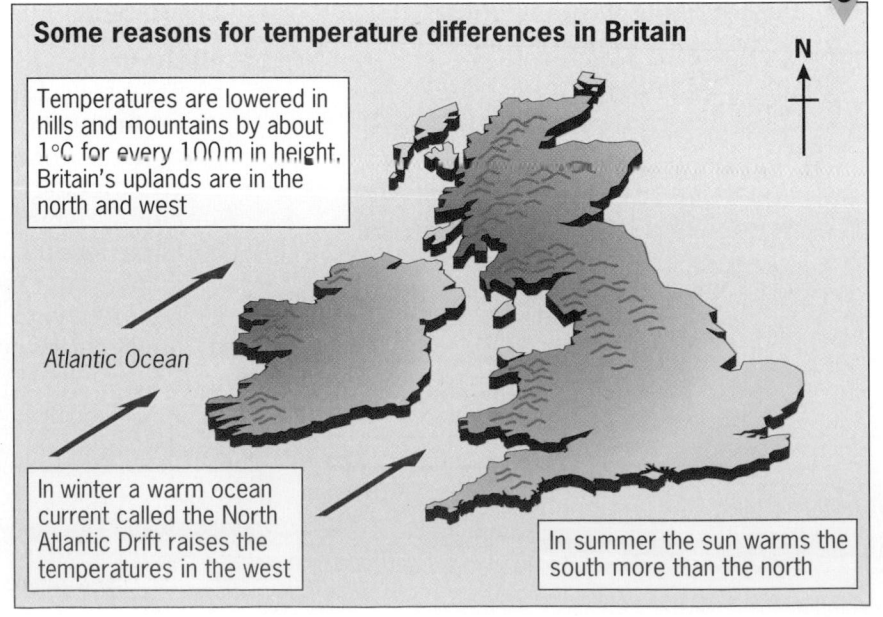

C

Some reasons for temperature differences in Britain

N

Temperatures are lowered in hills and mountains by about 1°C for every 100m in height, Britain's uplands are in the north and west

Atlantic Ocean

In winter a warm ocean current called the North Atlantic Drift raises the temperatures in the west

In summer the sun warms the south more than the north

Rainfall

In Britain we can expect rain at any time of the year. Although winter is wetter than the summer, seasonal differences in rainfall are very small.

As map **D** shows, however, the amount of rainfall varies considerably from place to place and the greatest differences are between the east and the west.

D

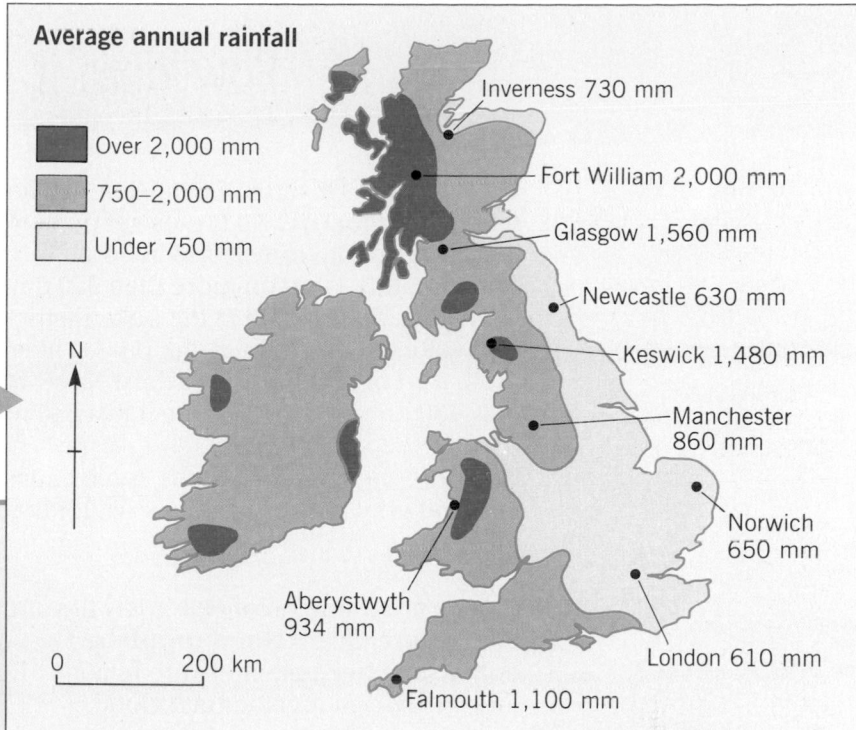

Average annual rainfall

Over 2,000 mm
750–2,000 mm
Under 750 mm

N

Inverness 730 mm
Fort William 2,000 mm
Glasgow 1,560 mm
Newcastle 630 mm
Keswick 1,480 mm
Manchester 860 mm
Norwich 650 mm
Aberystwyth 934 mm
London 610 mm
Falmouth 1,100 mm

0   200 km

Activities

1 What is the difference between weather and climate?

2 a) Write out and complete the following sentence to describe summer temperatures in Britain.

> Summers in Britain are _____ than winter. The warmest weather is in the _____ and temperatures get lower (decrease) towards the _____ .

b) Write a similar sentence to describe winter temperatures.

3 Why are there temperature differences in Britain? Think of **three** reasons and write them in your work book.

4 a) List the **three** wettest and the **three** driest towns from map **D**. Give your answers in order with the wettest first.

b) With the help of a simple diagram, describe the difference in rainfall from east to west. Give actual figures in your answer.

5 a) Make a large copy of map **E**.

b) Match the following climate descriptions to areas Ⓐ, Ⓑ, Ⓒ and Ⓓ and write them on your map. Ⓐ has been done on the map to help you.
● Warm summers, cold winters, dry
● Mild summers, mild winters, wet
● Warm summers, mild winters, quite wet
● Mild summers, cold winters, dry

c) Suggest reasons for the climate of area Ⓐ.
d) Mark where you live on your copy of map **E**.
e) Describe the climate there and suggest reasons for it.

E

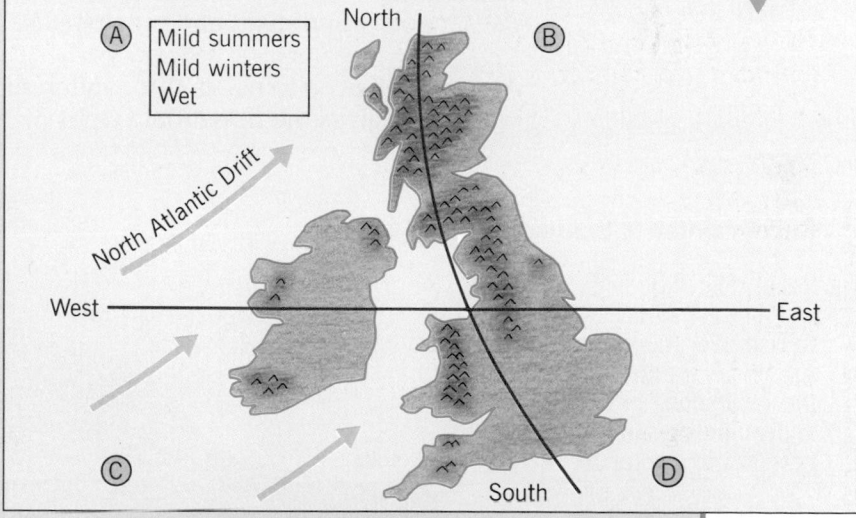

Ⓐ Mild summers / Mild winters / Wet

North

Ⓑ

North Atlantic Drift

West — East

Ⓒ

Ⓓ

South

Summary

Britain's climate varies from place to place and from season to season. Heating from the sun, ocean currents, and the height of the land are some of the reasons for these variations.

How does it rain?

The Atacama Desert in South America has had no rain for over 400 years yet parts of the Amazon rain forest, also in South America, have rain on more than 330 days each year. Seathwaite in the Lake District, the wettest place in England, has on average 3,340 mm of rain per year, whilst Newcastle, only 130 km away, may expect just 630 mm.

What are the reasons for this, what causes rain and why are some places wetter than others?

Clouds are made up of extremely tiny drops of moisture called **cloud droplets**. They are only visible because there are billions of them crowded together in a cloud.

Clouds form when moist air rises, cools and changes into cloud droplets. This is **condensation**. A cloud gives rain after these tiny cloud droplets grow thousands of times larger into raindrops which then fall to the ground.

Look at diagram **A**. It shows how rain is formed. The process is always the same: air rises, cools, condenses and precipitates.

Air can be forced to rise in three different ways. This gives the three main types of rainfall: **relief, convectional**, and **frontal**. These are shown in diagrams **B, C** and **D**.

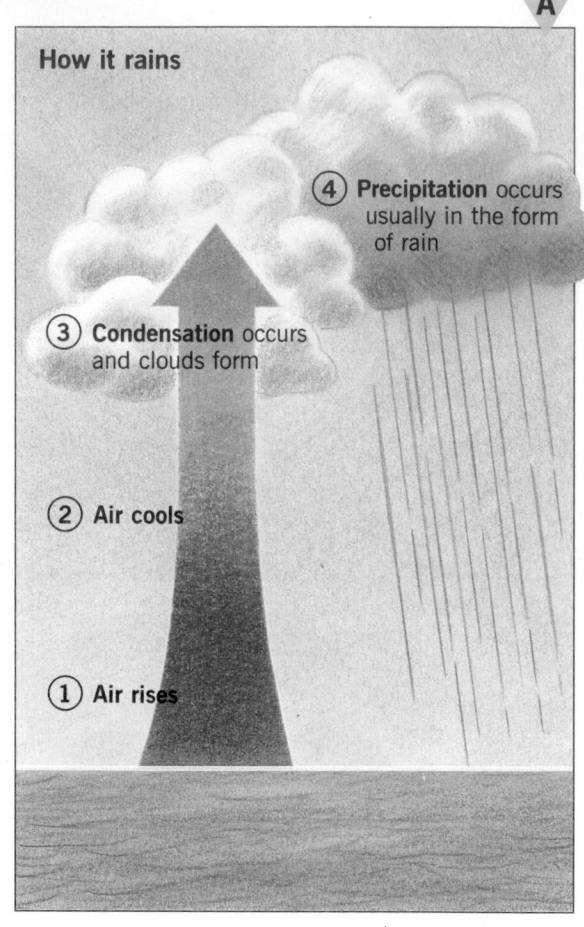

A

How it rains

4. **Precipitation** occurs usually in the form of rain

3. **Condensation** occurs and clouds form

2. **Air cools**

1. **Air rises**

B

Relief rainfall in the north of England

Relief rainfall occurs when moist air is forced to rise over mountains. As it rises it cools and the rainmaking process shown in diagram **A** comes into operation.

Relief rainfall is quite common in Britain especially in the west where most of the high land is located.

Cloud and rain

Air rises over Lake District mountains

Air descends and warms

Rain stops

North Sea

Warm moist air

• Seathwaite

Irish Sea

Newcastle

Lake District

West

East

C

Convectional rainfall

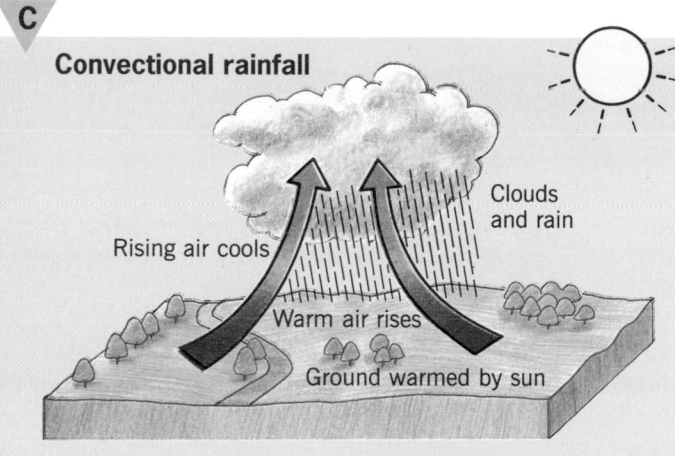

Rising air cools

Clouds and rain

Warm air rises

Ground warmed by sun

When the ground surface is heated by the sun, the air above it is warmed up. This air rises and as it cools down clouds form and rain follows. The showery weather and thunderstorms of a British summer are this type of rainfall.

D

Frontal rainfall

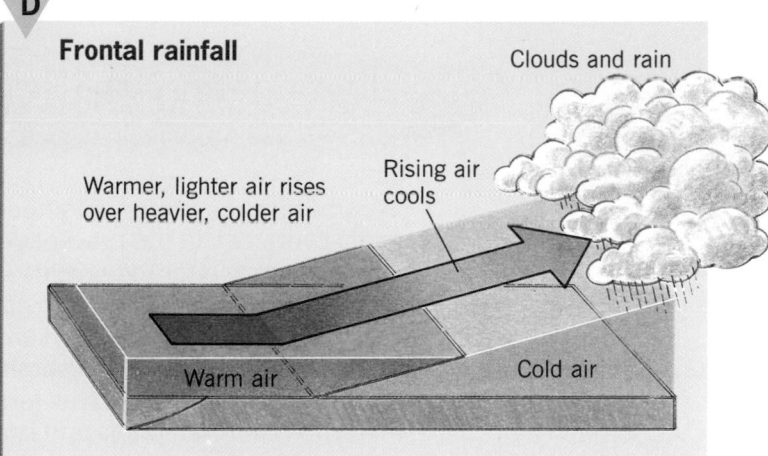

Clouds and rain

Warmer, lighter air rises over heavier, colder air

Rising air cools

Warm air

Cold air

When a mass of warm air meets air at a lower temperature, it rises up and over the colder, heavier air. Once it is made to rise, cloud and rain will follow due to the process shown in diagram **A**.

The place where warm air and cold air meet is called a **front**. Frontal rainfall is very common in Britain throughout the year and especially in winter.

Activities

1 Match the beginnings of these labels to their correct endings.

Clouds are	rain, snow and other forms of moisture in the sky.
Precipitation is	when water vapour changes to water.
Condensation happens	made up of tiny drops of moisture called cloud droplets.

2 With the help of a labelled diagram, describe how it rains.

3 a) Make larger copies of the three diagrams below.
 b) For each diagram explain how it rains by adding labels at points ①, ②, ③ and ④.
 c) Add colour to make your diagrams clearer.
 d) Underneath each of your diagrams give a brief reason for the air rising.
 e) Give each diagram a title.

4 Explain why Seathwaite is wetter than Newcastle. Use diagram **B** to help you.

Summary

Rain is caused by moist air rising and cooling. The three types of rainfall produced in this way are relief, convectional and frontal.

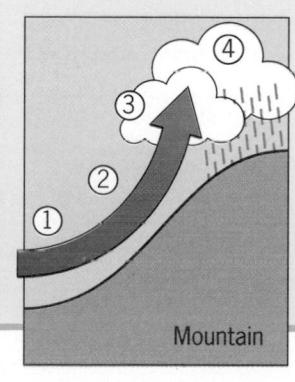

④ ③ ② ①

Mountain

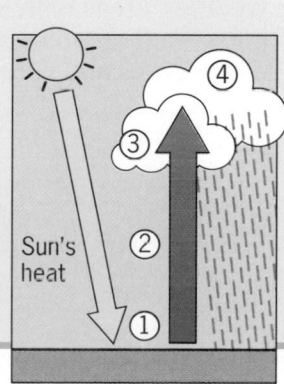

④ ③ ② ①

Sun's heat

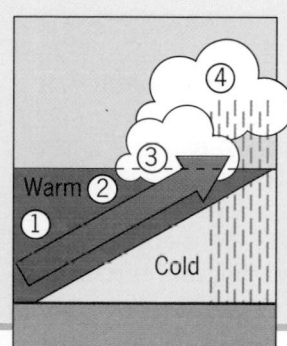

④ ③ Warm ② ①

Cold

Forecasting the weather — anticyclones

Weather has an important effect on our lives. Every day in the newspapers and every evening after the television news there is a **weather forecast**. Forecasts can tell us in advance what the weather will be. For many of us they are of passing interest but for some people such as farmers, fishermen, aircraft pilots and builders the forecasts are very important because the weather affects their work and even their safety.

Map **A** is a typical newspaper weather map. Notice how easy it is to read the weather using the picture symbols.

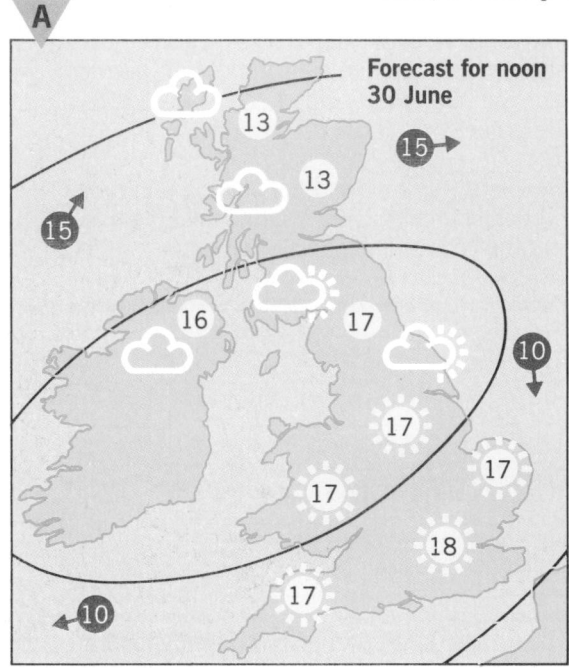

A Forecast for noon 30 June

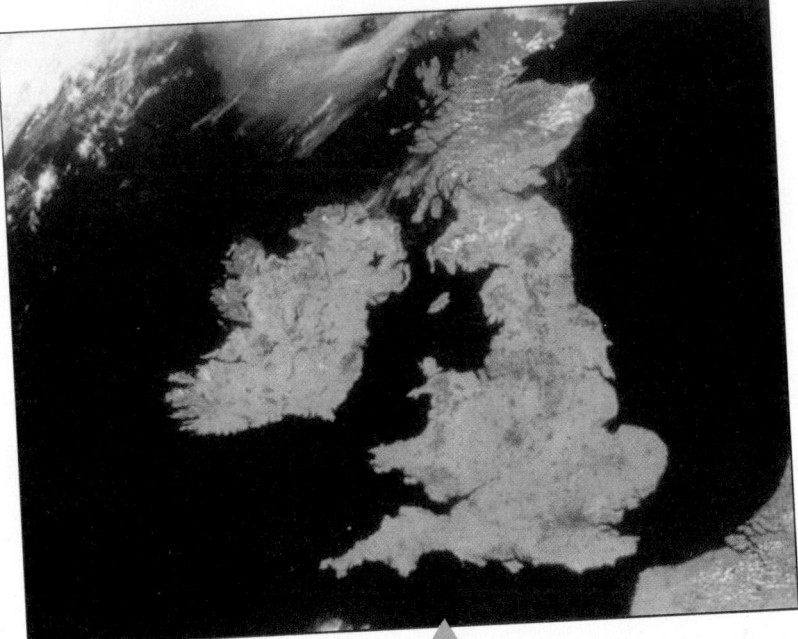

B Satellite photo of an anticyclone

How do weather forecasters know what the weather will be like tomorrow? How can they tell if it will be wet or dry, or hot or cold?

Forecasting is very complicated and lots of information and advanced computers are needed to make good forecasts. In recent times, satellites have become particularly useful because they can see weather systems many kilometres away.

Photo **B** has been taken from a satellite. It shows Britain with very little cloud overhead and clearly enjoying a fine sunny day. Photos like these are taken every few hours and by looking back over several of them, the movements of the weather systems can be worked out, and forecasts made.

The weather system in photo **B** is an **anticyclone**. It occurs because of changes in the air pressure. The weight of air pressing down on us from above is called pressure. This pressure varies from place to place and results in the development of pressure systems. Areas with above average pressure (high pressure) are called anticyclones and usually give good weather. Areas with less than average pressure (low pressure) are called depressions and usually give poor weather.

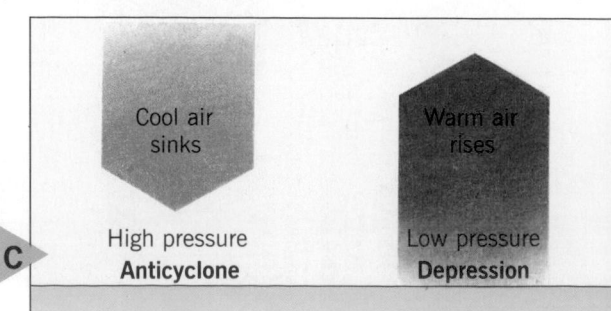

Cool air sinks

High pressure
Anticyclone

Warm air rises

Low pressure
Depression

C

D

Features of an anticyclone

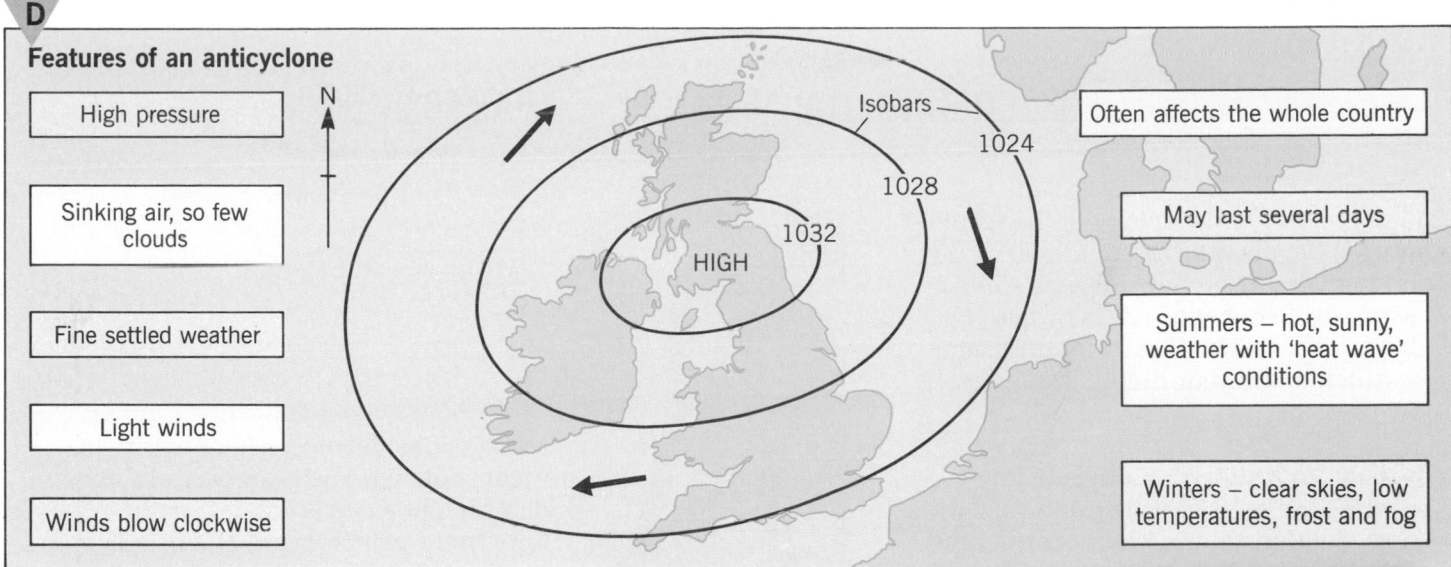

| High pressure |

| Sinking air, so few clouds |

| Fine settled weather |

| Light winds |

| Winds blow clockwise |

N

Isobars

1024

1028

1032

HIGH

| Often affects the whole country |

| May last several days |

| Summers – hot, sunny, weather with 'heat wave' conditions |

| Winters – clear skies, low temperatures, frost and fog |

Activities

1 From map **A**, give the weather that is forecast for the place where you live.

2 **a)** When do you think it would be useful for you to know the next day's weather?

   b) Make a list of people who need the weather forecast. For each person explain why they need to know about the weather.

3 How do satellites help in forecasting weather conditions?

4 **a)** Make a sketch of an anticyclone like the one in diagram **D** above.

   b) Next to your sketch, write out the paragraph below and fill in the blank spaces with the following words:

E

Weather in a winter anticyclone

5 Copy and fill in table **F** to show the weather features of an anticyclone.

• LONG   • LARGE   • HIGH   • COOL
Anticyclones are areas of _____ pressure which form when _____ air sinks. They usually cover _____ areas and give _____ periods of fine settled weather.

F

	Summer	Winter
Temperatures		
Cloud cover		
Wind speed		
Wind direction		
Rain		
Other features		

Summary

Knowing what the weather will be like can be useful to us. Anticyclones can bring good weather and may be forecast with the help of satellites.

E X T R A S

1 Use photo **E** to describe the weather of an anticyclone in winter.

2 Study map **A** on page 24 giving the newspaper weather forecast. Write a weather forecast to be read out on the radio for the same day. Your forecast should be about 100 to 150 words in length.

Forecasting the weather — depressions

All too often we seem to hear the weather forecast begin with 'Today will be cloudy, and rain already in the west will spread eastwards to cover all areas by late afternoon . . .'. The reason for this is that for much of the year Britain is affected by low pressure.

As diagram **A** shows, at times of low pressure the air is usually rising. As it rises it cools, condenses and clouds form. Low pressure areas are called **depressions**. Depressions are the most important weather systems affecting Britain and they bring with them clouds and rain.

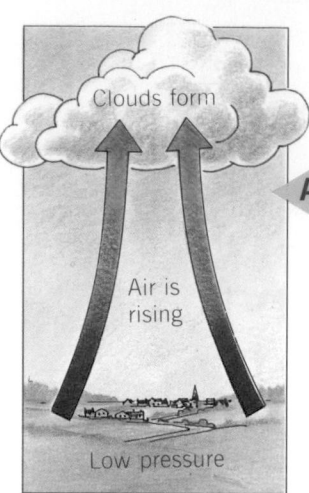

A

Depressions develop where warm air meets cold air. The boundary of the two different air types is called a **front**. Along a front there will be cloud and usually rain. Diagram **B** shows the features of a depression. The isobars are lines that join up areas of equal pressure and they help us to see the shape of the depression.

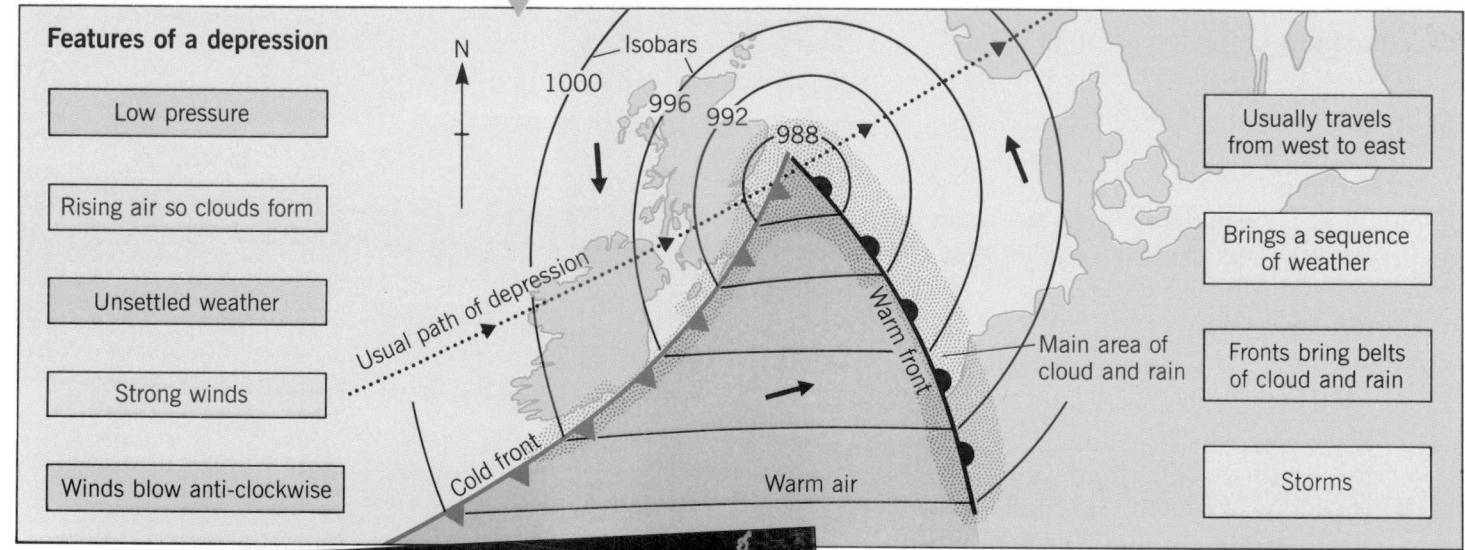

B

Features of a depression

- Low pressure
- Rising air so clouds form
- Unsettled weather
- Strong winds
- Winds blow anti-clockwise

- Usually travels from west to east
- Brings a sequence of weather
- Fronts bring belts of cloud and rain
- Storms

Isobars 1000 996 992 988

Usual path of depression

Cold front

Warm front

Warm air

Main area of cloud and rain

C Satellite photo of a depression

Depressions are huge areas of low pressure measuring many hundreds of kilometres across. They show up very clearly on satellite photographs as great swirls of cloud that look like gigantic catherine wheel fireworks. The fronts are easily recognised as areas of thick white cloud arranged in an upside down 'V' shape. The centre of the depression is normally just above or a little behind the point of the 'V'.

Look at photo **C** which shows a depression approaching Britain. Can you work out which areas are the fronts and where the centre of the depression might be? With help from diagram **B** can you work out which is the area of warm air? What sort of weather does that area seem to have?

Depressions usually form over the Atlantic Ocean and move across Britain from west to east. With help from satellite photographs, weather forecasters can work out the direction they are travelling and how fast they are moving. From this information they can produce quite accurate weather forecasts. Diagram **D** shows how the weather changes as a depression passes over Britain. Notice the changes in the weather that occur in the area where you live.

▷ D A depression passing over Britain

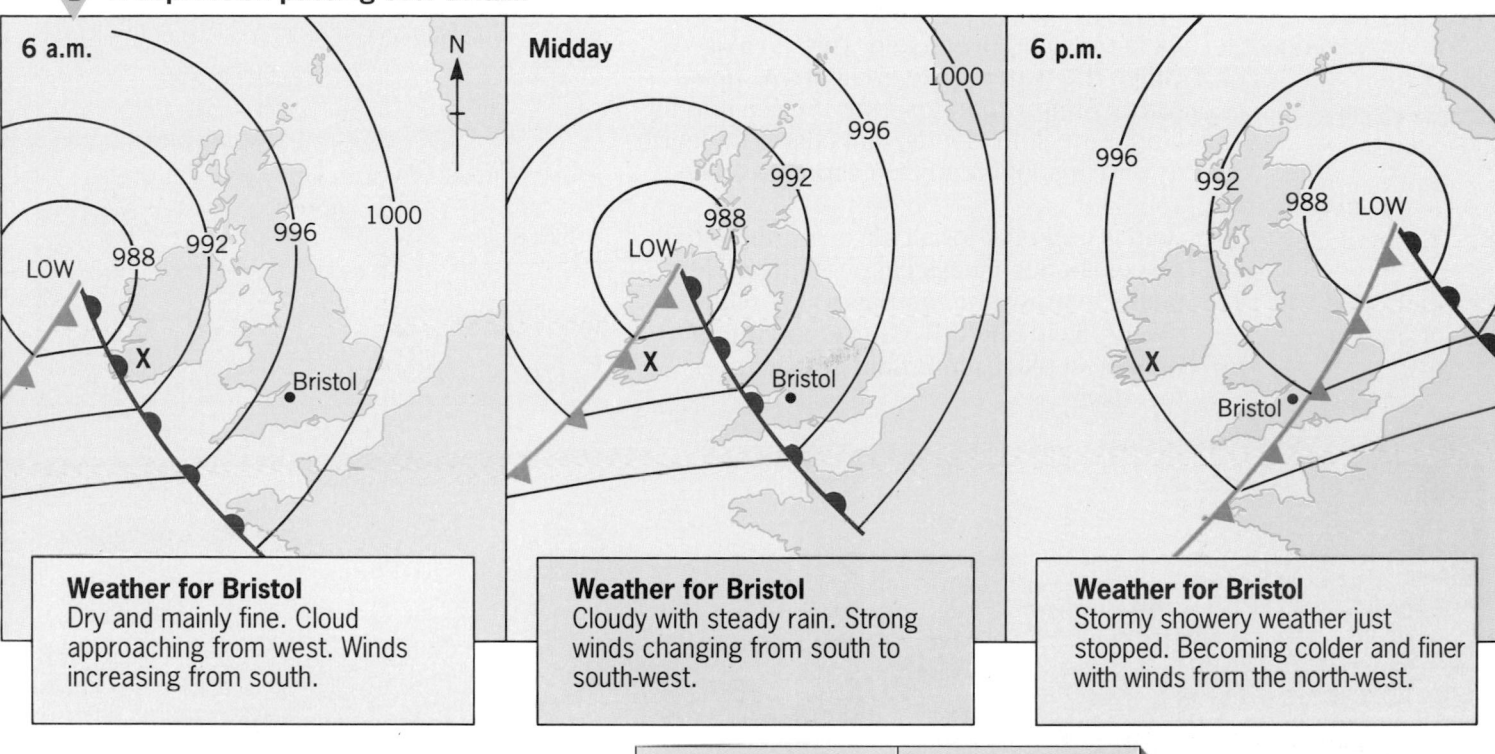

Weather for Bristol
Dry and mainly fine. Cloud approaching from west. Winds increasing from south.

Weather for Bristol
Cloudy with steady rain. Strong winds changing from south to south-west.

Weather for Bristol
Stormy showery weather just stopped. Becoming colder and finer with winds from the north-west.

General features	Weather

Activities

1 The words below have been jumbled up. Unscramble the words and fill in the blank spaces in the following paragraph.

NIRA SATE DULOC OWL TEWS SERIS

Depressions are areas of _____ pressure which form when air _____ . They usually move across Britain from _____ to _____ and bring most of our _____ and _____ .

2 With the help of a labelled diagram, explain why depressions bring cloud and rain.

3 Make a labelled sketch of a depression like the one shown in diagram **B**. Underneath your sketch make a copy of the table at the top of the next column.

Complete the table to show the main features of a depression.

4 From diagram **D**:
   a) Describe the weather at place **X** for 6 a.m., 12 midday and 6 p.m.
   b) Explain why the weather has changed.
   c) At what time will the warm front be over the place where you live?
   d) Describe the weather you may get at that time.

E X T R A

   a) Trace the outline of Britain from photo **C**.
   b) Mark and label the following:
   - warm front
   - cold front
   - warm air
   - centre of the depression.
   c) Shade the area of cloud and rain along the fronts.
   d) Describe the weather over Britain.

Summary

Depressions are the most common weather system affecting Britain. They are low pressure areas and bring stormy winds, cloud and rain.

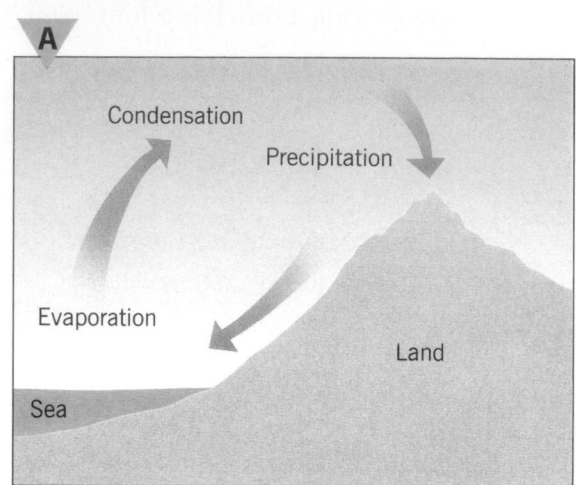

What happens when rain reaches the ground?

The question 'How does it rain?' was answered on pages 22 and 23. Rain is part of a never-ending cycle in which water is used over and over again. This cycle is called the **water cycle**. Diagram **A** shows how water evaporates from the sea and the land, turns into clouds, and falls to the earth as rain or snow ready to evaporate again.

Rain is essential for all life on earth. Some places do not always get enough rain for plants to grow and animals to live. Other places, as in photo **B**, can get too much rain. Most places in Britain get rain every few days.

A

Condensation

Precipitation

Evaporation

Land

Sea

B

What happens when rain reaches the ground is very important to us. When it rains some of the water may lie on the surface. It forms pools which later dry up as the water evaporates.

Some of the rain may slowly sink in to the ground. This water may be used by plants. Some of the water may drain away over the surface of the ground or through the soil to end up in **rivers**.

Whether the rain lies on the surface, sinks into the soil or flows over the surface depends upon the **slope** and the **surface** of the ground. Diagram **C** shows two different types of **slope**. The steeper the slope the more likely it will be that water will flow over the surface.

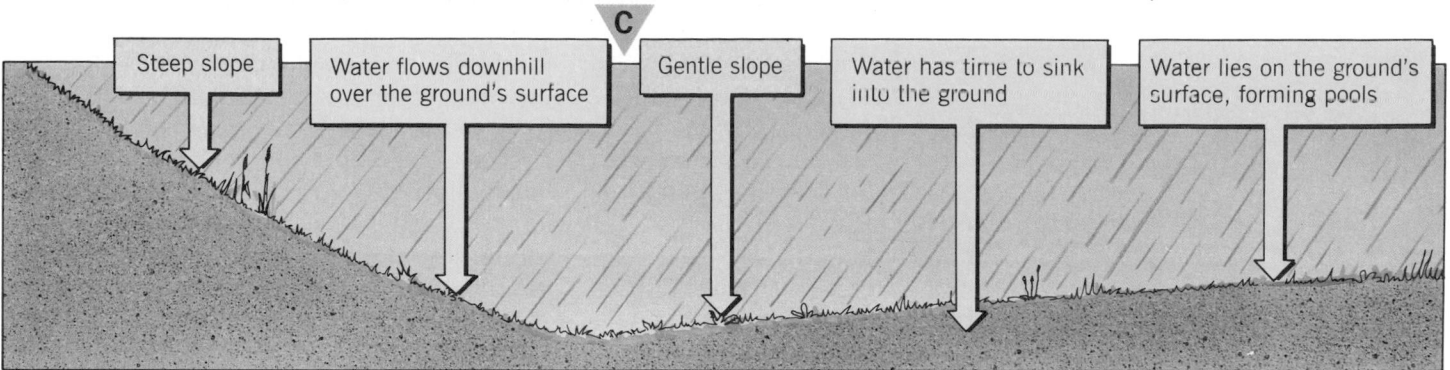

C

| Steep slope | Water flows downhill over the ground's surface | Gentle slope | Water has time to sink into the ground | Water lies on the ground's surface, forming pools |

Your school grounds may have different types of **surface**. Diagram **D** shows four pupils pouring the contents of four watering cans onto four different surfaces. You will probably already know what will happen to any water poured onto the tarmac and the sand. A grass surface protects the soil. It will take some time for water poured onto the grass to reach the soil and sink into it. Water poured onto bare, unprotected soil will soon sink into the ground.

D

Tarmac   Sand   Grass   Bare soil

Activities

1 Working in pairs and using photo **B**, list some of the problems that may result from too much rain. Clues – think about housing, transport, crops and animals.

2 Which one of sentences **a)** and **b)** below best describes what happens to rain on a steep slope? Which one of the sentences best describes what happens to rain on a gentle slope?
  a) Rain forms pools on the surface giving it time to sink into the ground.
  b) Rain flows downhill over the surface of the ground.

3 There are four types of surface shown in the diagram **D**. Copy out and complete table **E** below, putting each type of surface next to the correct statement.

	E
	Surface
Water lies on the surface and does not sink into the ground.	
Water sinks very slowly into the ground.	
Water sinks quite quickly into the ground.	
Water sinks very quickly into the ground.	

Summary

What happens to rain when it reaches the ground depends on the type of slope and surface upon which it falls. Most of the rain usually ends up in rivers.

29

What is a river basin?

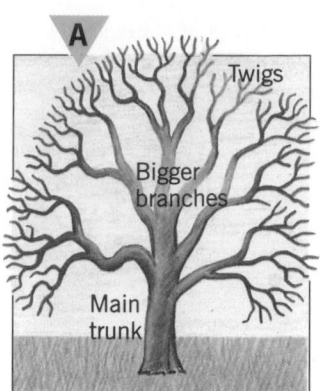

A

Twigs

Bigger branches

Main trunk

If you look at the top of a large tree you will see lots of twigs. Twigs are small branches. If you follow these downwards, as in diagram **A**, you will see these twigs joining to form branches. These branches in turn join to form one big trunk.

A **river basin** (drainage basin) is like a tree. It has lots of small **streams** which join to

form **tributaries** which later join to form the main **river** (diagram **B**). When it rains, most of the water slowly drains into streams, then into tributaries and finally into the main river. A river basin is the area of land drained by a main river and its tributaries. The area of highland marking the edge of the basin is called a **watershed**.

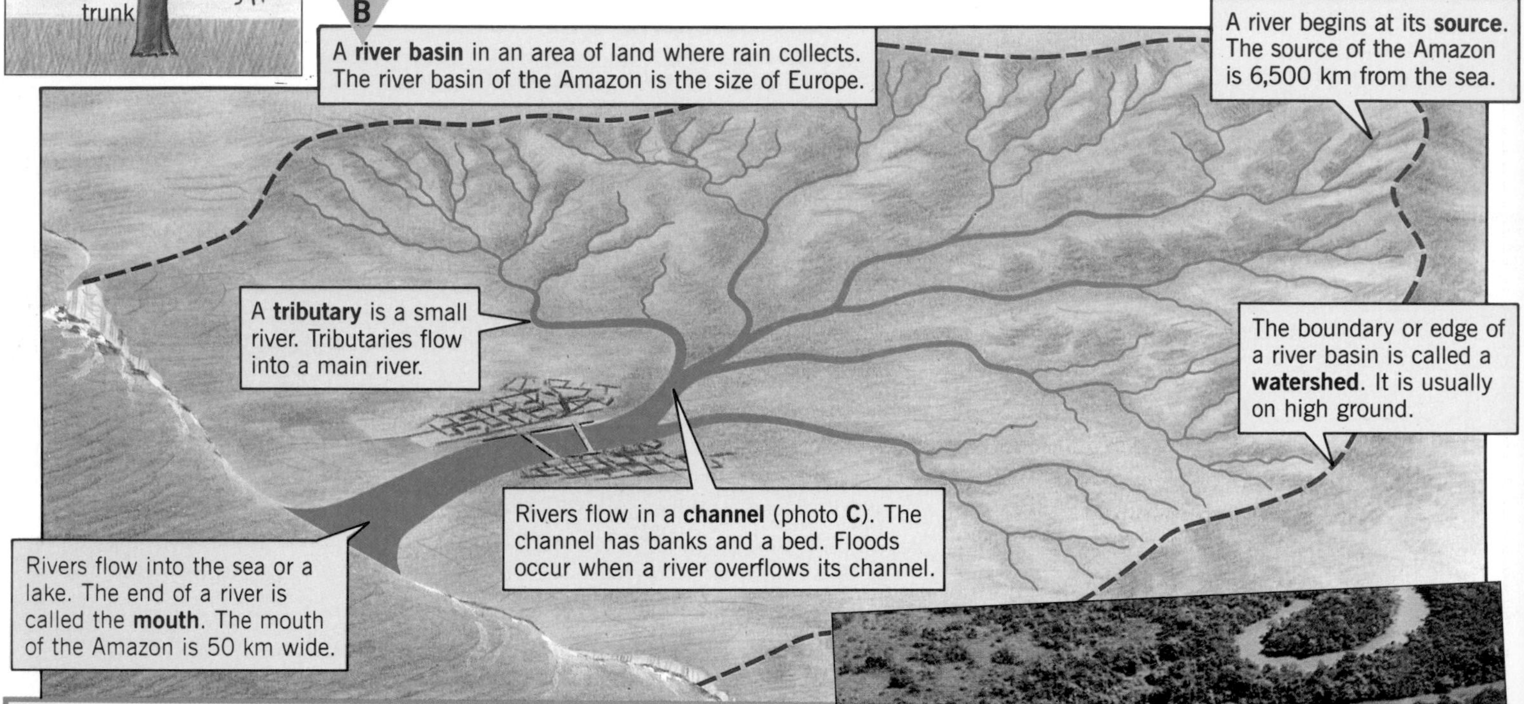

B

A **river basin** in an area of land where rain collects. The river basin of the Amazon is the size of Europe.

A river begins at its **source**. The source of the Amazon is 6,500 km from the sea.

A **tributary** is a small river. Tributaries flow into a main river.

The boundary or edge of a river basin is called a **watershed**. It is usually on high ground.

Rivers flow in a **channel** (photo **C**). The channel has banks and a bed. Floods occur when a river overflows its channel.

Rivers flow into the sea or a lake. The end of a river is called the **mouth**. The mouth of the Amazon is 50 km wide.

Activity

Diagram **B** shows a river basin. There are two lists below. One gives words used to describe parts of river basins and the second gives their meanings. Match up the two lists.

A watershed	is where a river begins
The source	is where the river flows
A river basin	is where a river flows into a lake or the sea
A tributary	is an area of highland forming the edge of a river basin
A channel	is a stream or small river flowing into a main river
The mouth	is an area of land drained by a river and its tributaries

C River Amazon

Where are the world's most important rivers?

Activities

Thirteen important world rivers are, in alphabetical order, the Amazon, Colorado, Danube, Ganges, Mississippi, Murray-Darling, Nile, Rhine, St Lawrence, Volga, Yangtze, Zaire (Congo) and Zambezi.

1 Fit the names of these rivers into crossword **D** on the right. The number of letters in each word will help you to fit them into the puzzle. For example, the Murray-Darling, which has been done for you, was the only word with 13 letters. It could only fit into that one place.

2 With help from map **E** below, sort the rivers into groups under the headings: *Africa, America, Asia, Australia* and *Europe*.

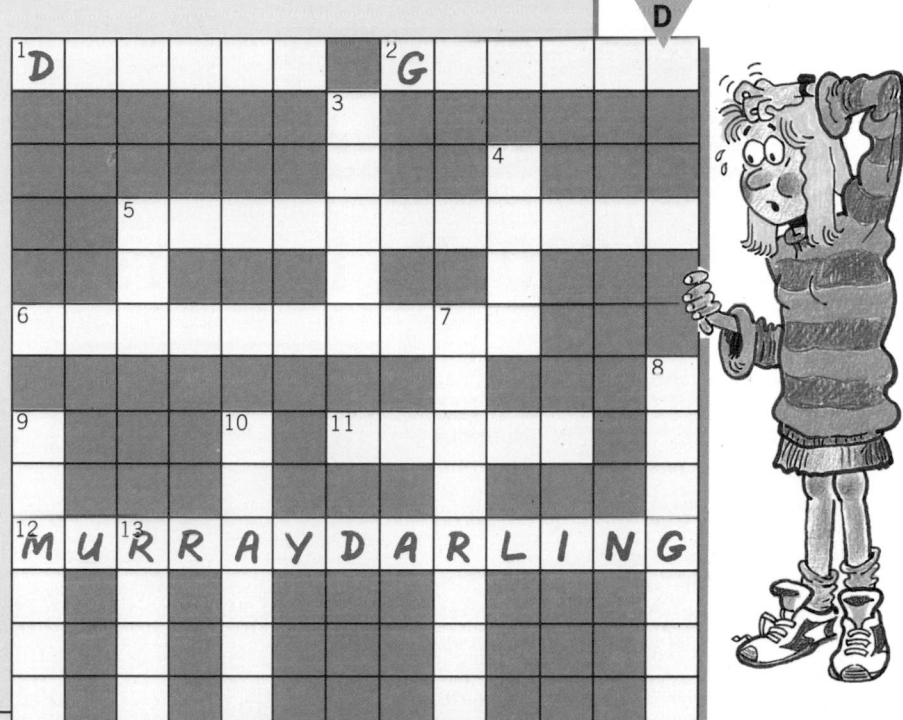

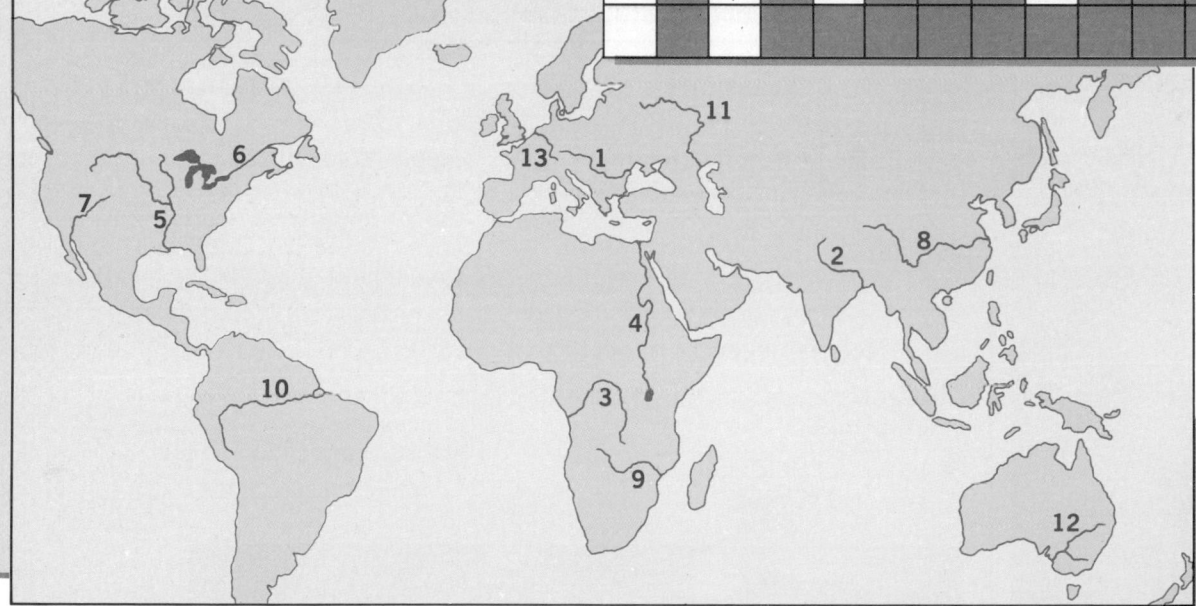

Summary

Rain collects in rivers in a river basin. Rivers have their source in highland areas and flow in a channel to the sea or to a lake.

E X T R A S

1 The three longest rivers in the United Kingdom are the Severn, the Thames and the Trent. Name **one** city on each of these rivers.

2 Match the 13 rivers named in question **1** above with a country through which they flow. Some flow through several countries, so choose only **one** important country.

What are the results of a flood?

A

সাপ্তাহিক জনমত **Janomot Newsweekly** 5 September, 1988

1,000 die in worst ever floods

The heaviest monsoon rains ever to hit Bangladesh have left over 1000 people dead and 25 million homeless. Up to 80 per cent of the country is at least one metre deep in floodwater. The rice crop has been lost and 35 million people now face starvation. The chief export crops of sugar cane and jute have also been ruined. The only dry places to live are on roof tops – but even these are not safe as snakes have also sought refuge here. Water and electricity have both been cut off.

Transport

Railways and bridges have been swept away. Nearly all of the country's roads are impassable. Dhaka airport is under water, preventing foreign help from arriving.

Disease Threat

With most of the country's water supply contaminated, the threat of disease is real. Hospitals are already full of cases of dysentery and diarrhoea. Yesterday 500 cholera cases were admitted to Dhaka hospital.

Help is urgently needed

The government announced today that they need:

- boats and helicopters to reach stranded villages,

- food to replace the lost rice crop,
- medicines,
- water purification tablets,
- blankets.

What causes flooding in Bangladesh?

A flood occurs when there is too much water for a river to carry away in its river channel. The river overflows and covers any flat surrounding countryside.

Bangladesh has floods every year – but they seem to be getting worse. The country relies on the heavy monsoon rains to flood the rice fields, but too much rain can destroy the crop as well as the homes of the farmers. In four monsoon months Bangladesh can get as much rain as London gets in two years! Some of the causes of flooding in Bangladesh are shown in diagram **B**.

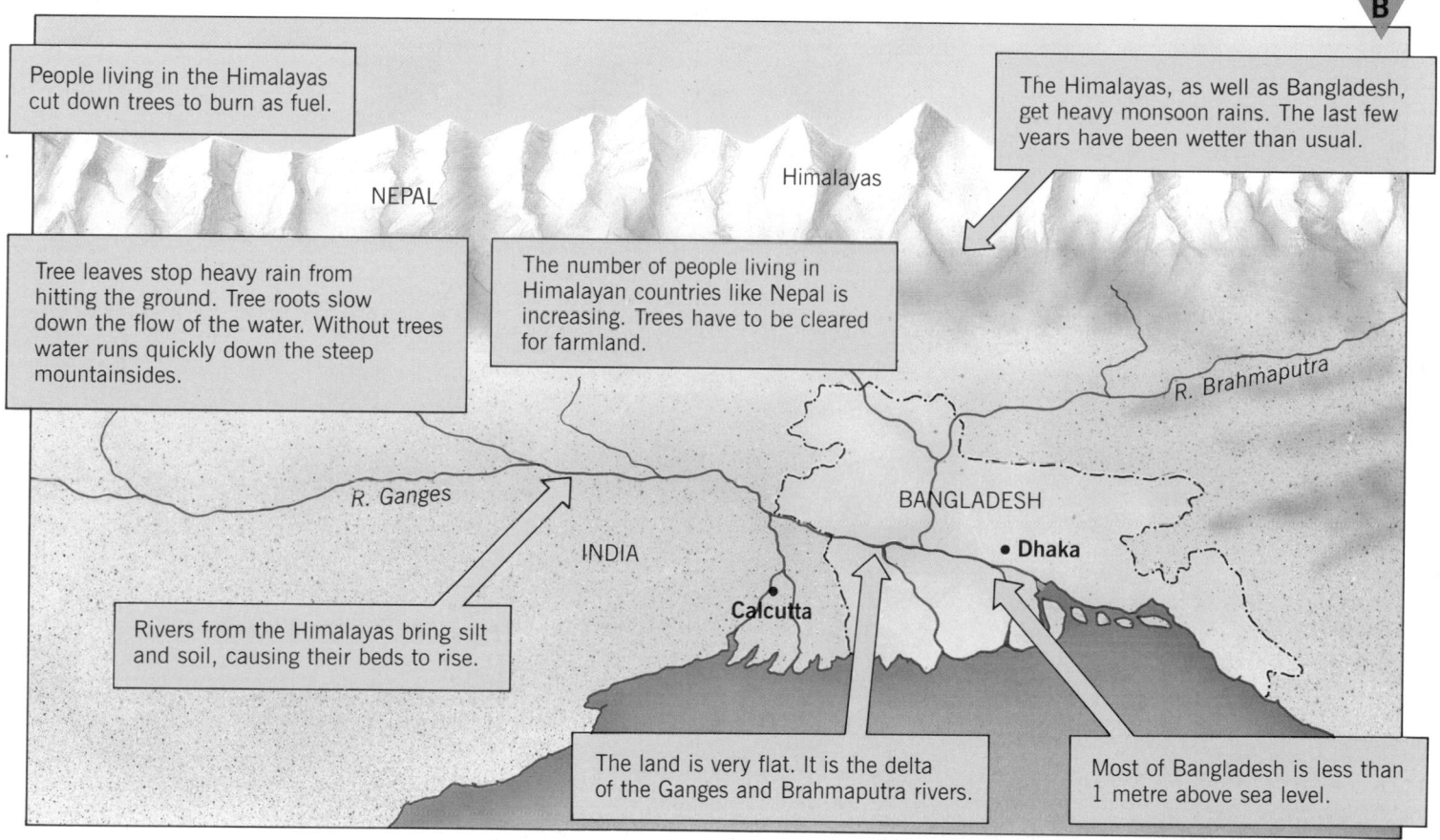

B

People living in the Himalayas cut down trees to burn as fuel.

The Himalayas, as well as Bangladesh, get heavy monsoon rains. The last few years have been wetter than usual.

Tree leaves stop heavy rain from hitting the ground. Tree roots slow down the flow of the water. Without trees water runs quickly down the steep mountainsides.

The number of people living in Himalayan countries like Nepal is increasing. Trees have to be cleared for farmland.

Rivers from the Himalayas bring silt and soil, causing their beds to rise.

The land is very flat. It is the delta of the Ganges and Brahmaputra rivers.

Most of Bangladesh is less than 1 metre above sea level.

NEPAL Himalayas R. Brahmaputra INDIA R. Ganges BANGLADESH • Dhaka Calcutta

Activities

1 Find Bangladesh, India, Nepal, the Himalayas and the rivers Ganges and Brahmaputra on a map in your atlas.

2 Read the front page of the newspaper in diagram **A**. How did the 1988 flood affect people living in Bangladesh?

3 The cause of annual (yearly) flooding in Bangladesh is partly due to natural reasons and partly due to human activities. Copy out the table below and complete it, using information given in diagram **B**.

Causes of flooding in Bangladesh	
Natural reasons	*Human activities*

Summary

Flooding can seriously affect people's lives. Floods may result from natural events or from human activity.

What causes floods?

There are many causes of floods. Sometimes a flood has only one cause, often there are several reasons. The main causes of floods are given on map **A**. As this map shows, floods can occur in many different parts of the world. The examples chosen show that flooding can affect **river basins**, and **coastal areas**.

In many parts of the world floods seem to be occurring more often and they also seem to be increasing in size. This is blamed on human activity. Two ways in which humans may increase the risk of flooding is by building more towns and cities (**urbanisation**) and by cutting down trees (**deforestation**). The effects of urbanisation and deforestation are shown on diagram **C** and in the photos in **B**.

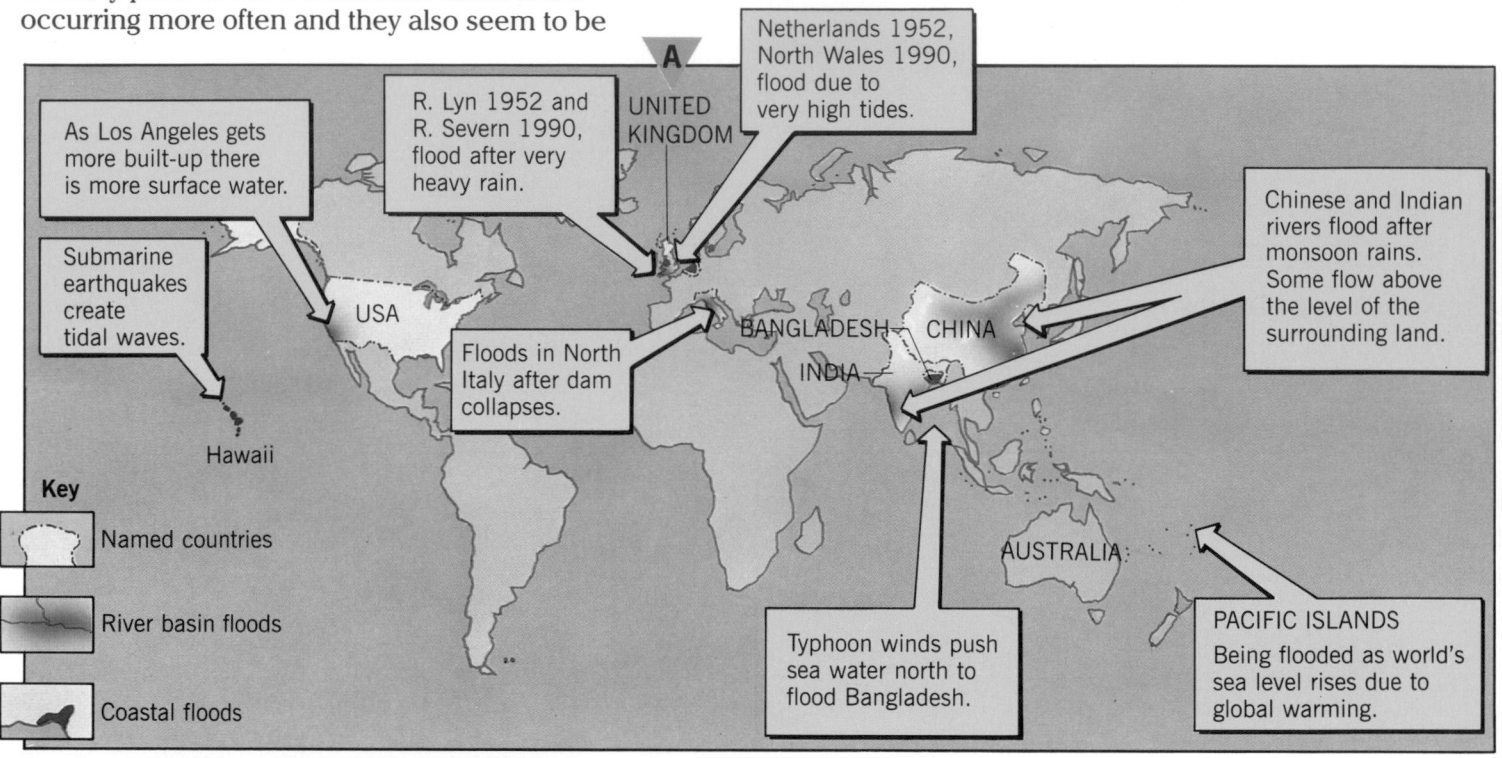

A

Netherlands 1952, North Wales 1990, flood due to very high tides.

As Los Angeles gets more built-up there is more surface water.

R. Lyn 1952 and R. Severn 1990, flood after very heavy rain.

UNITED KINGDOM

Submarine earthquakes create tidal waves.

USA

Floods in North Italy after dam collapses.

BANGLADESH CHINA

INDIA

Chinese and Indian rivers flood after monsoon rains. Some flow above the level of the surrounding land.

Hawaii

AUSTRALIA

Key

Named countries

River basin floods

Coastal floods

Typhoon winds push sea water north to flood Bangladesh.

PACIFIC ISLANDS
Being flooded as world's sea level rises due to global warming.

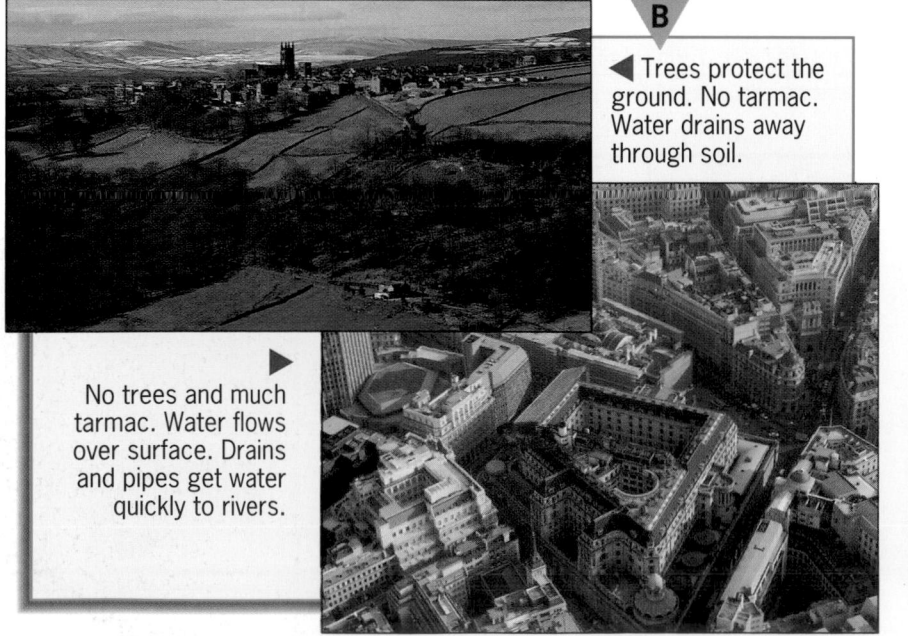

B

◀ Trees protect the ground. No tarmac. Water drains away through soil.

No trees and much tarmac. Water flows over surface. Drains and pipes get water quickly to rivers. ▶

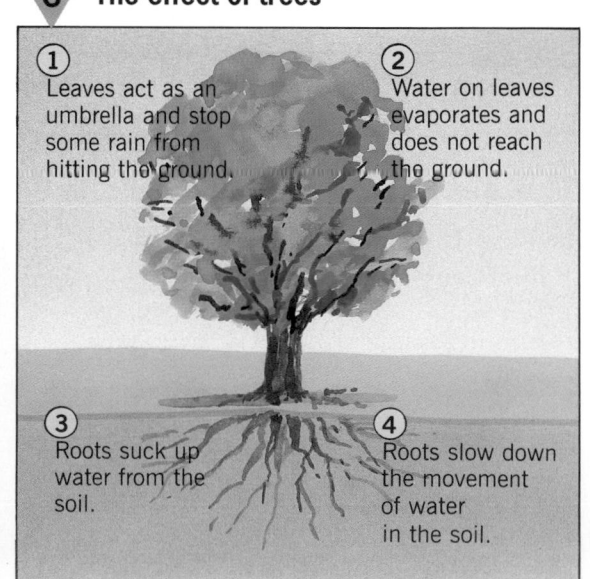

C The effect of trees

① Leaves act as an umbrella and stop some rain from hitting the ground.

② Water on leaves evaporates and does not reach the ground.

③ Roots suck up water from the soil.

④ Roots slow down the movement of water in the soil.

How can the risk of flooding be reduced?

The reasons for trying to reduce the risk of floods may depend upon several factors.

- Places which flood frequently are more in need than places which only flood occasionally.

- Small floods may be a nuisance which have to be endured. Perhaps nothing can stop very big floods.

- Attempts to stop floods will be greater where lives and property of many people are at risk.

- The methods used will depend upon the wealth of a country. For example, poorer countries like Bangladesh cannot afford expensive dams like those in the USA.

Diagram **D** shows some responses to floods.

D

"We can only hope and pray the river does not flood."
"I've got my fingers crossed"

"We made the river deeper by taking silt from its bed."
"We put the silt on the banks to make them higher."

"We did not need the land for farming so we planted trees"
"When the trees grow they should reduce flooding."

"The dam will hold back the flood water."
"It will control the river."

Activities

1 Using **B**, give **three** reasons why the risk of floods increases as the size of towns and cities increases.

2 Diagram **E** shows the same place as diagram **C** but with the trees cut down. Copy out diagram **E** and add the missing labels.

3 Diagram **D** shows four responses to floods.
   a) Which **two** responses will be the cheapest and which **two** will be the safest?
   b) Which **two** responses are more likely to be those made by the governments of:
      i) Bangladesh,
      ii) the United Kingdom?
   c) Give reasons for your answers to **a)** and **b)**.

E X T R A

Name a river near you which used to, or still may flood. Find out what methods have been used to try to prevent it from flooding. Have these methods been successful? If not, what else may be done?

E

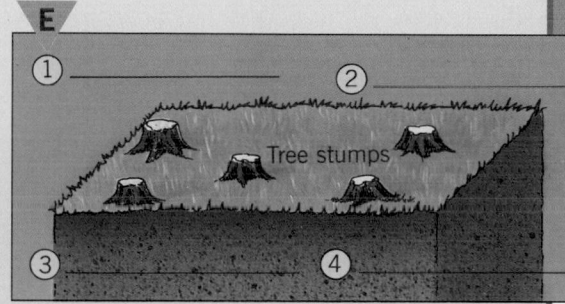
① _____ ② _____
Tree stumps
③ _____ ④ _____

Summary

There are several different causes of floods. There are several methods of trying to reduce the risk of floods.

How does the water cycle work?

The water cycle is when water is used over and over again in a never-ending cycle (diagram **A**, page 28). The amount of water in the cycle always stays the same. Some of the water may be **stored** in the sea, in the air and on the land. Later some of this water will be **transferred** (moved) around the cycle. The main stores and transfers in the cycle are shown in diagram **A**.

The water cycle can be very complicated but its main features are shown in diagram **B**. Notice that water can be moved in different forms – as vapour, rain, snow or hail. Some of the geographical terms used on this diagram are long and will be new to you. Chart **C** on the next page explains what these words mean.

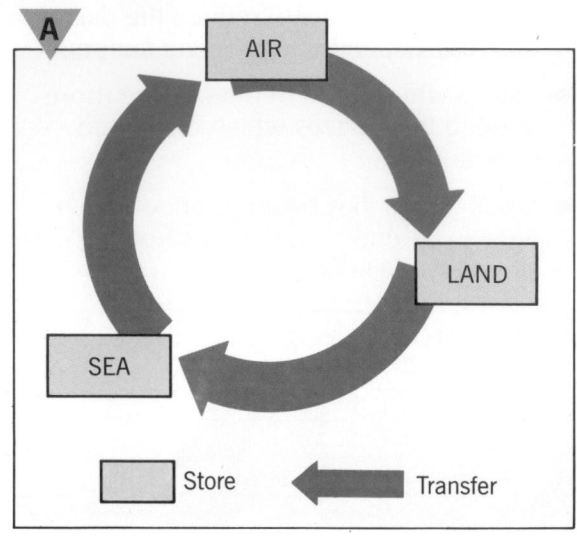

A

AIR

LAND

SEA

☐ Store   ⬅ Transfer

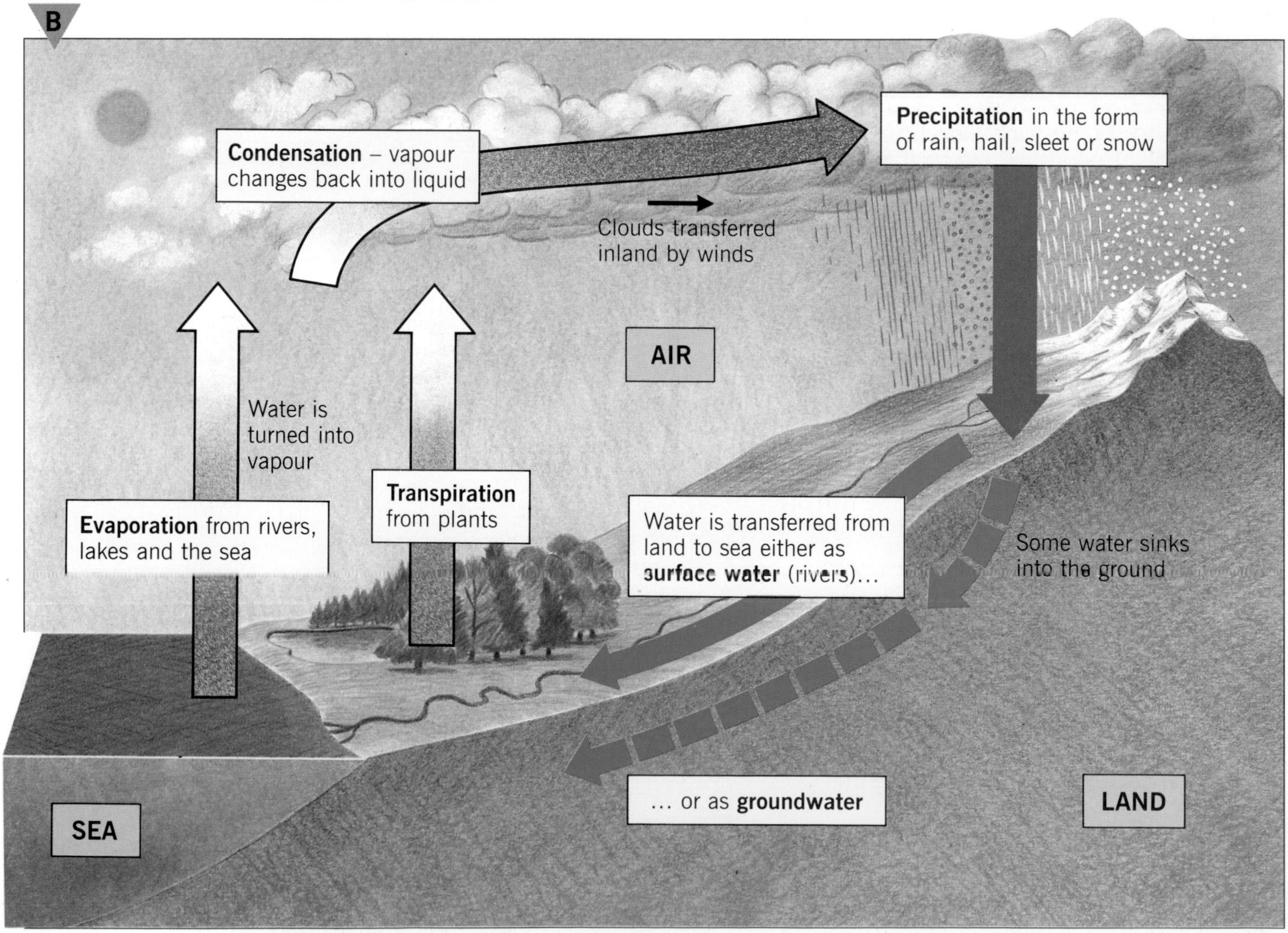

B

Condensation – vapour changes back into liquid

Precipitation in the form of rain, hail, sleet or snow

Clouds transferred inland by winds

AIR

Water is turned into vapour

Transpiration from plants

Evaporation from rivers, lakes and the sea

Water is transferred from land to sea either as **surface water** (rivers)…

Some water sinks into the ground

… or as **groundwater**

SEA

LAND

C

Evaporation		The transfer and change of water from the ground into water vapour in the air. Water vapour is an invisible gas.
Transpiration		The transfer and change of water from plants into water vapour in the air.
Condensation		Water vapour in the air changes back into a liquid. It forms small droplets which are visible as cloud.
Precipitation		The transfer of water from the air to the land. Water can fall to earth as rain, hail, sleet or snow.
Surface water		The transfer of water back to the sea over the ground surface. It is called surface run-off. It is easiest to see where it forms rivers.
Groundwater		The transfer of water through the ground back to the sea.

Activities

1 Diagram **D** shows part of the water cycle. Draw the diagram and boxes. Choose your answers from the following:

condensation

evaporation

groundwater

precipitation

surface water

transpiration

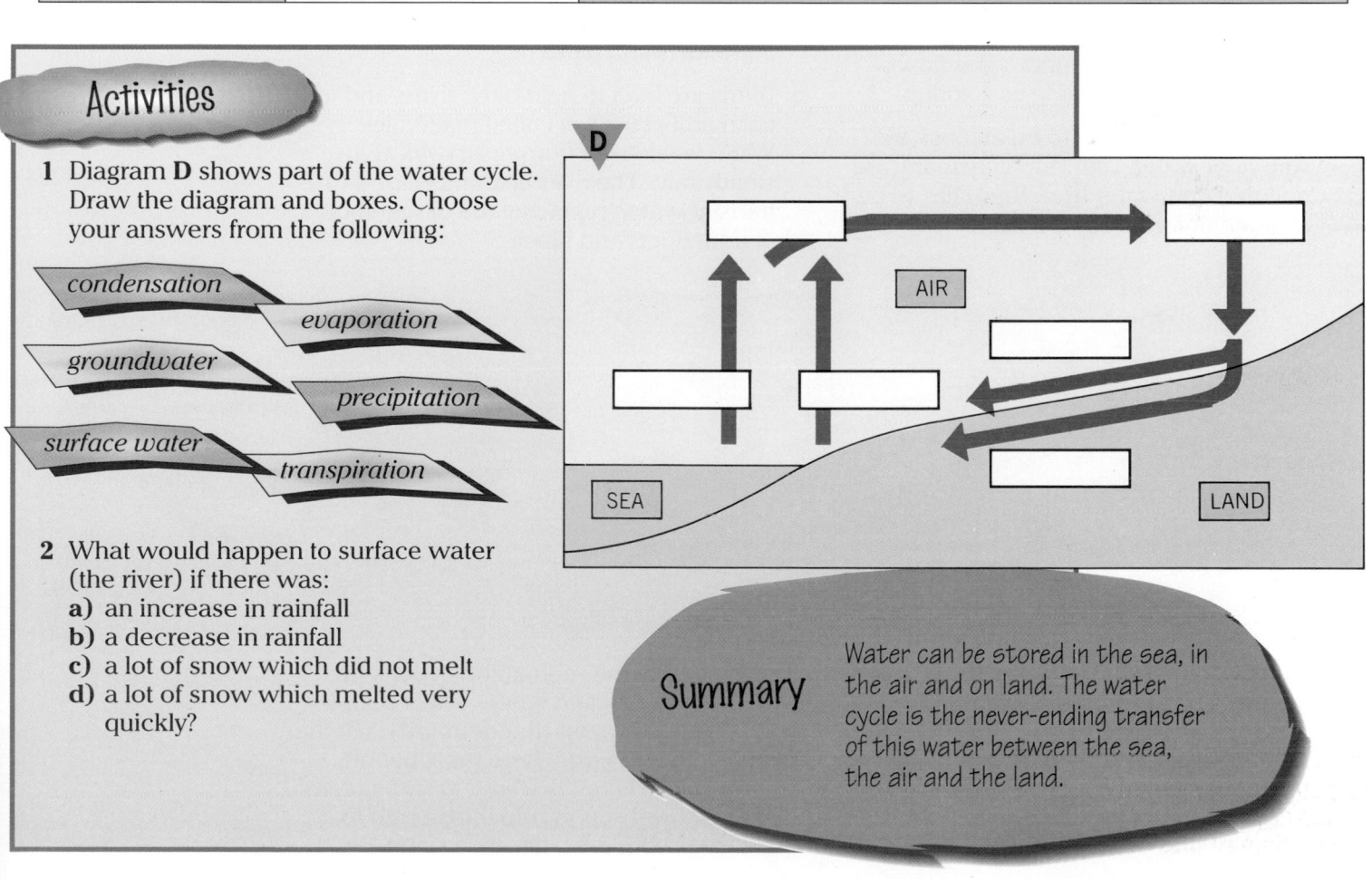

2 What would happen to surface water (the river) if there was:
   a) an increase in rainfall
   b) a decrease in rainfall
   c) a lot of snow which did not melt
   d) a lot of snow which melted very quickly?

Summary Water can be stored in the sea, in the air and on land. The water cycle is the never-ending transfer of this water between the sea, the air and the land.

How can supplies of fresh water be obtained?

What are the main sources of fresh water?

With over three-quarters of the earth covered in water there should be plenty for plants, animals and people. Unfortunately over 97 per cent of that water is in the seas and oceans (diagram **A**). As this is salt water it cannot be used by life on land. To make matters worse, three-quarters of the fresh water is held in storage as ice or snow (diagram **A**). This water can only become available if the world's glaciers and icecaps melt.

How do we get reliable supplies of fresh water in Britain?

Diagram **B** shows five main ways. These are listed below.

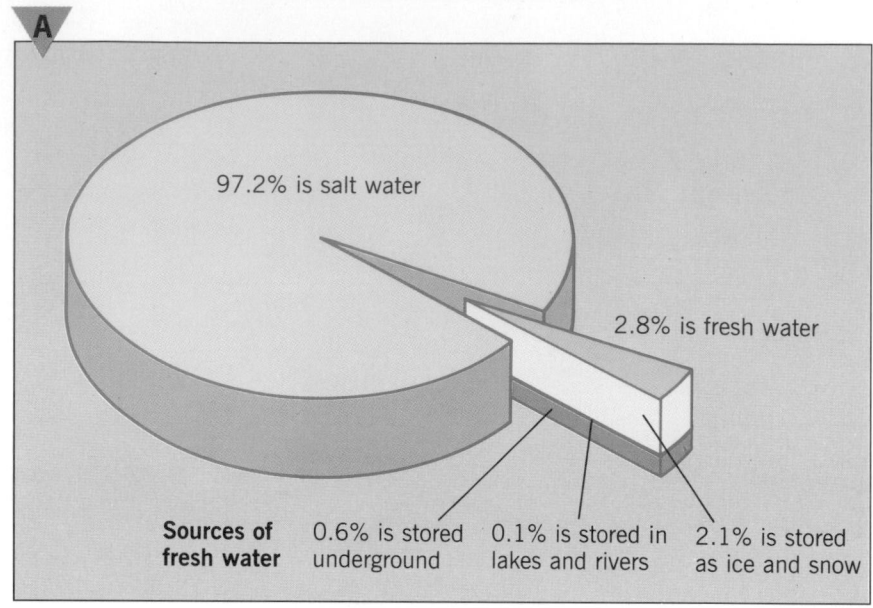

A

97.2% is salt water

2.8% is fresh water

Sources of fresh water   0.6% is stored underground   0.1% is stored in lakes and rivers   2.1% is stored as ice and snow

1 Most of the available fresh water is stored underground in rocks. It may be obtained by sinking wells and boreholes.

2 Sometimes underground water flows naturally out of a hillside as a spring.

3 Rivers would appear to be an obvious source of water. Unfortunately many are polluted and water from them has to be cleaned before it can be used.

4 Lakes form natural stores of water on the earth's surface. Water from them may be sent (transferred) to large cities by aqueducts and pipes.

5 Dams are built to hold back rivers and to form artificial lakes called reservoirs. Water is released from reservoirs at a steady rate. The river channel is used to transfer water, replacing the old method of aqueducts and pipes.

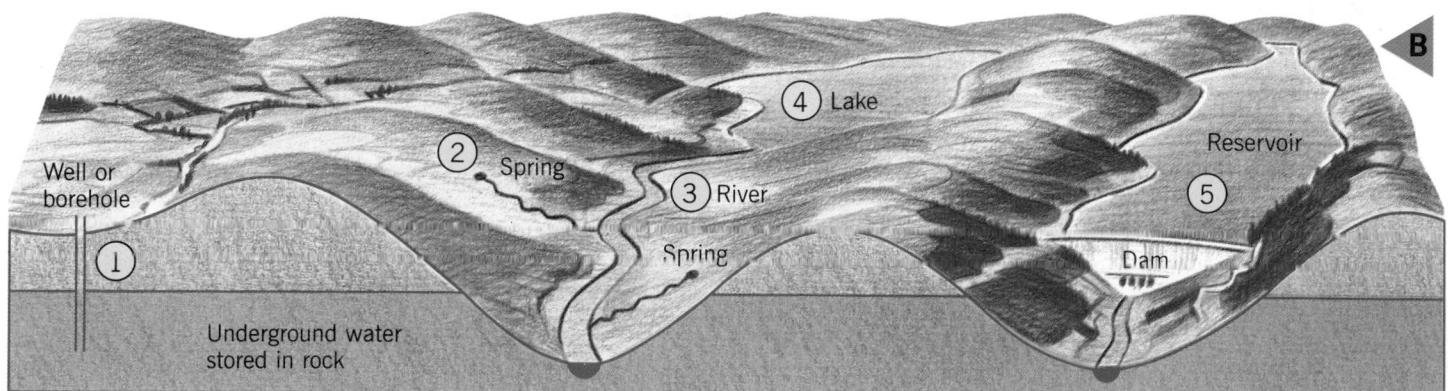

B

Well or borehole
①
Underground water stored in rock

② Spring
③ River
Spring
④ Lake

⑤ Reservoir
Dam

How is water transferred from one area to another?

Although in Britain we get far more rain than we need, it does not always fall where it is needed. Diagram **C** and the rainfall map on page 21 show that most rain (the **supply**) falls in the mountainous parts of north and west Britain where fewer people live. The biggest need (the **demand**) is in the flatter south and east where most people live. Therefore water is stored in those areas with the largest supply and transferred to those areas with the biggest demand.

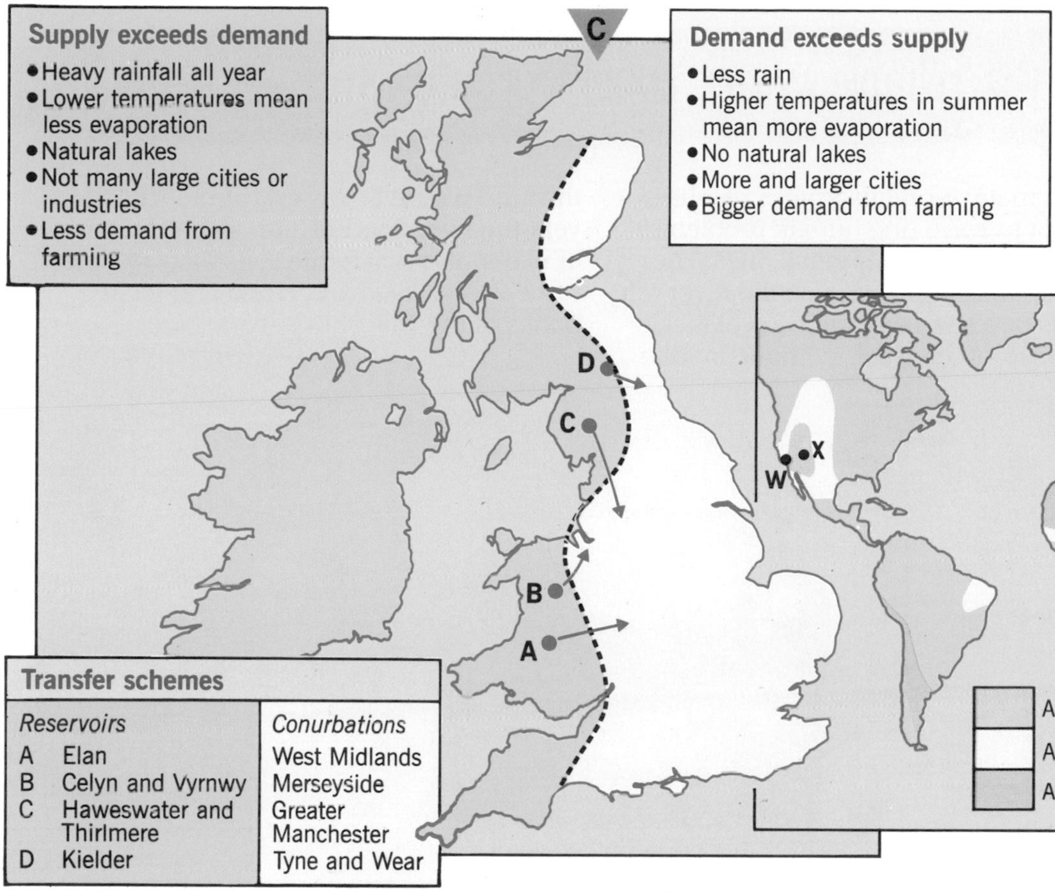

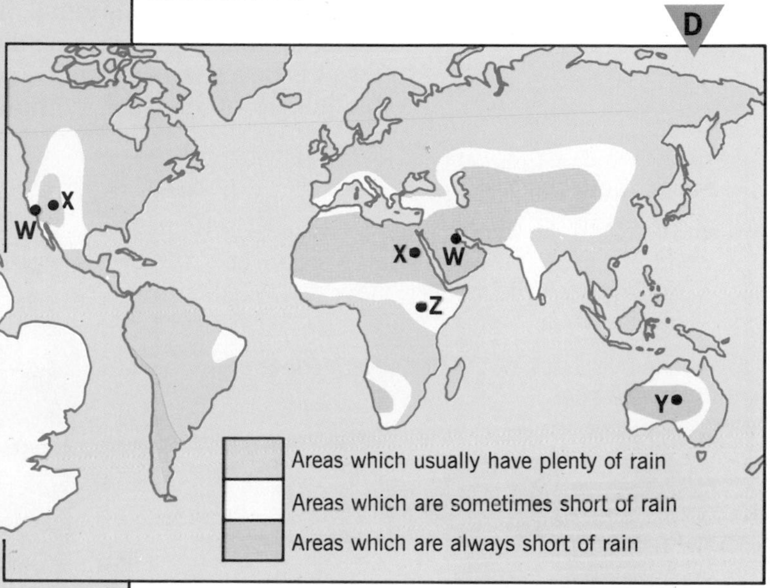

Supply exceeds demand
- Heavy rainfall all year
- Lower temperatures mean less evaporation
- Natural lakes
- Not many large cities or industries
- Less demand from farming

Demand exceeds supply
- Less rain
- Higher temperatures in summer mean more evaporation
- No natural lakes
- More and larger cities
- Bigger demand from farming

C

D

Transfer schemes

Reservoirs		Conurbations
A	Elan	West Midlands
B	Celyn and Vyrnwy	Merseyside
C	Haweswater and Thirlmere	Greater Manchester
D	Kielder	Tyne and Wear

Areas which usually have plenty of rain

Areas which are sometimes short of rain

Areas which are always short of rain

Diagram **D** shows other possible methods of getting supplies of fresh water. Areas **W** (Saudi Arabia and California) have enough money to turn salt water from the sea into fresh water (desalination). This is very costly. Areas **X** (Nile and Colorado Valleys) have large dams built on rivers flowing across deserts. Area **Y** (Central Australia) obtains water from deep underground (artesian wells). Area **Z** (Ethiopia and northern Kenya) relies on overseas aid to sink deep wells.

E

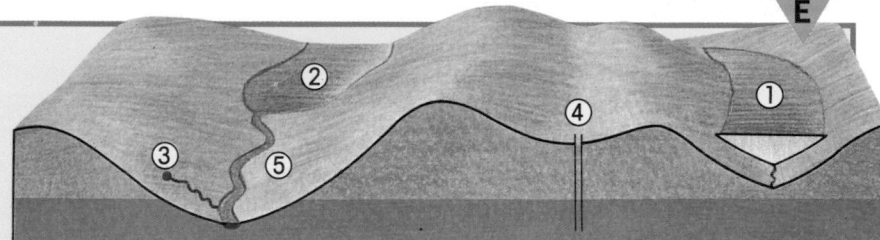

Activities

1 Draw a bar graph to show the sources of fresh water on earth.

2 Diagram **E** shows five possible ways of getting fresh water. These have been labelled ① to ⑤.
   a) Copy the diagram. Name the five ways of getting fresh water.
   b) Which **three** ways use water found naturally? Which **two** of these ways are most likely to provide clean water?
   c) By which **two** ways can water only be used with human assistance? Which of the two is cheaper?

3 a) Why is the supply of fresh water greater in Wales than the demand for fresh water?
   b) Describe two ways by which Wales transfers surplus water to England.

1 Why is the demand for water greater than the supply in south-east England?

2 Design a poster to show the people living in south-east England that they need to save water during dry summers. The poster should be colourful, interesting and eye-catching.

E X T R A S

Summary

There are limited sources of fresh water on earth. These sources are not always found where the water is needed. Several methods are used to try to provide a reliable supply of fresh water.

How can providing a reliable water supply create other problems?

There are many world examples of where an attempt to solve one human problem can create new environmental ones. The building of the Aswan Dam on the River Nile in Egypt is one such example. Egypt is said to be the 'gift of the Nile'. Without the Nile the land would be desert (photo **A**). Each year the river flooded and covered the land in water and rich fertile soil. Many people have always lived and worked along the banks of the Nile.

Facts about the Nile

- The Nile is the world's longest river. It flows 6,690 km (4,160 miles) from its source on the Equator to its mouth in the Mediterranean Sea.

- The river basin of the Nile covers one-tenth of all Africa.

- During its 1,520 km (950 mile) journey through Egypt it has no tributaries and hardly ever gets any rain.

A

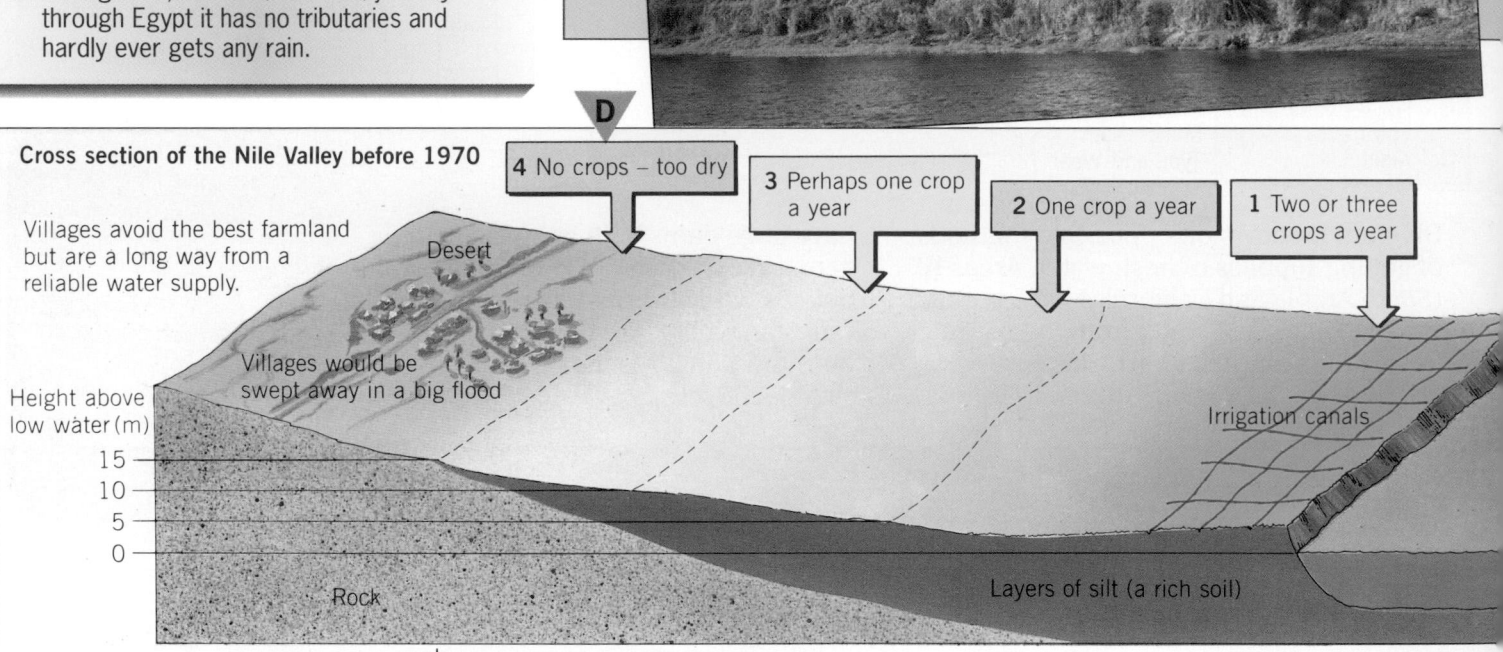

D

Cross section of the Nile Valley before 1970

4 No crops – too dry

3 Perhaps one crop a year

2 One crop a year

1 Two or three crops a year

Villages avoid the best farmland but are a long way from a reliable water supply.

Desert

Villages would be swept away in a big flood

Irrigation canals

Height above low water (m)

15
10
5
0

Rock

Layers of silt (a rich soil)

Area of fertile land often only one kilometre wide

Activities

1 Why is Egypt called 'the gift of the Nile'?

2 Before 1970 what were
   a) the advantages and
   b) the disadvantages
   of the River Nile to Egypt?

3 Diagram **E** shows the land farmed by four different farmers (**A, B, C, D**).

a) The following are four statements made by each farmer. Match the statements with the correct farmer.

- 'I get enough water all year. I do not have to worry about the flood.'

- 'The flood has not reached my fields. How will I feed my family?'

Only the land next to the Nile had a reliable, regular supply of water. Land further away from the river needed to be irrigated. **Irrigation** is the artificial watering of the land. Two old ways of watering the land are still in use today.

1   The shaduf (photo **B**) is a long pole. At one end is a bucket which is dipped into the river, and at the other end is a heavy weight. The weight makes it

easier to swing the full bucket round to the irrigation channel.

2   The saquia (photo **C**) is a wheel with small buckets fixed to it. The wheel is turned by animals and water is scooped up from the river in the buckets. As the wheel turns, the water is tipped into the irrigation channel.

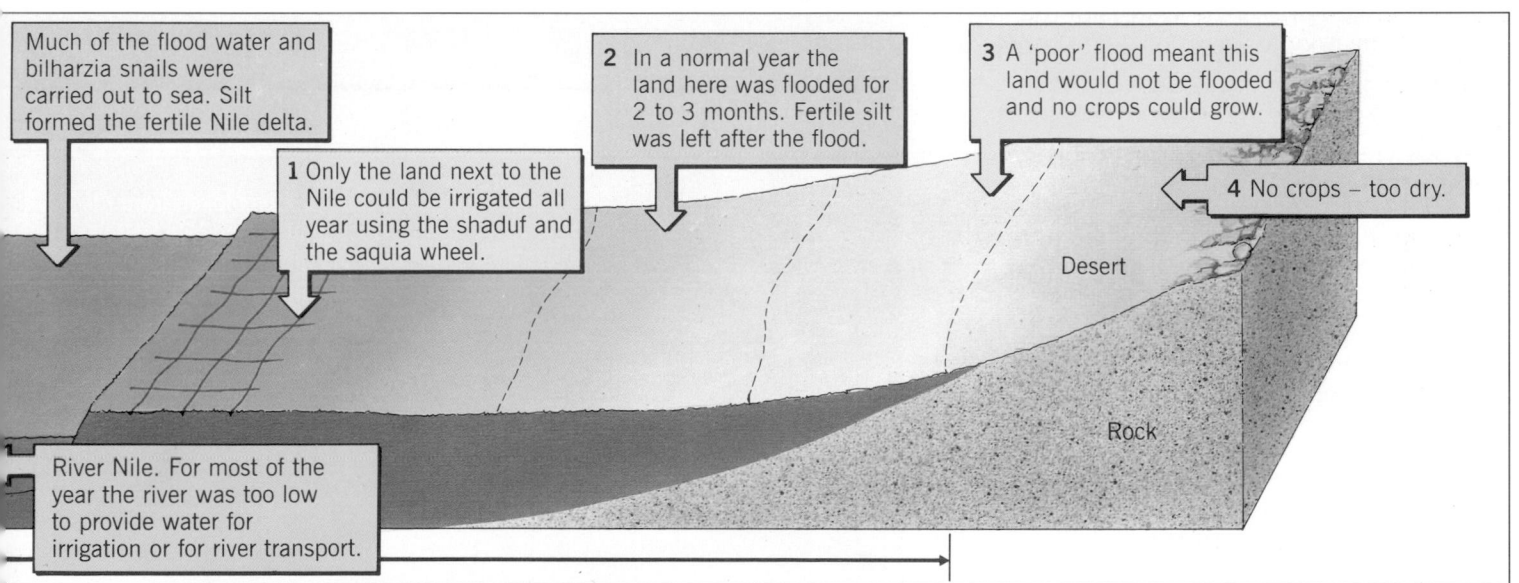

Much of the flood water and bilharzia snails were carried out to sea. Silt formed the fertile Nile delta.

1 Only the land next to the Nile could be irrigated all year using the shaduf and the saquia wheel.

2 In a normal year the land here was flooded for 2 to 3 months. Fertile silt was left after the flood.

3 A 'poor' flood meant this land would not be flooded and no crops could grow.

4 No crops – too dry.

Desert

Rock

River Nile. For most of the year the river was too low to provide water for irrigation or for river transport.

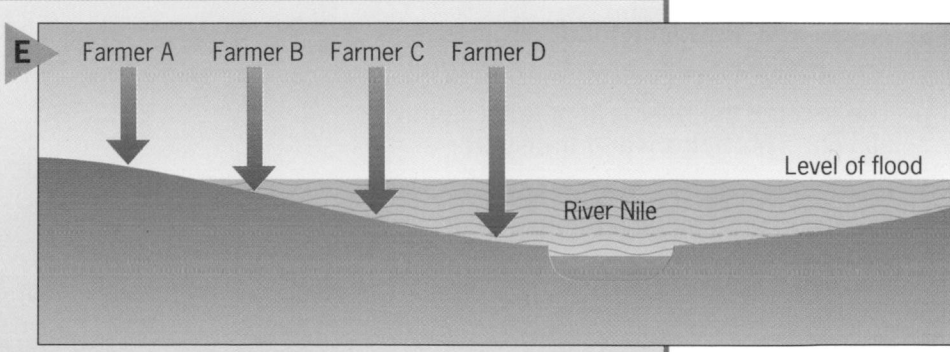

E   Farmer A   Farmer B   Farmer C   Farmer D

Level of flood

River Nile

- 'The flood only just reached my fields. I will be able to grow a few crops.'

- 'My fields have been flooded long enough to give me very good crops.'

b) What could be done to try to solve the problems?

How can providing a reliable water supply create other problems?

The Aswan Dam

For centuries the Egyptians had wanted to control the flow of the Nile. For two or three months each year it flooded the land. For much of the year it flowed at a low level. There were several ways in which the Nile could be controlled – the Egyptians decided to build a large dam at Aswan and to create a big lake behind it.

The dam is a multipurpose scheme. This means it was built for several different reasons. Two main reasons were to prevent serious flooding in the Nile Valley, and to provide water all year round for Egyptians and their crops and animals. The dam is 3 km long, took ten years to build and was opened in 1970 (photos **A** and **C**). Lake Nasser, which formed behind the dam, is 550 km in length. As the waters of the lake rose, many people were forced to move home.

What are the advantages of the Aswan Dam?

1 Water can be stored in the lake and is available for irrigation all year round.

2 More land can be irrigated.

3 With water always available, two or three crops can now be grown in a year.

4 The dam produces electricity. This provides power for villages, cities and industry as well as for new diesel pumps used for irrigation.

5 Villages along the Nile now have a reliable supply of water.

6 As the Nile no longer floods, villages near to its banks are safe from the flood risk.

7 The level of the river is kept fairly steady all year. This helps water transport.

8 Lake Nasser stocks fish, creating jobs for fishermen and helping to provide a better diet.

A

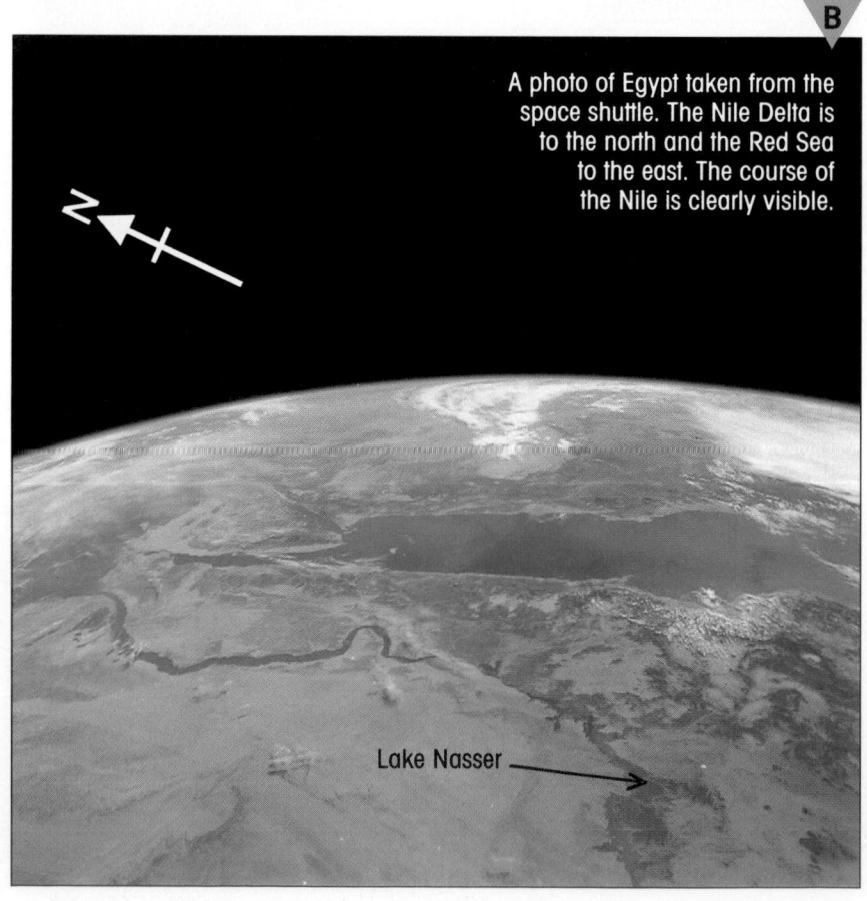

B

A photo of Egypt taken from the space shuttle. The Nile Delta is to the north and the Red Sea to the east. The course of the Nile is clearly visible.

Lake Nasser

What environmental problems has the Aswan Dam created?

1 As no more silt (soil) is deposited the land is becoming less fertile.

2 Fertiliser has to be added to the soil to keep it fertile. This costs the farmers money.

3 Fertiliser is polluting the Nile.

4 Without a supply of silt the delta, one of the most fertile places in the world, is getting smaller.

5 Lake Nasser is filling with silt.

6 As water snails are no longer swept out to sea, bilharzia, the disease they spread, is increasing. If the disease is not treated people can die from it.

7 Water from irrigation soon evaporates in the heat, leaving salt in which crops cannot grow.

8 As fewer nutrients reach the sea there is less food for fish and so there are fewer fish to be caught.

C

HIGH DAM AUTHORITY

LONGITUDINAL SECTION ALONG

MAX. HEIGHT OF THE DAM 111 m.
DAM LENGTH AT THE CREST 3830 m.
DAM WIDTH AT THE BASE 980 m.
DAM WIDTH AT THE TOP 40 m.
NO. OF THE MAIN TUNNELS 6
NO. OF TUNNEL BRANCHES 24
NO. OF TURBINES 12
MAX. POWER OF TURBINE 175000 kw.
MAX. DISCHARGE OF TURBINE 346 m³/sec
LENGTH OF STORAGE LAKE 500 km
RESERVOIR AREA 6000 km²
TOTAL CAPACITY OF THE RESERVOIR 162,000 million

Activities

1 Give **two** reasons why the Aswan Dam was built.

2 Imagine you are a conservation officer in Egypt. Write a letter to a friend in Britain explaining some of the environmental problems caused by the Aswan Dam.

3 Diagram **D** gives the views of eight people affected by the building of the Aswan Dam. Which **four** have benefited from the dam? Which **four** are now worse off?

E X T R A S

Try to find out how water is provided for irrigation in **either** the Colorado Valley, USA **or** the Indus Valley in Pakistan.

Find out how countries like Saudi Arabia obtain fresh water from desalination plants.

D

Since the dam was built my income has declined. We do not catch as many fish.

Mediterranean fisherman

Many more people now suffer from bilharzia than 20 years ago.

Old Egyptian doctor

The Lake seems to get shallower every year. That is very worrying.

Manager of the Aswan Dam

We have to produce a lot of fertiliser for the farmers. I employ many people.

Manager of a fertiliser factory

Tourists can now sail up and down the Nile all year.

Nile ferry boat owner

I can grow more crops now there is water all year around.

Fellah or peasant farmer

I can fish in the lake. I earn money and eat better.

Lake Nasser fisherman

I have to buy fertiliser to keep any crop yield lush. Also I have to buy diesel to power my water pump.

Fellah or peasant farmer

Summary

Attempts to improve and manage environments can sometimes cause new and unexpected problems.

What are settlements and why do they grow?

A **settlement** is a **place** where people live. It can be as small as a village or as large as a city. Many settlements in Britain began, or **originated**, a long time ago – some even in Roman times.

For a settlement to grow there had to be a special reason why it should be built in the first place. This is called a **function**. The four photos on these two places show four different functions of settlements in Britain.

> The market is in a square. Around the square are banks, pubs, shops and offices used by farmers and other people when they visit the market.

Photo **A** is of a **market** town. Market towns were needed when most people in Britain were farmers. They were a place where farmers could buy seed, tools and animals and sell their grown crops and animals. The function of market towns was buying and selling.

A

B

Photo **B** is of an **industrial** town. Industrial towns grew up much later than market towns. The function of an industrial town was to make (manufacture) things in factories. Some of the early factories used goods sold by farmers, such as wool, to make things. Other factories made things needed by farmers, such as machines.

> The tall chimneys and large buildings belong to factories. Factories are found in industrial (manufacturing) towns.

The towns in photos **C** and **D** both grew up to help and serve people living in market and industrial towns.

Photo **C** shows a **port**. It brings in goods from overseas countries which are needed on local farms and in factories. Later the port will send products from these farms and factories back overseas. Goods or products that are brought into a country are called **imports**. Goods that are sent overseas are called **exports**.

Photo **D** shows a **holiday resort**. People from nearby settlements come here to relax and enjoy themselves.

Some settlements still have their original function but others have changed. Dover had a castle to try to stop people invading Britain. Now it is a port to help people come into Britain. Larger settlements, like London, have had more than one function, e.g. market, port, industry and now as a centre for holidays and business.

> A harbour is a sheltered place for ships. A port is where the harbour is surrounded by docks, warehouses, roads and railways.

Activities

1 Complete the following definitions by matching the beginnings on the left with the correct ending from the list on the right.

A settlement	is where people buy and sell things
A function	is where goods are brought into and sent out of a country
A market town	is a place where people live
An industrial town	is where people go on holiday to relax
A port	is where people make things
A resort	is the reason why a town was first built

> People go to holiday resorts like this one to swim in the sea and relax on the beach. They stay in hotels and need things to do (entertainment).

2 a) What was the original function of your local town or city?

b) What are its functions today?

Summary

For a settlement to grow up (originate) in the first place, it had to have a special use (function). Different settlements grew up with different functions.

How were the sites for early settlements chosen?

When we use the word **site** we mean the actual place where a village or town grew up. A site was chosen if it had one or more natural advantages. Diagram **A** shows eight natural advantages. The more natural advantages a place had the more likely it was to grow in size.

A

Protection. Good views from a hilltop give you warning if you are about to be attacked.

Plenty of water. Needed for drinking, cooking and washing. Water might come from a river, spring or well.

Building materials. Needed wood or stone. Useful to be near a wood or a rocky hillside.

Supply of wood. Needed for fires for warmth and to cook on.

Not too much water. Sites must not flood or be marshy.

Rivers. Easy to cross either on foot at a ford or by a bridge.

Shelter. A south facing slope will have more sun and will be protected from the cold north wind.

Flat land. Easier to build on, for growing crops and travelling to other towns.

'Is this a good place to build a village?'

'Is this a good place to build a town?'

Activities

1 Write down the meaning of the word 'site'.

2 Landsketch **B** shows an area in Ancient Britain. On it, labelled **A, B, C, D** and **E**, are five possible sites for a village.
   a) Suggest at least **one** natural advantage of each site.

   b) Suggest at least **one** natural disadvantage of each site.
   c) Which site would you choose? Give **three** reasons for your choice.

3 Try to find out what were the natural advantages of the site of your own town or village.

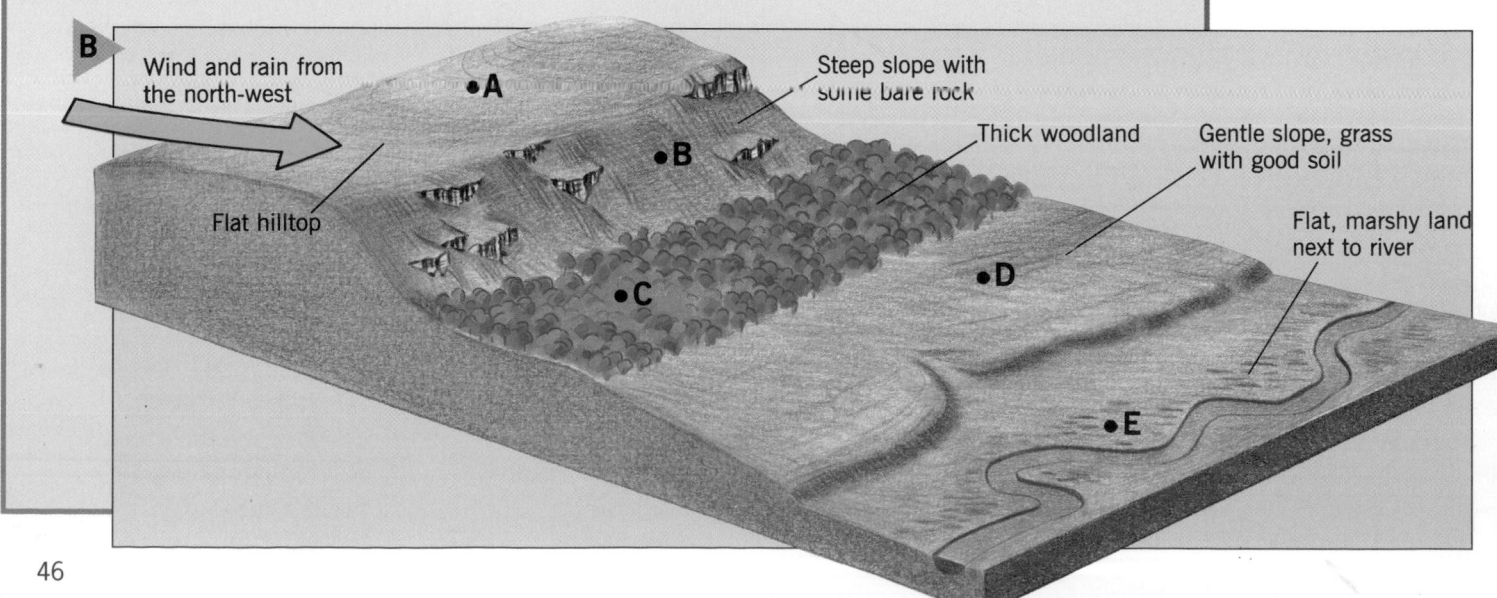

B

Wind and rain from the north-west

Steep slope with some bare rock

Thick woodland

Gentle slope, grass with good soil

Flat hilltop

Flat, marshy land next to river

•A

•B

•C

•D

•E

What do we mean by settlement patterns?

By a **settlement pattern** we mean the shape of the settlement. The shape of early villages and towns was usually influenced by the surrounding area.

Photo **C** shows farms and buildings which are spread out. This is a **dispersed** pattern, often found in upland areas of Britain. People who live here need a lot of land to earn a living.

Photo **D** shows a village where all the buildings are grouped together. This is a **nucleated** settlement. People often used to group together for protection. This pattern is common in flatter, lowland parts of Britain.

Photo **E** is a **linear** settlement. Because the hillsides are steep, houses are built in a line along the gentler slopes of the valley.

C

E

Activities

1 Make a simple copy of map **F**. Put each of these three labels – *dispersed, nucleated, linear* – next to the settlement pattern it describes.

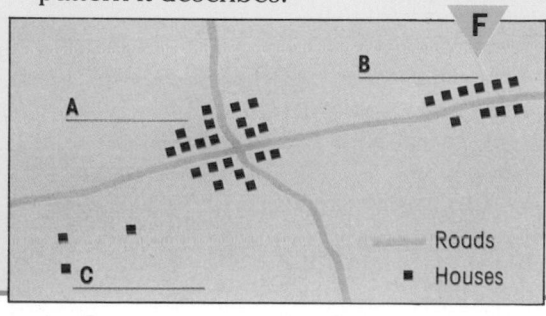

F

A

B

C

Roads
■ Houses

2 Look at photos **C, D** and **E**. Write **two** lines about each one to describe the **shape** of the settlement in each of the photos.

E X T R A

London became a big city because its site had many natural advantages. Try to find out what these advantages were.

Summary

Early sites for settlements were chosen because of natural advantages such as a good water supply, dry land, defence, shelter, farmland and building materials. The shape of early settlements was often decided by the surrounding area (environment).

What are the benefits and problems of settlement growth?

In Britain most people are urban dwellers living in towns and cities. These settlements grew very quickly in the last (nineteenth) century. This was when large numbers of people moved there to work. Today Britain's cities are no longer growing in size. However, in many overseas countries people are still moving to cities in large numbers. This is because they believe that many **benefits** come from living and working in cities. Moving there will improve their **quality of life**.

Drawing **A** shows some of the benefits which people hope to find in large towns and cities.

- There are more houses and flats to buy or to rent.
- There are more jobs which are better paid.
- Food supplies are more reliable, with many shops giving a greater choice.
- It takes less time and money to travel to work and to shops.
- There are more and better services, such as schools and hospitals.
- Urban areas have 'bright light' attractions, such as discos, concerts and sporting activities.

For people already living in cities, life is often less attractive. Living and working in cities creates many **problems**. Drawing **B** shows some of the problems found in British cities.

B

Old housing

Disused factories

SITE TO LET

Pollution

Traffic congestion, pollution and noise

Crime and vandalism

JOB CENTRE VACANCIES

High prices

Litter and rubbish dumping

Unemployment

Homelessness

- Traffic causes congestion, accidents, noise and air pollution.
- Old roads are too narrow for lorries and buses; new roads take up much land.
- Old houses and factories need urgent, expensive repairs or they are left empty.

- There is waste land where houses and factories have been pulled down.
- Crime, vandalism and litter make cities dangerous and unpleasant.
- Land is very expensive to buy, in and near the city centre.

Activities

1 a) Make a copy of the table below. List the **three** things which you think are best about living in cities, and the **three** things you think are the worst.

Cities		
Good news	Bad news	

b) Do you think there is more good news or bad news?

2 If you had to move from where you live, would it be to a bigger or a smaller settlement? Give reasons for your answer.

E X T R A S

1 Try to find out what has been done in your local town or city to try to reduce
  a) traffic problems
  b) pollution
  c) crime, vandalism and litter.

2 Suggest other ways in which these three problems may be overcome.

Summary

Many people move to large cities because they see benefits in living and working there. However, as these settlements become older and bigger, many problems are created.

How do settlements change with time?

No town or village remains the same for ever. Over a period of time the following may all change:

1 the **shape** of a settlement
2 the **function** of a settlement
3 the **land use** of a settlement
4 the **number** and **type** of people living in the settlement.

Villages are small in size so it is often easier to see these changes in them than it is to see changes in a large town or city.

What was a typical village like in the 1890s? Although no two villages are the same, most have several things in common. Diagram **A** shows a typical village about one hundred years ago. In the centre there was

often a village green. Buildings were grouped closely together (nucleated) around this green forming a **core**. Roads were usually narrow lanes. Most houses were small terraced cottages. The people who lived in them would probably have been born in the village. Most would have worked on local farms. As houses and farms were built at different times they would have different styles and building materials.

How has the village changed by the 1990s? Diagram **B** shows the same village today. The village has grown larger and has many new buildings. It has become **suburbanised**. This means it has become similar to the outskirts of larger towns.

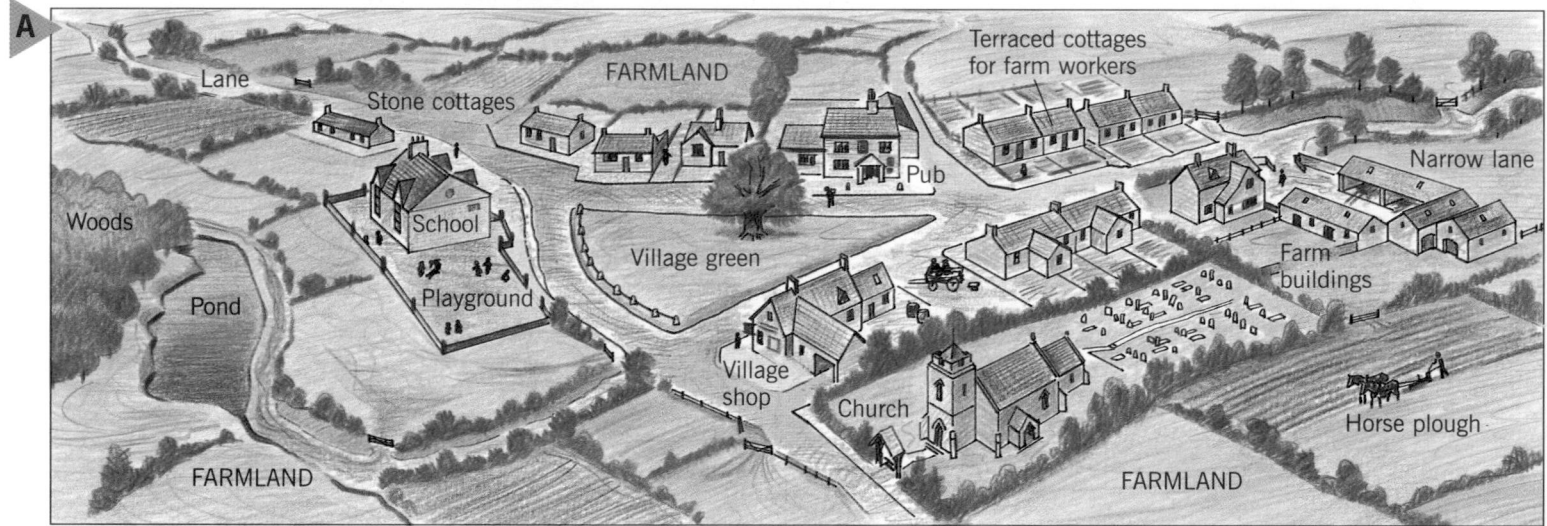

A
Lane · Stone cottages · FARMLAND · Terraced cottages for farm workers · Woods · School · Pub · Narrow lane · Village green · Pond · Playground · Farm buildings · Village shop · Church · Horse plough · FARMLAND · FARMLAND

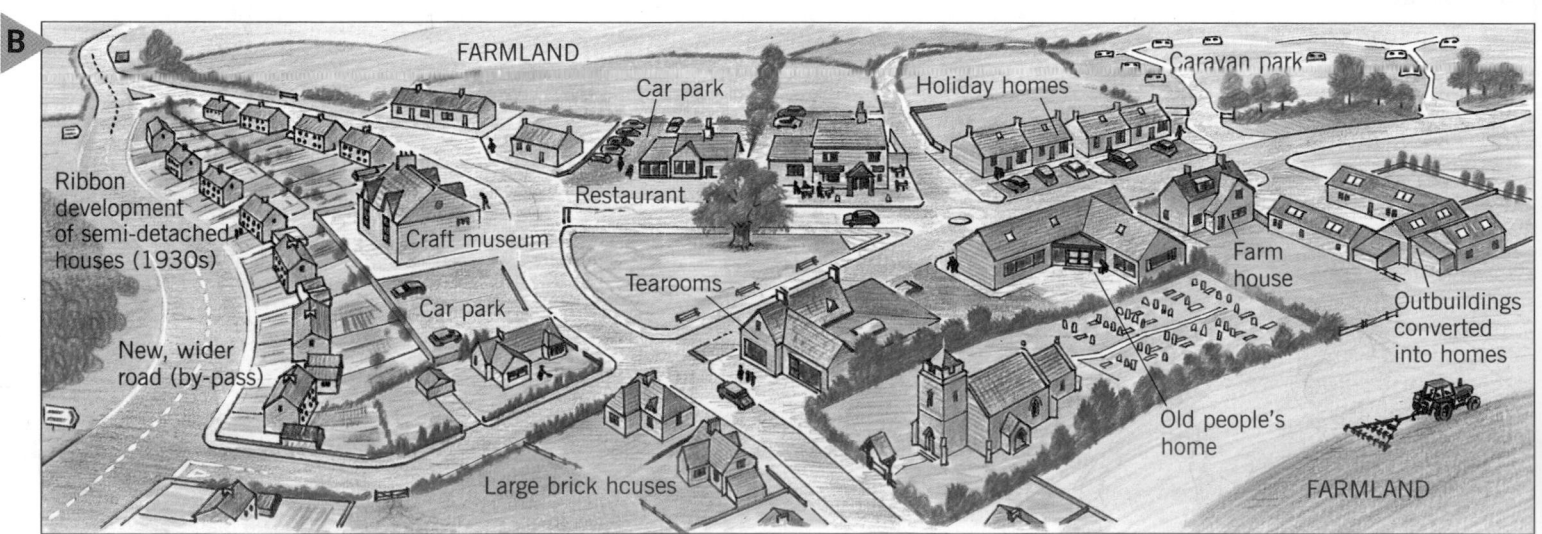

B
FARMLAND · Car park · Holiday homes · Caravan park · Ribbon development of semi-detached houses (1930s) · Restaurant · Craft museum · Tearooms · Farm house · Car park · Outbuildings converted into homes · New, wider road (by-pass) · Old people's home · Large brick houses · FARMLAND

Activities

1 Write down the meaning of
   a) shape
   b) function
   c) land use
   when talking about a settlement.

2 **Spot the differences!** List at least **ten** differences between the village in the 1890s and the village in the 1990s.

3 The changes to the village will have affected different groups of people in different ways. Look at the pictures of some of these groups of people shown below. Match up the pictures with the statements below numbered **1** to **8**.

   For example:
   Young married couple = statement **2**

How groups may be affected

1 I might have to close as most people have cars to shop in town.

2 We are just married and cannot afford an expensive house.

3 The extra noise frightens away the wildlife.

4 To get customers I have to provide food for townspeople. Villagers only want a drink.

5 I made money by selling my land so that houses could be built. Now people walk on the land I still own.

6 With all the new houses I have plenty of work to do.

7 I have to travel 10 km to school. At night there is nothing to do.

8 I came here for peace and quiet. Now I cannot drive into town and there are no buses.

Farmer

Shopkeeper

Bird-watcher

Teenager

Young married couple

Restaurant owner

Elderly person

Builder

E X T R A S

1 Activity **2** asked you to find the differences in the village between the 1890s and the 1990s. Why do you think changes have been made in:
   a) the number and type of houses
   b) the use of buildings around the green
   c) the use of the land around the village
   d) the roads?

2 It has been suggested that the woods should be cleared so that an estate of expensive houses can be built.
   a) Which groups of people will like this change?
   b) Which groups of people will be against this change?
   Suggest reasons for your answers.

Summary

Settlements change over a period of time. These changes can affect:

- the size and shape of the settlement
- the environment, e.g. new roads, larger villages
- the lives of people living in the settlement.

Why are there different land use patterns in towns?

We have seen (page 44) that when each town first began to grow it had one particular use or function. Towns and cities of today often have several different functions. The main functions are **commerce** (shops and offices), **industry** (factories), **residential** (flats and houses) and **open space** (parks). As each function tends to be found in a particular part of a town, then a pattern of land use develops. Although no two towns will have exactly the same pattern of land use, most have similar patterns. When a very simple map is drawn to show these similarities in land use it is called an **urban model**. A model is when a real situation is made simple so that it is easier to understand.

The model in diagram **A** shows a line (**transect**) from a city centre to the city boundary. It shows four main types of land use. It is suggested that this pattern developed because:

1 The oldest part of a town was in the middle. As the town grew, larger new buildings were built on its edges.
2 Land in the city centre is expensive to buy. This is because many different land users would like this site and so compete for it. Usually the price of land falls towards the edges of a town.

As a result, differences in land use can be shown by a series of **circles** drawn around the city centre (diagram **B**).

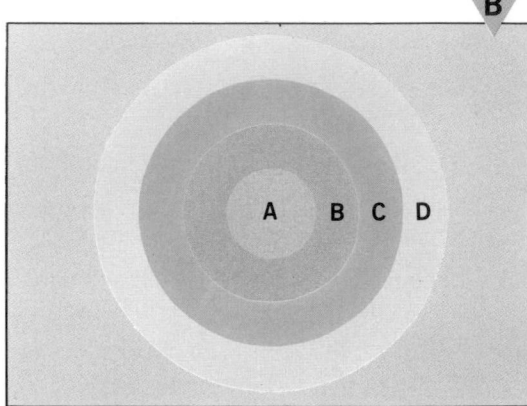

B

A B C D

A

Zone A

The centre of the town was the first place to be built. It is full of shops, offices, banks and restaurants. There are very few houses here.

It is now called the central business district (**CBD** for short). Most cities have been modernised.

Zone B

This zone used to be full of large factories and rows of terraced housing built in the last century. Houses were small because land was expensive.

This zone is called the **inner city**. Today many of the big factories have closed and the oldest houses have been modernised or replaced.

Activities

1 Copy out the following sentences using the correct word from each pair in brackets.
- The centre of a town is called the (ABC/CBD).
- It has many (large/small) shops and tall blocks of (flats/offices).
- There are (a lot of/few) houses and (much/little) open space.

E X T R A

2 a) Copy diagram **B** (page 52). Colour in the four areas. Give the diagram a title.
b) Add to the drawing the name of each area – *CBD, inner city, inner suburbs* and *outer suburbs*.
c) Name **one** part (district) of your local town that fits each area.

Using your local newspaper, try to find adverts of houses for sale in **Zones B, C** and **D**. How does this compare with diagram **A** and activity **3**?

3 a) Make a larger, simple copy of diagram **C** which shows differences in houses in three different parts of a town.
b) **Zone C** has been done for you. Now complete **Zones B** and **D** using the correct words from the following list.

- detached
- old
- gardens
- garages
- large
- terraced
- new
- no gardens
- no garages
- small

Summary

Land in a town can be used in different ways. Land use depends upon the main function of that part of a town. The main function, or land use, of an area may result from its age, the cost of land and the lines of communication.

C

Zone B

Zone C
Semi-detached | Garage
Garden | Inter-war, 1930s | Medium-sized

Zone D

Zone C

This zone is nearly all houses built in the 1920s and 1930s.

This zone is called the **inner suburbs**.

Zone D

This zone has many large, modern houses as well as some council estates. Recently small, modern industries and large shops have been built here. There are often areas of open space.

Countryside

Houses and shops and new industry are here because the land is cheaper. This is the **outer suburbs**.

Why does land use in towns change?

Land use in towns changes over time. City centres are modernised to attract more people, while open space on the outskirts is turned into housing estates and large shopping centres.

Inner city areas were often built over one hundred years ago. Naturally they have aged in that time. Houses became too old and cramped to live in and factories closed down. The inner cities had to change. Photos **A** and **B** show an inner city area in London in the early part of this century.

A

London's docks in 1926. London used to be the world's biggest port. In 1965 it still employed 28,000 dockers. There was plenty of work even if it was hard, dirty and poorly paid. Another 90,000 people worked in repairing ships, in transport and in factories using goods unloaded in the port.

B Houses were small and packed closely together. They did not have indoor toilets, hot water or bathrooms. Yet they were cheap enough for poorly paid workers to afford and created a strong 'Eastenders' community spirit.

C London's Docklands

In 1981 the London Dockland Development Corporation (LDDC) was set up. It began by clearing the old docks and houses. Old warehouses were turned into expensive flats. Old industries were replaced by those using high technology, such as newspapers, and by the office blocks of financial firms. The city airport and Docklands Light Railway were built. The environment is being improved and the use of the land is changing. Photo **C** shows part of this area in 1995.

How does this affect people?

Between 1967 and 1981 all of London's docks closed. Goods arriving in the port now came in big boxes called **containers**. As they were loaded and unloaded by cranes the dockers were not needed. The new container ships were too big to sail up the Thames to London. As the docks became derelict many dockers, factory workers and their families moved away to find work and better quality housing.

Diagram **D** shows how the recent changes in this area have affected different groups of people. Some groups have lived here all their lives, other groups have only just moved in.

D

Losers

Winners

Elderly people

Shopping is expensive. Money is spent on houses and offices, not on hospitals and old people.

The LDDC

We have changed the face of London. We have created 20,000 new homes and 10,000 new jobs. The environment is becoming cleaner.

Local shopkeepers

All these newcomers mean more trade – especially as they are wealthy with money to spend.

Young married couples

We will have to move as we cannot afford to buy a new flat. A cheap flat is over £100,000.

Former dockers

The new jobs are no use to us. We have not got the right skills. We will have to move away.

Social workers

The community atmosphere has gone. The 'yuppies' who buy the luxury flats do not mix with local people.

Financial company

We moved here because of cheap land. It only takes ten minutes to travel into central London. There is high quality housing.

School leavers

We are being trained to use computers. We should be able to get a job locally and so we can stay in the area.

Activities

1 Table **E** below shows changes in jobs in the London Docklands between 1978 and 1990. Plot this information as a bar chart. 1978 has been done for you on diagram **F**.

E

	1978	1981	1990
Manufacturing	43%	41%	21%
Services	51%	52%	73%
Building	6%	7%	6%

F

Employment changes 1978–1990

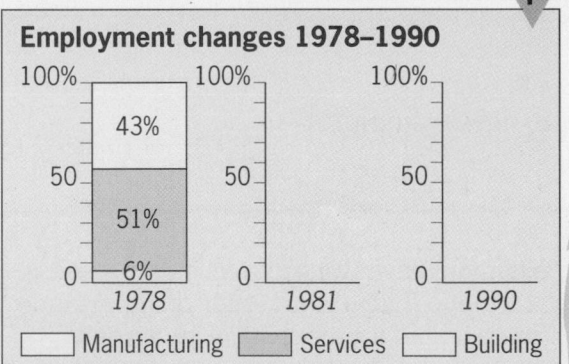

1978: 43%, 51%, 6%

☐ Manufacturing ☐ Services ☐ Building

2 Divide your class into eight groups. Each group represents one of the groups named in diagram **D**.
   a) Decide if your group is a winner or a loser.
   b) Decide why your group is a winner or a loser.
   c) Choose one person to speak for your group.
   d) If your group is a **winner** say which changes you think have improved the area.
   If your group is a **loser** say what changes you would like to see take place.

Summary

As time passes, the functions and land uses of different parts of a town will change. These changes affect different groups of people in different ways.

What is a settlement hierarchy?

Activities

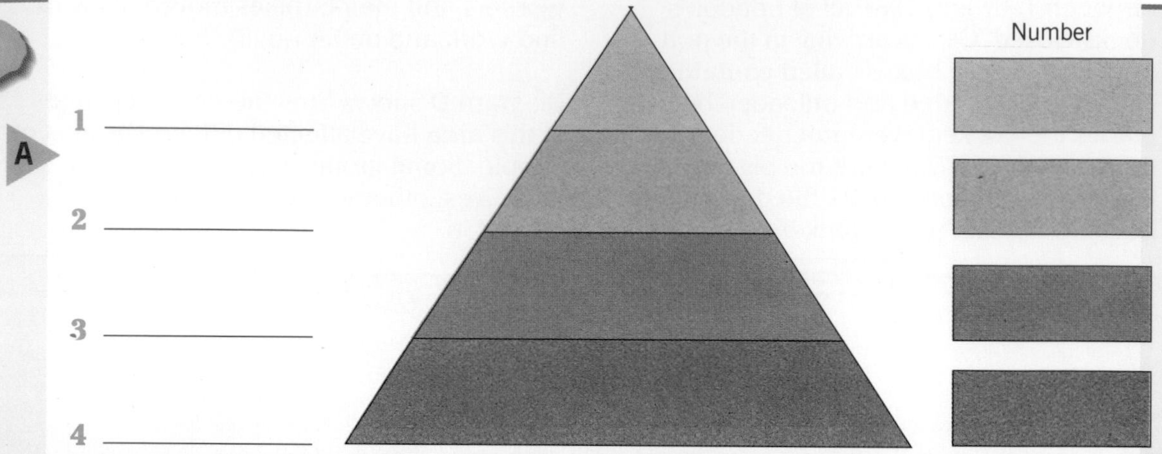

A
1 _____

2 _____

3 _____

4 _____

Number

1 The school hierarchy

a) Copy the school hierarchy **A**.

b) In a school, the headteacher is very important because he or she makes decisions which affect everyone else. Put the following people in order of importance on the lines marked **1, 2, 3** and **4** above. The most important one goes first.

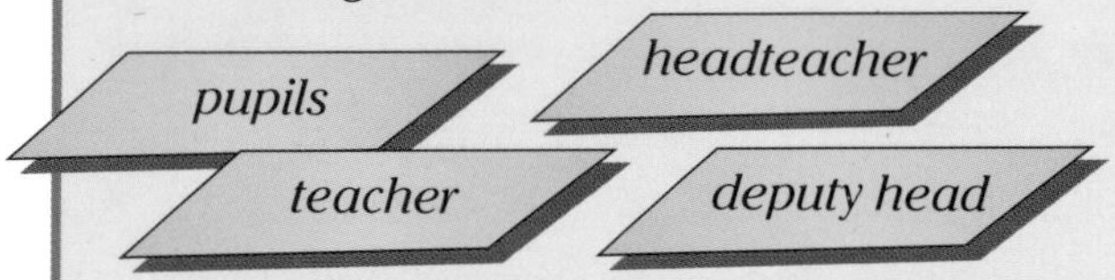

pupils

headteacher

teacher

deputy head

c) In the boxes next to the pyramid add the numbers of pupils, headteachers, teachers and deputy heads in your school.

d) What is the link between the importance and size of each group?

2 a) Copy the hierarchy **B** below. Give it a title.

b) Put the following settlements in order of their size and importance on the lines marked **1, 2, 3** and **4** below. Put the largest and most important first.

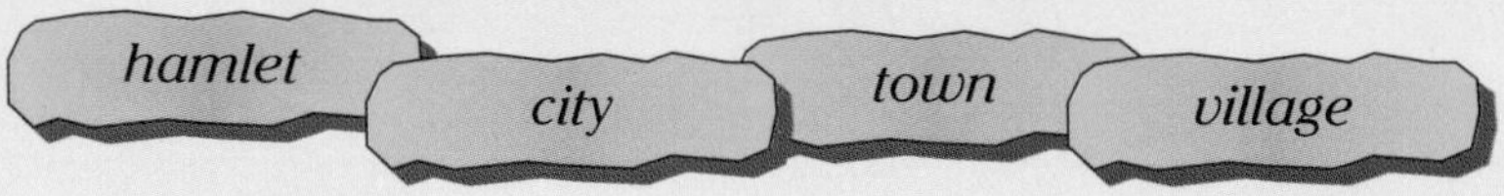

hamlet   city   town   village

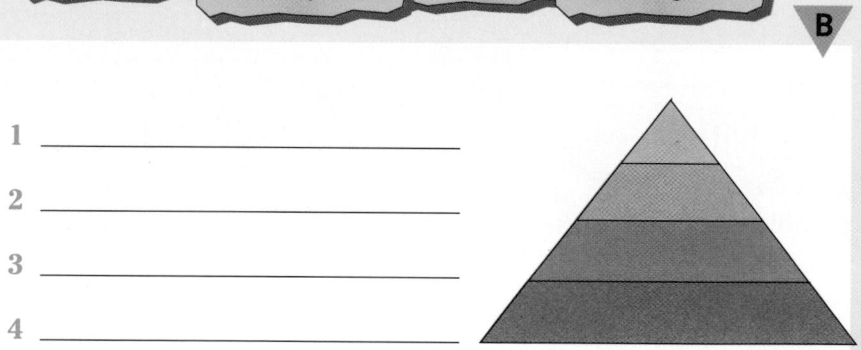

B

1 _____

2 _____

3 _____

4 _____

What you have done in activities **1** and **2** is to arrange things in an order of importance. This is called a **hierarchy**. A settlement hierarchy is when places are put in order.

It is possible to use three different methods to get a settlement hierarchy.

The three methods can be tested by making a simple statement about each one. These three statements are given in the following activities section.

1 Count the number of each type of settlement in an area, and look at their distance from each other.

2 Work out the size of each settlement. This could either be the size of the area (land) it covers or the size of its population (the number of people living in it).

3 Find out the range and number of functions and/or services it provides. A service is something which helps people, e.g. health centre, buses.

Activities

1 **The larger the settlement the further it is away from another large settlement.** Look at map **C** and write down the average (**mean**) distance between the
- villages
- towns
- cities on the map.

2 **The larger the settlement the fewer there are of them.**
  a) Look at map **C** and count the number of
  - villages
  - towns
  - cities on the map.

  b) Look at table **D**. Column **1** names five types of settlement. Column **2** suggests the minimum number of people living in each settlement. Copy out the table, matching up the two columns.

3 **The larger the settlement the more services it will have.**
  Table **E** shows a settlement hierarchy based on services.
  a) Use the Ordnance Survey (OS) map and its symbols on pages 108 to complete table **F** below.
  b) Draw the correct Ordnance Survey symbol in the space below each column heading.
  c) When you have completed the table, put the five places in order of importance. The one with the most services goes first.

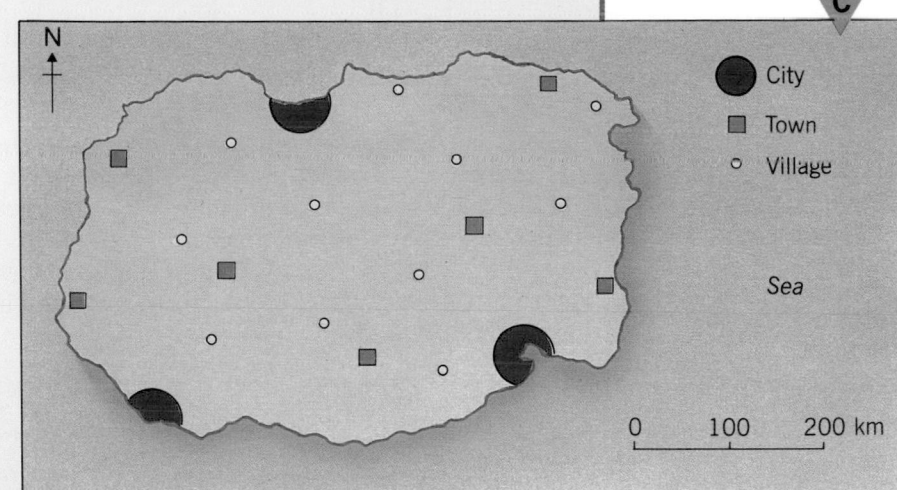

N

| | |
| City |
| Town |
| Village |

Sea

| 0 | 100 | 200 km |

D

Column 1	Column 2
City	200
Town	5
Village	100,000
Hamlet	10,000
Farm	25

E

Settlement	Services
Hamlet	Perhaps none
Village	Church, post office, public house, shop for daily goods, small junior school
Town	Several shops, churches and senior school, bus station, supermarket, doctor, dentist, banks, small hospital and football team
City	Large railway station, large shopping complex, cathedral, opticians and jewellers, large hospital and football team, museum

F

Settlement	Post offices	Churches	Main roads	Telephones	Inns, public houses	Railway/ bus station	TOTAL
Foxton							
Central Cambridge							
Haslingfield							
Grantchester							
Harston							

Summary

Settlements found in any given area will vary in size and function. These settlements can be arranged in order of importance to give a hierarchy.

Is there a shopping hierarchy?

Types of shopping areas can also be organised in a hierarchy. At the base of the pyramid are shopping centres which sell **low order goods**. These centres are small. They tend to sell **convenience goods** such as food and newspapers, which may be needed every day.

At the top of the pyramid are centres selling **high order goods**. These centres are large. They may sell either **specialist** and **comparison goods** like furniture which are not needed very often, or they sell in bulk.

Map **A** shows the shopping pattern for a typical British town or city. Notice the location of the four main types of shopping centre.

○ Corner shops

These are found in old inner city areas and date from the last century. They sell low order goods to people living in nearby streets. As the shops are small, they can only stock a small range of goods. These are often sold in small amounts but at a high price.

○ Shopping streets

There are two types. The older type lie alongside main roads near the city centre. Shops are usually low order or are large discount warehouses. The newer type are located in the suburbs. A row of low order shops and a few specialist shops serve a local housing estate. Shoppers may visit several times each week.

Motorway

Minor roads

City boundary

Major roads

■ Shopping malls

The city centre has traditionally had the largest shops selling high order goods. Shoppers come from all parts of the town, perhaps weekly, to buy goods in bulk from a supermarket or to compare the prices and quality of specialist goods. Many city centres now have undercover walkways, protected from traffic and the weather.

■ Out-of-town shopping centres

These are modern centres built on the edges of cities where land is vacant and cheaper. This allows space for hypermarkets and their large car parks. People can buy in bulk, perhaps two or three times a month. All their needs are under one roof.

Activities

1 Use the two word searches on the right to complete the table below. The words read across and down. There are ten words in each word search.

Some features, goods and services at shopping centres	
Low order centres	High order centres

2 a) Write one sentence to describe what is meant by a low order centre.

 b) Write one sentence to describe what is meant by a high order centre.

3 Copy out diagram **F**. Label it, 'An urban shopping hierarchy'. Put the terms below into the correct places:
 ● **Column 1** – middle order centre, low order centre, high order centre.
 ● **Column 2** – photo **B**, photo **C**, photo **D**.
 ● **Column 3** – the name of a shopping centre in your home area for each level in the hierarchy.

Low order centres

```
S O R H S B M I L K Z
M T S E P R V O N F R
Q C O R N E R S H O P
I L U P T A O W N O L
L U P Z R D B E C D O
N E W S P A P E R S C
D F G T Q I J T N K A
P O T A T O E S S O L
```

High order centres

```
S S P E C I A L I S T
H L Z D B Y W X V M C
O A Q R A C B D A L H
E F U R N I T U R E O
S E P O K H G N I K I
I N S U R A N C E F C
D C I T Y C E N T R E
K O B I G O E B Y A T
```

F

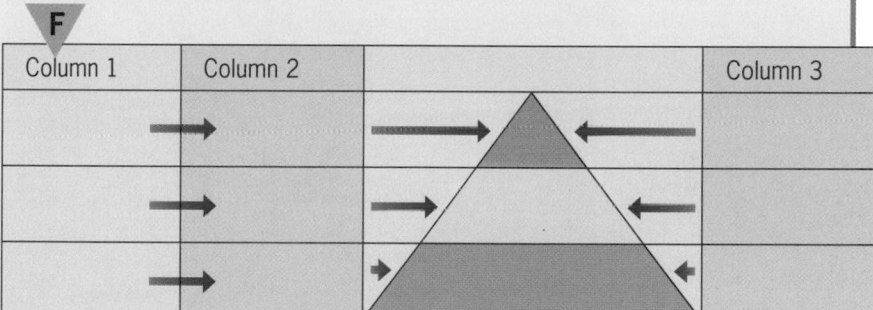

Column 1	Column 2		Column 3

E X T R A

You may be close enough to a shopping centre to visit it during a geography lesson. If you do you **must** go in groups and take great care when crossing roads.

Aim – to compare the shopping habits of people at your local shopping centre with those of people in the city centre.

Equipment – questionnaire, clipboard and pencil.

Method
a) Make up a questionnaire similar to the completed one on the right.
b) Politely ask at least 20 male and female shoppers of different ages the questions.
c) Share your answers with other groups.
d) Think of ways to illustrate your results.
e) Describe your findings.
f) Suggest reasons for differences between the results of your questionnaire and those of the one taken in the city centre.

Shopping survey

The numbers on the right show the result of asking 100 people in a city centre shopping area (mall) the following questions:

1 Do you shop here
 ● every day? 15
 ● two or three times a week? 15
 ● once a week? 50
 ● once a month? 20

2 Have you travelled
 ● less than 1 mile? 15
 ● between 1 and 2 miles? 20
 ● between 2 and 5 miles? 30
 ● over 5 miles? 35

3 Do you travel here
 ● on foot? 5
 ● by car? 75
 ● by bus? 15
 ● any other way? 5

4 Do you do most of your weekly shopping here?
 ● Yes 75
 ● No 25

5 What is the main thing you buy here?
 ● Food 30
 ● Clothes 40
 ● Furniture 10
 ● Domestic equipment 10
 ● Others 10

Summary

Shopping centres can also be arranged in a hierarchy. Each centre tends to be located in a particular part of a town. If all the shopping centres in a town are plotted on a map, it is likely that a recognisable pattern will appear.

Why are shops and offices found in city centres?

In most city centres land is used either for shops (**retailing**) or for offices (**commerce**). These two compete for land in the central business district (**CBD**) leaving little room for housing or open space. Shops include large department stores, nationwide supermarkets and specialist shops. Commercial buildings will include banks and building societies as well as offices belonging to insurance companies and local industrial firms.

The main advantage of the city centre is its **accessibility**. Most of the main roads leading into the city from the suburbs and surrounding areas meet at the city centre. It is therefore the easiest place for most of the people living in town to reach (diagram **A**).

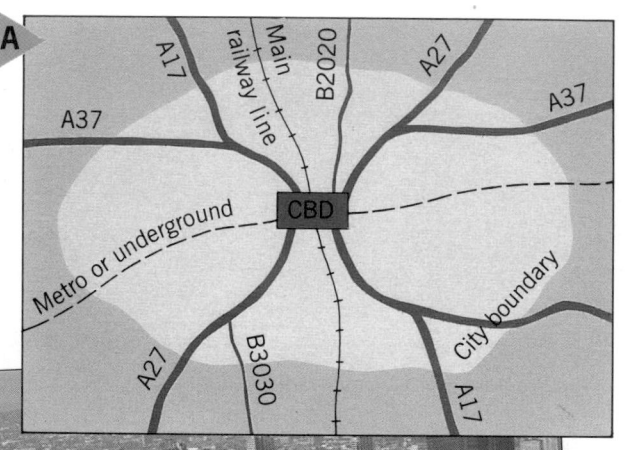

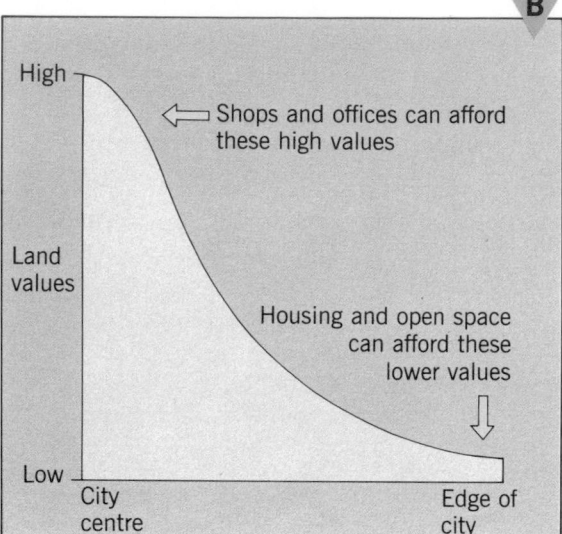

As so many people gather in the city centre, then shops and offices compete for **key** sites. This pushes up the price of land. This means only shops with big sales or offices making high profits can afford to buy or rent the land (diagram **B**).

In an attempt to save space and money many tall office blocks are built in the centre of large cities (photo **C**).

Activities

1 Name the main street, shopping area or mall in your local town or city.

2 Name **one** department store, **one** nationwide supermarket and **three** specialist shops found in it.

3 Name **three** different types of commercial building found in it.

Why are shops and offices moving to out-of-town sites?

Many new large shopping and office developments are being built in out-of-town centres. These are located on the edge of cities. Shopping centres often include large **hypermarkets** (photo **D**). Offices group together on **business** or **science parks**. Poster **E**, on the right, is an advert trying to attract firms to a business park on the edge of Swindon.

Blow away your worries...
Turn with the times...
Move to

WINDMILL PARK

- ◆ Modern buildings ◆ Landscaped grounds
- ◆ Close to the M4 ◆ Ample parking space
- ◆ Pleasant environment, clean air, quiet
- ◆ Room for expansion, land cheap
- ◆ Wide choice of housing nearby

Activities

1 Copy and complete table **F** using words and terms from diagram **G** below.

SHOP AND OFFICE LOCATION	
Edge of city advantages	City centre disadvantages

2 You are a business person. Write a short letter to a friend explaining why you are going to move your firm to a business park like the one in poster **E**.

EXTRA

Design a poster to show the advantages of using the shopping centre shown in photo **D**. Your poster should be attractive, interesting and give facts.

CHEAP LAND FEW HOUSES CROWDED NO PARKING SPACE
DIRTY CLEAN EXPENSIVE LAND
CONGESTED MANY NEW HOUSES PARKING SPACE
PLENTY OF SPACE NICE SURROUNDINGS
MODERN FACILITIES NEAR TO MOTORWAYS

Summary

City centres have traditionally been the main area for shops and offices. Recently out-of-town sites on the edges of cities have become the most favoured locations.

Which transport to use?

Transport is used to carry people and **goods** from one place to another. People need transport to go to work, to travel to the shops, to go on holiday and to visit friends. When people travel they are called **passengers**. When goods are moved from one place to another they are called **freight** or **cargo**. Coal, wheat and televisions are examples of goods that are often carried as freight or cargo.

The type of transport used depends on many things. The most important ones are distance, time, cost and the size of the things being carried. These points, and others, are shown in diagram **A**.

There are many different types of transport. Some are fast and some are slow. Some are cheap and some are expensive. Some are better for cargo than for passengers. Some serve only a few places whilst others can go almost anywhere. Diagrams **B, C, D** and **E** show some of the features of road, rail, sea and air transport.

A

Which transport?
Time
Cost
Distance
Value of goods
Size of goods
Weight of goods

B

Road transport

Includes:
- Cars
- Lorries
- Buses
- Motorbikes

Needs:
- Large amounts of land

Easy travel from place to place

Choose who to travel with

Cheaper than rail or air

Travel when you want to

Good for:
- Passengers
- Private use
- Freight
- Short distances
- Door to door journeys

Bad because:
- Slow
- Dangerous
- Exhaust fumes
- Traffic jams

C

Rail transport

INTERCITY

Includes:
- Passenger trains
- Freight trains

Needs:
- Track and stations

Comfortable

Cheaper than air

Reliable

Can work while travelling

Fast and safe

Good for:
- Medium length journeys
- Passengers
- Heavy and bulky goods
- Intercity use

Bad because:
- Expensive
- Villages poorly served

D

Sea transport

Includes:
- Passenger liners
- Ferries
- Hovercraft
- Cargo ships
- Oil tankers

Needs:
- Ports

Comfortable and relaxing

Carries very large cargo

Passengers well looked after

Cheaper than by air

Interesting and useful

Good for:
- Pleasure sailing
- Heavy and bulky goods
- Long distance travel

Bad because:
- Slow
- Few destinations

E

Air transport

Includes:
- Jet airliners
- Light aircraft
- Helicopters

Needs:
- Airports

Interesting and exciting

Fast

Handy

Comfortable and direct

Good for:
- Passengers
- Light goods
- Valuables
- Long distance travel

Bad because:
- Noise from airports
- Expensive
- High running costs
- Space for airports

Activities

1 a) How do you usually travel to school?
b) Which things from diagram **A** help you to choose that method of travel?

2 Give the meaning of each of the following:

transport

passengers

freight and cargo

3 a) Make a copy of table **F** below.
b) Match the best type of transport with each journey.
Tick only **one** box for each journey.
c) Choose any **two** journeys and explain your choice.

F

Journey	Road	Rail	Air	Sea
Short holiday to Spain				
Important letter to America				
Business trip to London				
Take coal to Japan				
Visit friends 10 km away				

Summary

There are many different types of transport. They all have advantages and disadvantages. When choosing which transport to use for a journey, it is important to think about distance, time, cost and what is to be carried.

Which route to take?

A straight line is the shortest distance between two places. Some roads and railways follow this most direct **route** and it is usually quick and cheap. More often a route will make twists and turns as it goes from one place to another. These are called **detours**. What are the reasons for this? Why don't all routes travel in straight lines?

Think about how you get to school. Almost certainly you will not travel in a straight line. Perhaps there are buildings or private land in the way. Maybe you have to cross a road or use a bridge to take you over a railway or stream. Meeting up with friends may also take you out of the way. Together, all these things affect which route you take from your home to school.

Some of the things affecting the route a road or railway takes are shown in diagram **A**. There are four different factors:

1 **Shortest route** – this is a straight line. It is the most direct and usually the quickest and cheapest way.

2 **Natural features** – these are obstructions like mountains, rivers, marshy land and coastal inlets. They may cause routes to detour from a straight line.

3 **Human needs** – these are things that people need, such as links between towns or by-passes to reduce traffic jams.

4 **Environmental concerns** – this is where the route taken may spoil the surroundings.

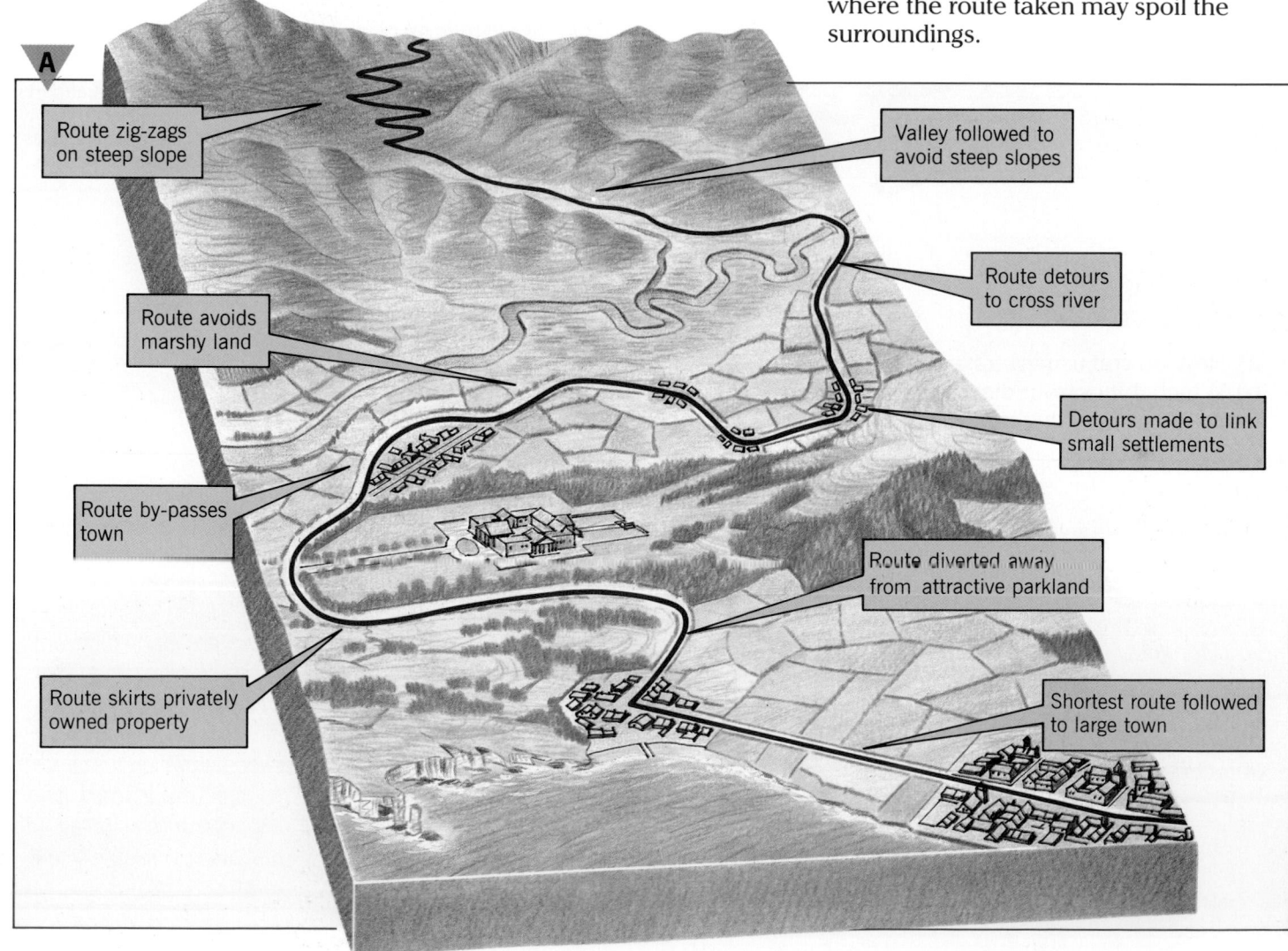

A

Route zig-zags on steep slope

Valley followed to avoid steep slopes

Route detours to cross river

Route avoids marshy land

Detours made to link small settlements

Route by-passes town

Route diverted away from attractive parkland

Route skirts privately owned property

Shortest route followed to large town

Photos **B** and **C** show two very different routes. The railway in Australia (photo **B**) is the longest straight section of track in the world and stretches an incredible 478 kilometres without a single bend. It is straight because there are no natural obstructions to avoid, no settlements to divert to, no worries about damaging the environment. It is a perfect example of a route that takes the shortest distance between two points. The road in Peru (photo **C**) is very different. It follows a valley but has to zig-zag to go up the sides of it, otherwise the road would be too steep. This is an example of a route affected by natural features.

B
Railway across the Nullarbor Plain, Australia

C
Road over the Andes Mountains, Peru, in South America

E

Factors affecting which route to take

① E.g.
② E.g.
③ E.g.
④ E.g.

Activities

1 Look at map **D** which shows the route that Claire takes to her school.
   a) Describe her route. Start with: *Claire leaves her house and turns right…*
   b) Give **three** reasons why she doesn't travel in a straight line from her home to the school.

2 Make a larger copy of all of diagram **E**.
   a) Give each box a suitable title.
   b) Add an example to each one.

3 Look at diagram **A** and list the things that affect the choice of route. Give your answers under these headings. The first one has been done for you.

> **Shortest route** – is a straight line between places. It is usually the quickest and cheapest.
> **Natural features** –
> **Human needs** –
> **Environmental concerns** –

D

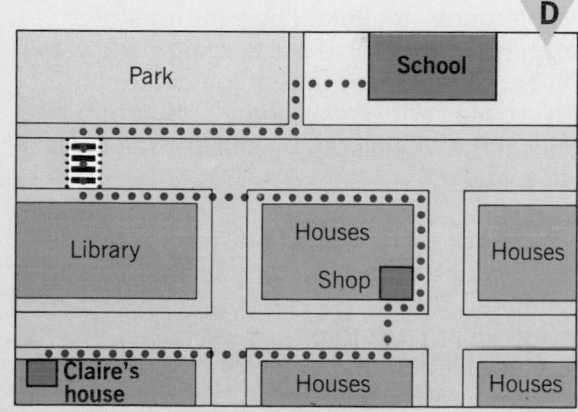

Park · · · · School

Library · · · Houses · Houses
· · · Shop

Claire's house · · · Houses · Houses

E X T R A S

1a) Draw a simple map to show your route to school.

b) List the reasons why you do not travel in a straight line.

Summary

The route a road or railway takes depends on physical, human and environmental factors. A straight line is the shortest route but it is often not possible to follow that route.

What is a network?

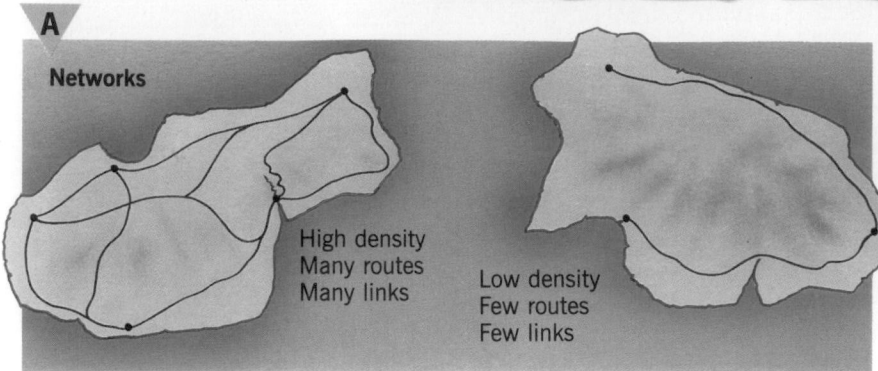

A

Networks

High density
Many routes
Many links

Low density
Few routes
Few links

When there are several routes in an area and they are linked together, they form a **network**. A **high density** network has many routes and many links. **Low density** networks have few routes and few links. A **link** is a connection.

Imagine living in a place with a very low density route network like the one in diagram **A**. It would be very difficult to get from one place to another. How would you get to school? How could goods be moved? The more routes there are, the easier it is to move about. The easier it is to move about the better the chance a place has of growing rich.

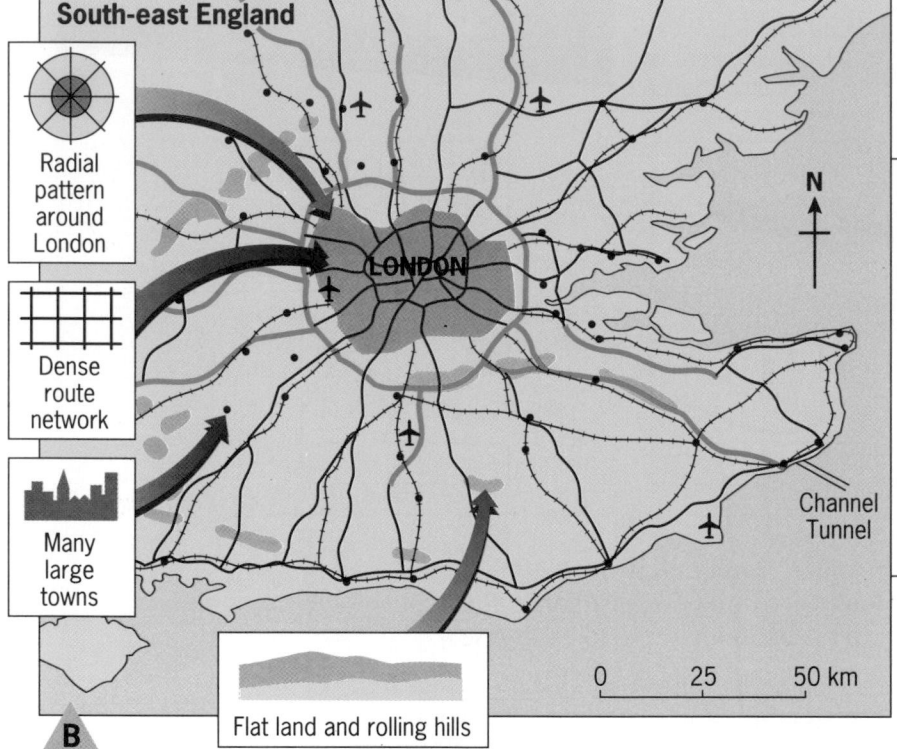

South-east England

Radial pattern around London

Dense route network

Many large towns

LONDON

Channel Tunnel

N

0   25   50 km

Flat land and rolling hills

B

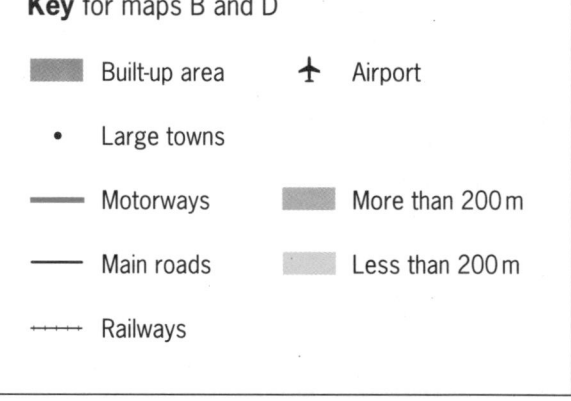

Key for maps B and D

▬ Built-up area   ✈ Airport

• Large towns

▬ Motorways   ▬ More than 200 m

▬ Main roads   ▬ Less than 200 m

┼┼┼┼ Railways

Look at map **B** which shows South-east England. It has the highest density road and rail network in Britain and is also the country's richest region. In this area there are very few places that are far from a motorway, main road or railway and all the settlements are linked by a number of routes. There is also a very clear pattern to the network. London is at the centre of everything with roads going both around the city and radiating out from it like the spokes of a wheel.

There are some simple reasons for this. Physically the area is quite flat and easy to build on. Settlements grew up long ago and were linked together by routes. These routes encouraged further settlement growth and that in turn caused even more routes to be built. Diagram **C** shows how this process is still going on.

C

Flat land, easy to build on

Many settlements

More routes needed

Network development in south-east England

More settlements

More routes needed

Routes easy to build

Study map **D** of Wales. Notice how different it is to South-east England. Is the road and rail network high density or low density? Why is this?

Now look at the area marked South Wales. The road and rail network here is high density. The reasons for this are mainly due to things that happened in the past.

The area has an interesting history. It developed many years ago as a mining area. There was a lot of coal and iron ore and these resources helped the growth of industry. Towns quickly grew up in the valleys and along the coast, and were gradually linked together by a network of roads and railways. Coal mining and some of the original industries have now declined but the pattern of roads, railways and settlements still remains.

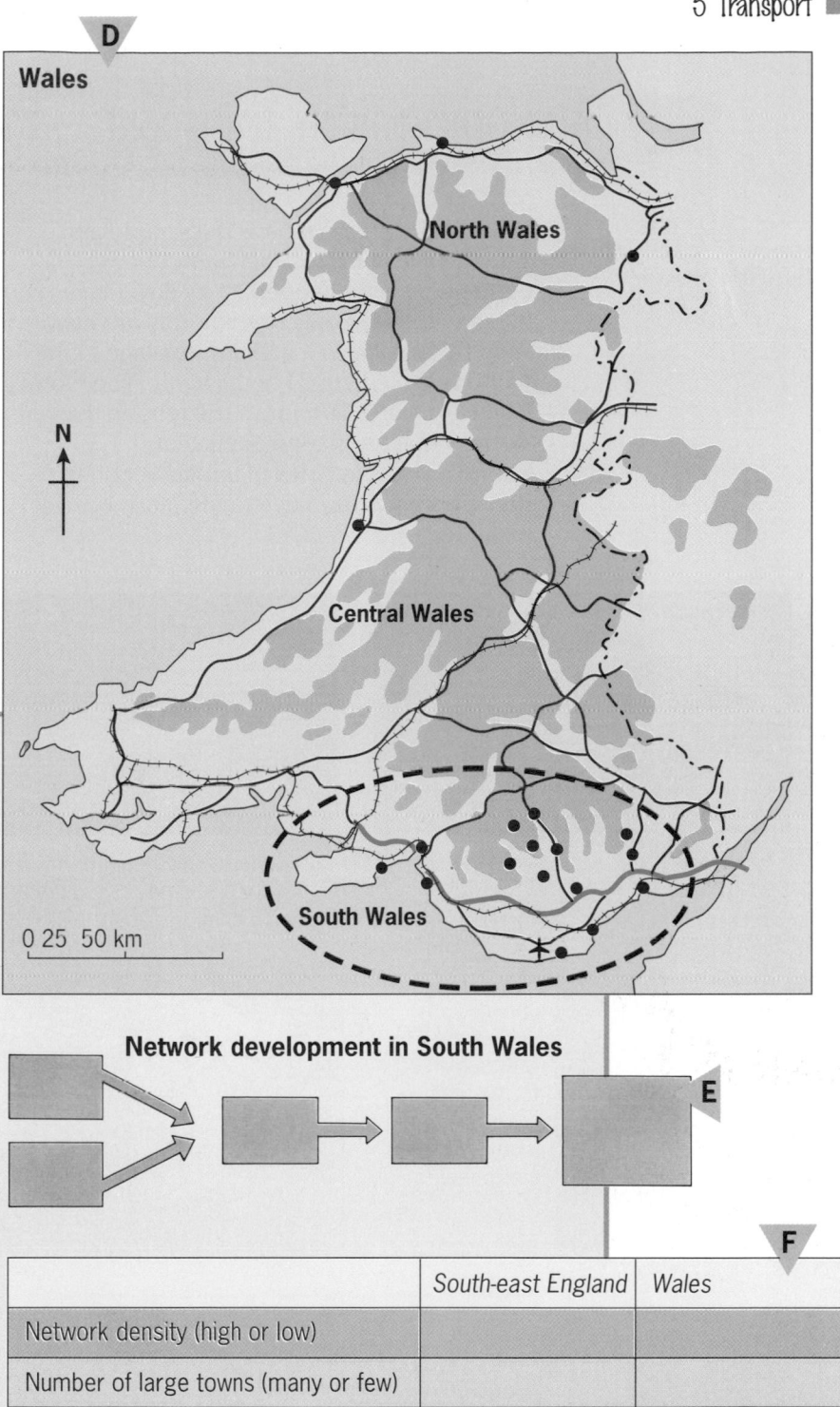

Activities

1 **a)** What is a network?
   b) What is the difference between a high density network and a low density network?

2 Make a larger copy of diagram **E** and add the following information to the correct boxes.
   ● High density road and rail network
   ● Industrial growth
   ● Development of towns
   ● Iron ore
   ● Coal

Network development in South Wales

E

3 **a)** Draw table **F** and fill it in to show the differences between South-east England and Wales.
   b) With help from the table, suggest reasons for the network density of Wales.

F

	South-east England	Wales
Network density (high or low)		
Number of large towns (many or few)		
Height of land (high or low)		

E X T R A

Look at diagram **C** which shows the development of high density road and rail networks in South-east England. Draw a similar diagram to show the development of networks in North Wales and Central Wales.

Summary A network is formed when routes are joined to other routes. The development of road and rail networks is closely linked to the growth of settlement in an area. Present day route patterns may be a result of conditions and activities in the past.

Developments in transport — the good news . . .

Changes in transport have been rapid and spectacular. Journeys that were once expeditions now happen every day. Places that were visited only by explorers are now seen by tourists. In the 1990s no place in the world is more than 24 hours away. The world is not shrinking. Distances still remain the same. What has happened is that improvements in types of transport and in transport networks have made places easier to get to.

A place that is easy to get to is said to be **accessible**. Accessibility depends on distance, the number of routes and links, travel is faster and the actual cost of a journey has decreased.

Better accessibility can bring many benefits. These include less time travelling, cheaper travel, a greater choice of holiday destinations, more markets for industrial products and increased trade.

A

French supertrain sets a world speed record of 270 km/h (168 m.p.h.)

Concorde reaches speed of 2,333 km/h (1,450 m.p.h.) and crosses Atlantic in 2 hrs 55 mins

Luxury coaches give more comfort at less cost

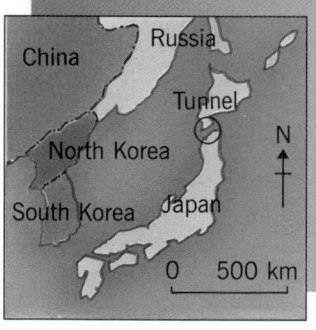

Japan's northern outpost linked to the main island by the world's longest rail tunnel

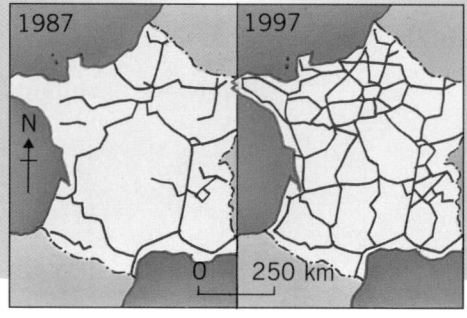

1987   1997

French plan massive growth in motorway system

Channel Tunnel halves crossing time

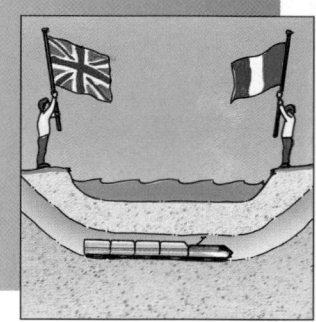

Activities

1 **a)** Copy and complete the accessibility crossword by adding five things that affect accessibility. *Clue*: the answers are all given in one sentence on this page!
 b) Give the meaning of accessibility.

2 From **A** above, give examples of transport improvements which will:
 a) reduce travelling times
 b) produce a better network.

A C C E S S I B I L I T Y

3 Describe an example of improved transport in the area where you live.

... and the bad news

Unfortunately, although developments in transport have brought many benefits, they have also brought problems. Sometimes transport is just too popular and the networks cannot cope. Roads get jammed, car parks fill up, trains are packed and airports burst at the seams.

Another more serious problem is the damage that transport can do to the environment. This is called **environmental pollution**. Pollution is dirt or noise or anything else that is damaging to an area. It may be harmful to people, to animals, to plants or to the surroundings as a whole. All forms of transport damage the environment in some way, but we need transport and transport improvements. So what we must do is to be very careful to balance the advantages of progress against the disadvantages of spoiling the world in which we live. We must try to increase the good news but reduce the bad news.

B

NEWTOWN JOURNAL
City fumes over car exhaust pollution

Morning News
Famous view spoilt by new car park

Evening Herald
New road threat to Amazon rain forest

The Oracle
Long delays expected as airport congestion gets worse

THE CHRONICLE
Residents to be heard over runway noise problem

THE DAILY GLOBE
Multiple crash closes over-used motorway

The Post
OIL SLICK REACHES BEACHES AS DOOMED TANKER SINKS

The Daily Times
Vineyards lost as French supertrain route gets OK

Weekender
10 mile traffic jam hits M25

WEEKLY LIFE
DELAYS AGAIN AS ROADWORKS RETURN

Activities

1 **a)** Unjumble the following words to give four types of pollution.

IAR	DNAL	TRAWE	SNIOE

   b) Give the meaning of the term **environmental pollution**.

2 Make a larger copy of diagram **C** and complete it using information from this page.

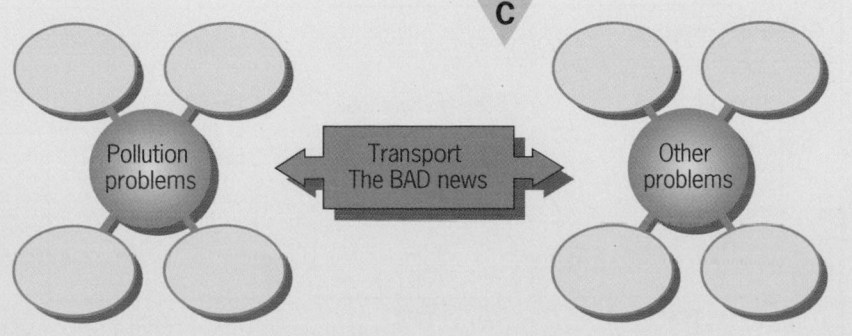

C

Pollution problems ← Transport The BAD news → Other problems

E X T R A

Imagine that a motorway is to be built very near to your house.
- List the advantages and the disadvantages that the motorway would bring.
- Would you be in favour of, or against, this development? Give reasons for your answer.

Summary

Developments in transport are happening all the time. An important advantage is improved accessibility. One major disadvantage is environmental pollution. Care must be taken to protect the environment from damaging transport developments.

Traffic in urban areas — why is it a problem?

Traffic is a serious problem in most urban areas. Large cities such as London, Paris and New York have over a million cars trying to move around in their central areas. Movement is often almost impossible. Perhaps worse than **congestion** is the problem of **pollution**. Exhaust fumes are poisonous and can seriously damage health. Some city workers are so concerned that they wear masks to protect themselves. So what can be done? What are the causes of the problem and why haven't they been solved?

A — What's the problem?

Look at any urban area and you will soon be able to answer that. Cars, buses and lorries are all over the place causing congestion and chaos. They produce lots of fumes, noise and danger. We live in an age of rapid transport yet vehicle movement in the cities is now actually slower than it was 80 years ago.

Loss of business and money

Traffic jams

Delays for police, fire service and ambulances

Harmful exhaust fumes

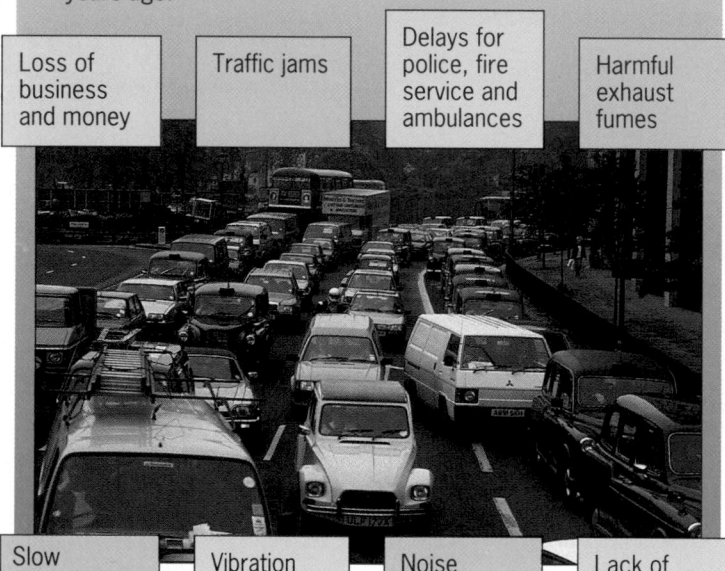

Slow movement of people and goods

Vibration from heavy lorries

Noise Danger from accidents

Lack of parking spaces

B — What's the cause?

Graph **B** shows one important reason. The number of cars has increased at a tremendous rate and there are now too many for cities to handle. Also, most city centres were designed and built before cars were invented. They are therefore just not suited to today's transport. The problem is worst in the morning and in the late afternoon when people are travelling to and from work. This is called the rush-hour.

Too many cars

Unsuitable roads

On-street parking

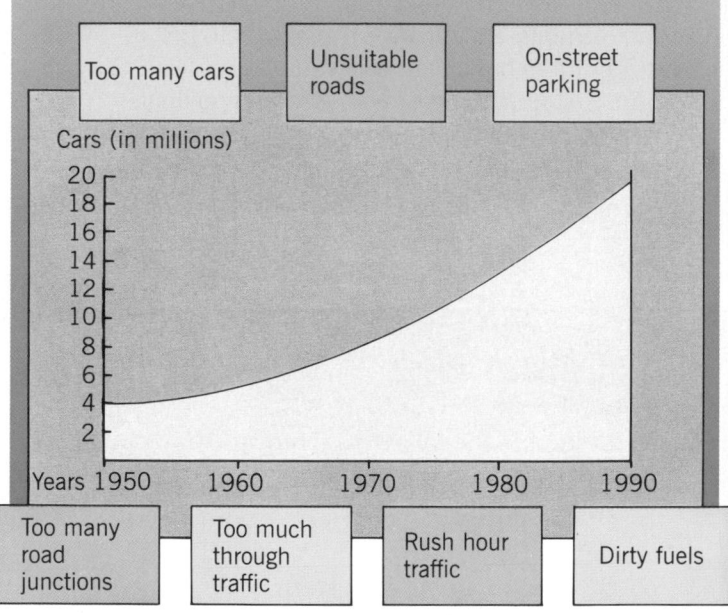

Cars (in millions)

Years 1950 1960 1970 1980 1990

Too many road junctions

Too much through traffic

Rush hour traffic

Dirty fuels

Activities

1. Look at the boxes on photo **A**. List what you think are the five worst problems caused by increased traffic in towns.

2. Look at graph **B**.
   a) How many cars were on Britain's roads in 1950? How many were there in 1990?
   b) Which of the graphs in **C** looks most like graph **B**? Use that description to describe the change in car numbers between 1950 and 1990.

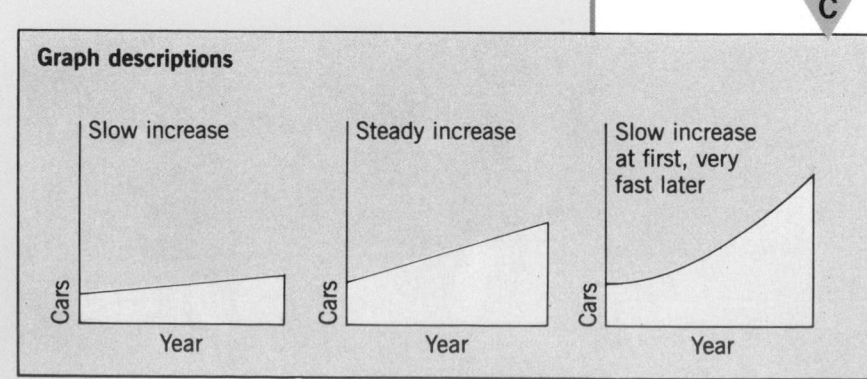

Graph descriptions

Slow increase — Cars / Year

Steady increase — Cars / Year

Slow increase at first, very fast later — Cars / Year

Is there a solution?

There are two main ways of approaching the problem. The first is to allow **private transport** to increase and make improvements to cope with larger amounts of traffic. The second is to restrict private transport and discourage motorists from bringing cars into town centres. This would mean improving **public transport** such as bus and train services.

In fact, the traffic problem is so big and complicated that no single solution will ever completely solve it. The best way is to try to reduce the worst parts of the problem by using several solutions together. Some ideas that have been tried are shown in diagram **D**. Can you think of any others?

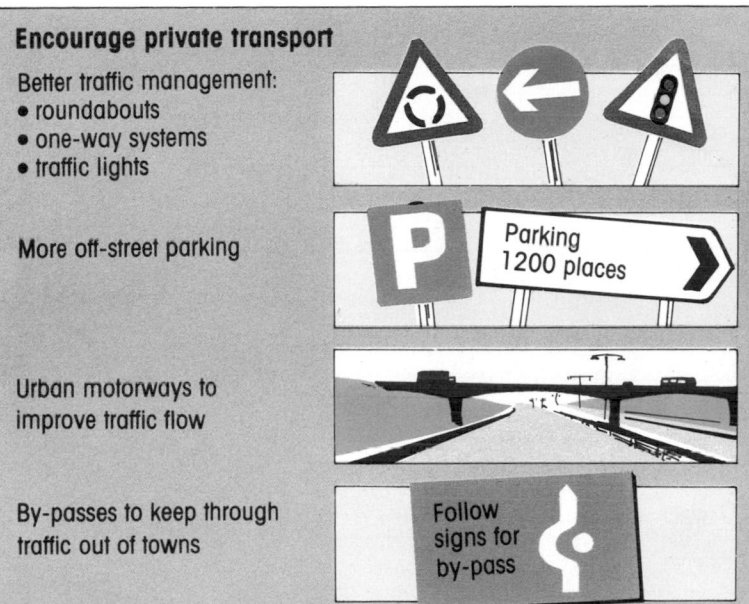

D

Encourage private transport

Better traffic management:
• roundabouts
• one-way systems
• traffic lights

More off-street parking

Parking 1200 places

Urban motorways to improve traffic flow

By-passes to keep through traffic out of towns

Follow signs for by-pass

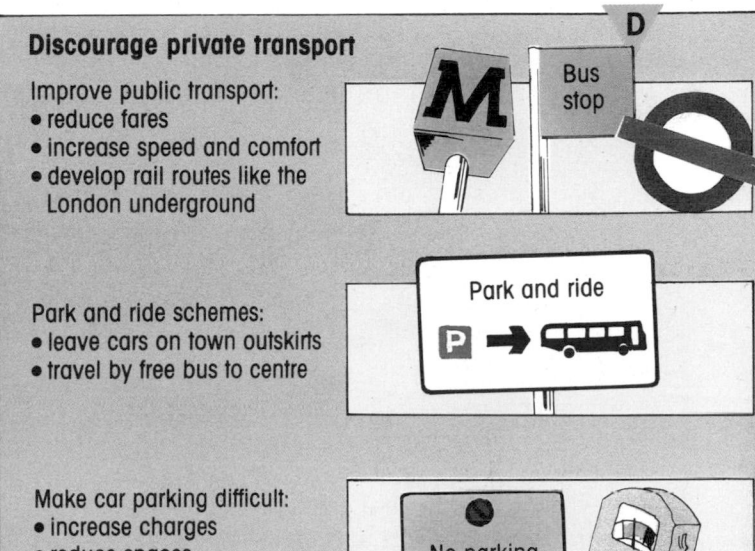

Discourage private transport

Improve public transport:
• reduce fares
• increase speed and comfort
• develop rail routes like the London underground

Bus stop

Park and ride schemes:
• leave cars on town outskirts
• travel by free bus to centre

Park and ride

Make car parking difficult:
• increase charges
• reduce spaces

No parking

Activities

1 a) What is meant by public transport?
   b) What is meant by private transport?
   c) Name each of the following types of transport and sort them out into *Public* and *Private*.

2 Draw a poster to discourage motorists from taking their cars into town centres.
   • Show the bad things about cars in town centres.
   • Show the other types of transport that can be used.
   • Colour your poster and make it interesting and attractive.

EXTRAS

1 Diagram **E** shows how private and public transport in towns affect each other. Copy and complete the diagram using the following phrases:

Fewer public transport users
Poorer quality public transport
Increase in car use

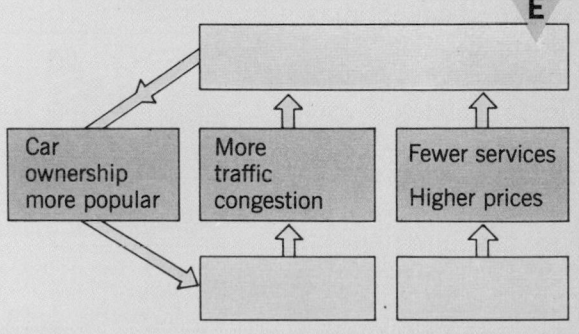

E

Car ownership more popular

More traffic congestion

Fewer services
Higher prices

2 Describe a traffic problem near your school or where you live. Suggest how the problem could be reduced.

Summary

Congestion and pollution are major problems in urban areas. The main causes of these problems are too many cars, rush-hour traffic and unsuitable road networks. Solving the problem is difficult but improved public transport may be the best solution.

Where should the by-pass go?

When a place becomes too crowded with vehicles (congested), a road can be built round it to take away some of the traffic. A road that is built to avoid a congested area is called a **by-pass**. Some by-passes are very long. The M25 which goes all the way round London is over 160 km (100 miles) long (see page 84). Most by-passes are much shorter than this.

Building a by-pass is not easy. Money has to be found, suitable routes planned out, and discussions held between people whom the route may affect. This is all very difficult and takes a long time.

A

Considerations	Red route	Blue route	Yellow route
Is the shortest route			
Avoids all the built-up area			
Avoids best farmland			
Avoids steep slopes			
Avoids marshy areas			
Avoids beauty spot			
Avoids parkland			
Needs fewest bridges			
Requires fewest trees to be cut down			
Serves the industrial estate			
Total			

Activities

1 Look carefully at diagram **B**. It shows an imaginary place called Keytown and some of the countryside around it.

Keytown was once a pretty, quiet village with narrow streets and an attractive central square. It is now busy, congested and can no longer cope with all the traffic going through it. It has been decided to build a by-pass to reduce the traffic going through the town centre.

Three possible routes have been suggested for the by-pass. Your task is to choose the best one.
  a) Copy table **A**, which shows some things that should be considered when choosing a by-pass route.
  b) Show advantages of each route by putting ticks in the *Red, Blue* or *Yellow* columns. More than one column may be ticked for each point.
  c) Add up the ticks to find which route has the most advantages.
  d) Which route would you choose? The one with the most advantages would be best.
  e) Give **two** disadvantages of your chosen route.
  f) Describe the route you have chosen. Start with, 'The by-pass leaves the main road at…'.

2 The *Yellow route* would be a popular choice because it follows a disused railway line and no property would need to be knocked down.

Work in pairs and suggest which of the people below would be against the *Yellow route*. Give reasons for your answer.

Walkers

Managers of factories on industrial estate

Residents of new housing estate

Hotel owner in Keytown

B

Keytown – suggested by-pass routes

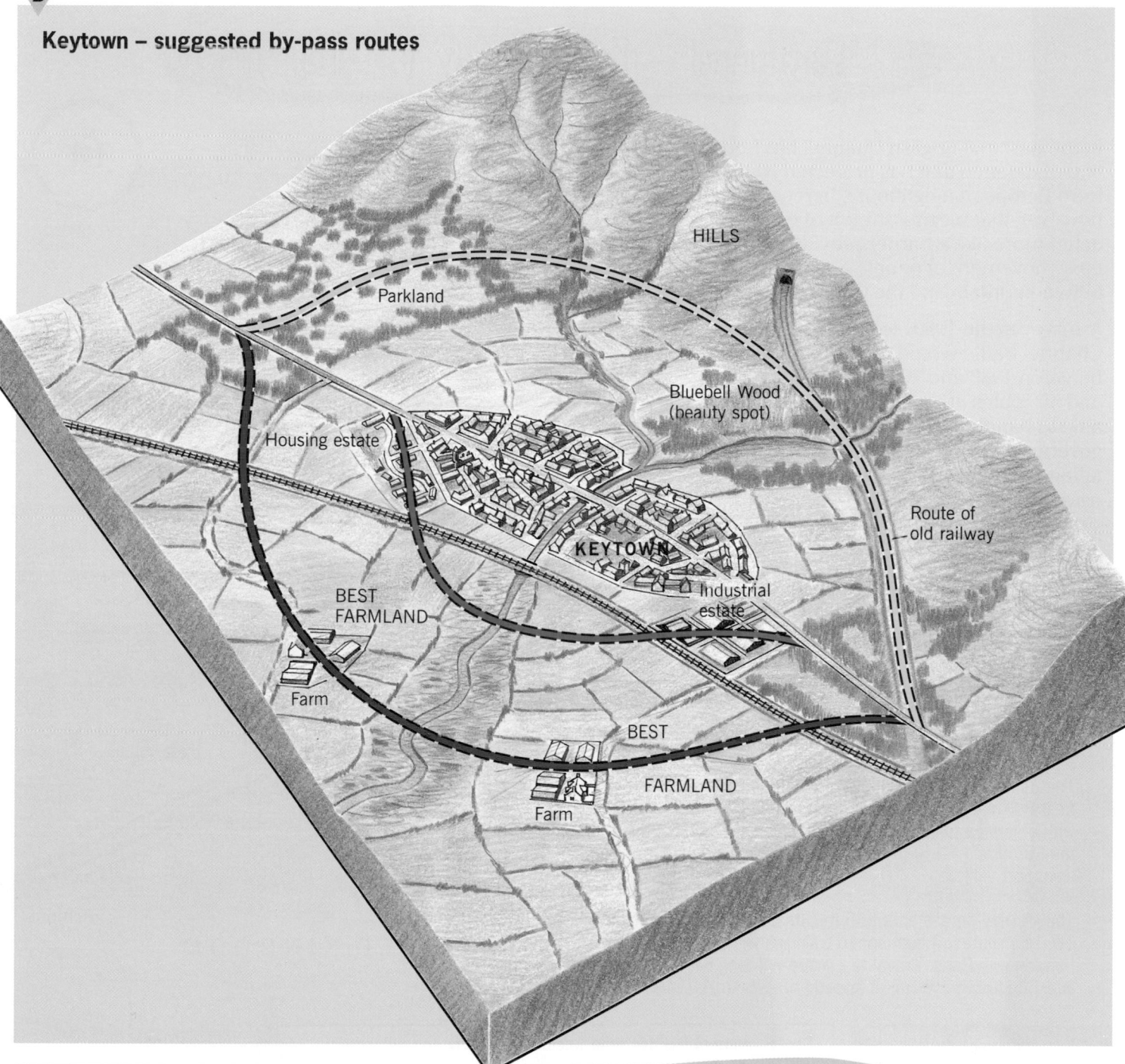

HILLS

Parkland

Bluebell Wood
(beauty spot)

Housing estate

Route of
old railway

KEYTOWN

BEST
FARMLAND

Industrial
estate

Farm

BEST

FARMLAND

Farm

E X T R A

Find out about a by-pass plan in your
local area.

- Draw a simple map to show where the
  by-pass goes.
- Briefly describe the route.
- Say why the by-pass was needed.
- Give the advantages and
  disadvantages of the route chosen.

Summary

A by-pass is one method of reducing
congestion in busy areas. Choosing
the route for a by-pass is very
difficult. Cost, the availability of land
and a concern for the environment are
important considerations. No route
will satisfy everyone.

Eurotunnel — the new way to Europe

In the past, the English Channel has been a line of defence that has protected Britain from European neighbours. In recent times, however, that narrow stretch of water has acted more like a barrier preventing the easy movement of people and goods between Britain and the Continent.

A survey in the 1980s forecast that cross-Channel traffic would more than double between 1983 and 2003. The existing sea and air routes at that time would not be able to handle that increase. In 1987 the governments of Britain and France finally agreed to build a **Channel Tunnel** to try to overcome the problem.

As diagram **A** shows, not everyone at the time was in favour of the tunnel. Eventually, however, after much delay it was completed and finally opened in May 1994. The tunnel provides a link between the transport networks of Britain and mainland Europe. It makes going to the Continent faster and easier. It also helps to improve tourism, trade, and industry.

A

The 1980s tunnel debate

(Many of these points are still valid today, years after the tunnel was opened.)

For

1 Road and rail networks of Britain and Europe joined

2 Faster travel

3 Trade and industry helped

4 Up to 35,000 new jobs created

5 Up to 1,500 lorries a day taken off the roads – this means less congestion and less pollution

6 No delays due to bad weather

7 The tunnel is a symbol of unity between Britain and Europe

The tunnel is about 50 km long and runs between terminals near Folkestone and Calais. There are two separate rail tunnels with a service tunnel between them (see sketch **D**). Fast trains – the Eurostar – carry through traffic, and special shuttle trains transport vehicles.

The journey time is about 35 minutes and trains leave every 10–15 minutes. A high speed train link will eventually connect London with Paris. Travel to Europe will then be on a fast InterCity train travelling at speeds of 225 km/h (140 m.p.h).

LONDON
Chatham
Maidstone
Motorway
High speed train
Ashford

UNITED KINGDOM

Hastings

ENGLISH CHANNEL

B

EURO TUNNEL

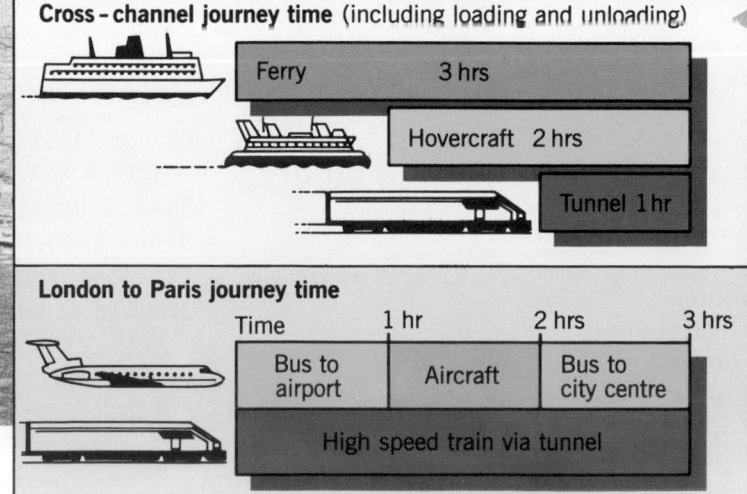

C

Cross-channel journey time (including loading and unloading)

Ferry	3 hrs
Hovercraft	2 hrs
Tunnel	1 hr

London to Paris journey time

Time	1 hr	2 hrs	3 hrs
Bus to airport	Aircraft	Bus to city centre	
High speed train via tunnel			

Against

1 Tunnel waste material spoils the environment

2 Massive rail terminals look ugly

3 Animals may get through the tunnel and bring in diseases such as rabies

4 Extra traffic causes congestion and pollution

5 New road and rail links use up land and damage the surroundings

6 Job losses in ports and ferry companies

7 Benefits go mainly to the already prosperous areas of the South East – that money could be better spent helping areas with high unemployment

Activities

1 a) Which two Channel ports does the tunnel run between?

b) How long is the Channel Tunnel route?

c) How are people and vehicles transported through the tunnel?

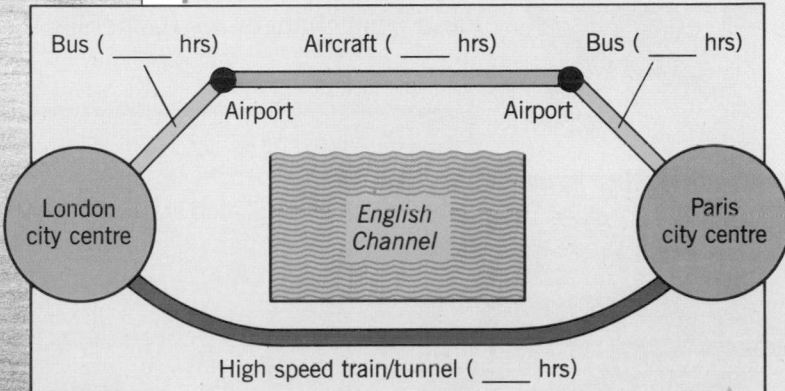

Bus (____ hrs)   Aircraft (____ hrs)   Bus (____ hrs)

Airport   Airport

London city centre   English Channel   Paris city centre

High speed train/tunnel (____ hrs)

E

2 a) Make a copy of diagram **E**.

b) Using bar chart **C**, write in the times spent in the bus, aeroplane and train.

c) With help from your completed diagram, say which would be the easiest and most relaxing journey to make between London and Paris. Give reasons for your answer.

3 Give three ways in which the tunnel project could:
- damage the environment
- help create jobs.

4 Suggest why the following people might be against the Channel Tunnel project.
- Villagers near Folkestone.
- Channel ferry crews.
- Farmers near the high speed train (TGV) route to Paris.

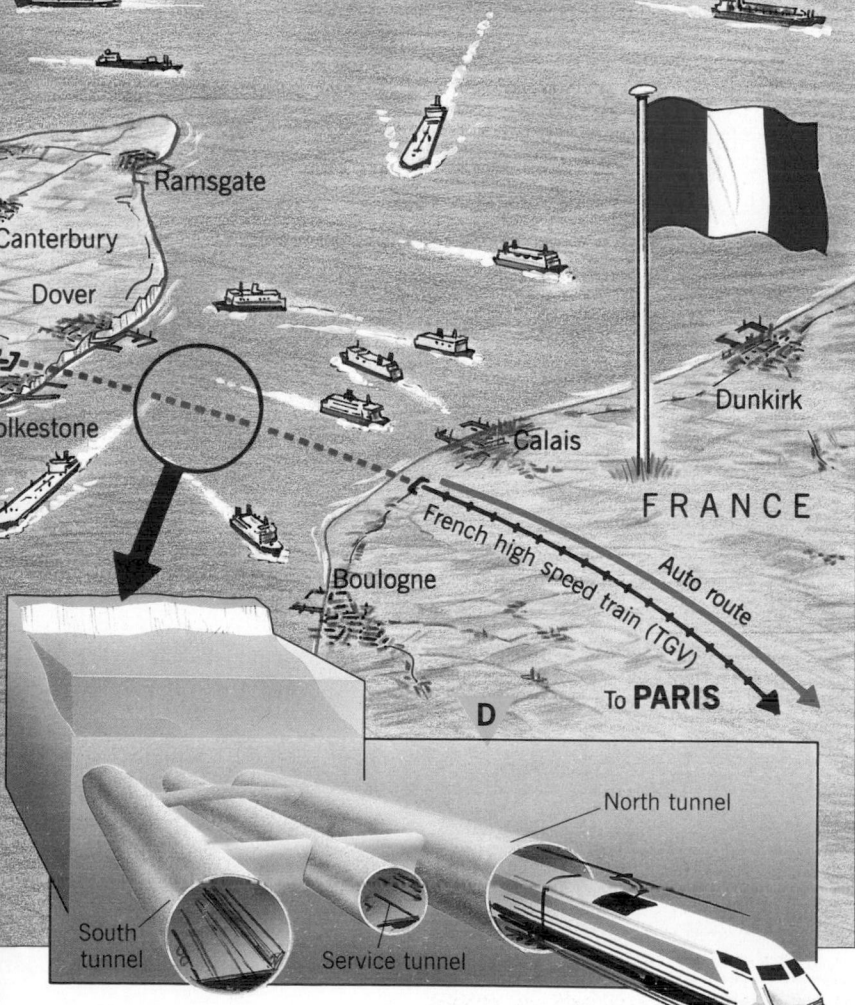

Ramsgate

Canterbury

Dover

Folkestone

Dunkirk

Calais

FRANCE

French high speed train (TGV)

Auto route

Boulogne

To **PARIS**

D

North tunnel

South tunnel

Service tunnel

Summary

The Channel Tunnel brings the road and rail networks of Britain and mainland Europe together. This increases accessibility and helps improve trade and industry. Many people are worried about the damaging effects the tunnel project can have on their lives and surroundings.

What is your image of a region?

In this unit examples are given from two different regions. One of them may be the region you live in, or it may be similar to your region. They will give you an idea of how to study a region, what a region is like and what changes are happening there.

The Greater London region lies inside the circle made by the M25 motorway. The land is **lowlying** and has few hills. Most of the land has been built upon. It is the largest **urban** area in the UK. People from many different ethnic groups live here. Each group has its own language, religion and culture. The majority in these groups were born in the UK and are British.

Area (thousand km) ➡ 1½
Population (million people) ➡ 6 ¾
Average number of people in a grid square ➡ 4,000

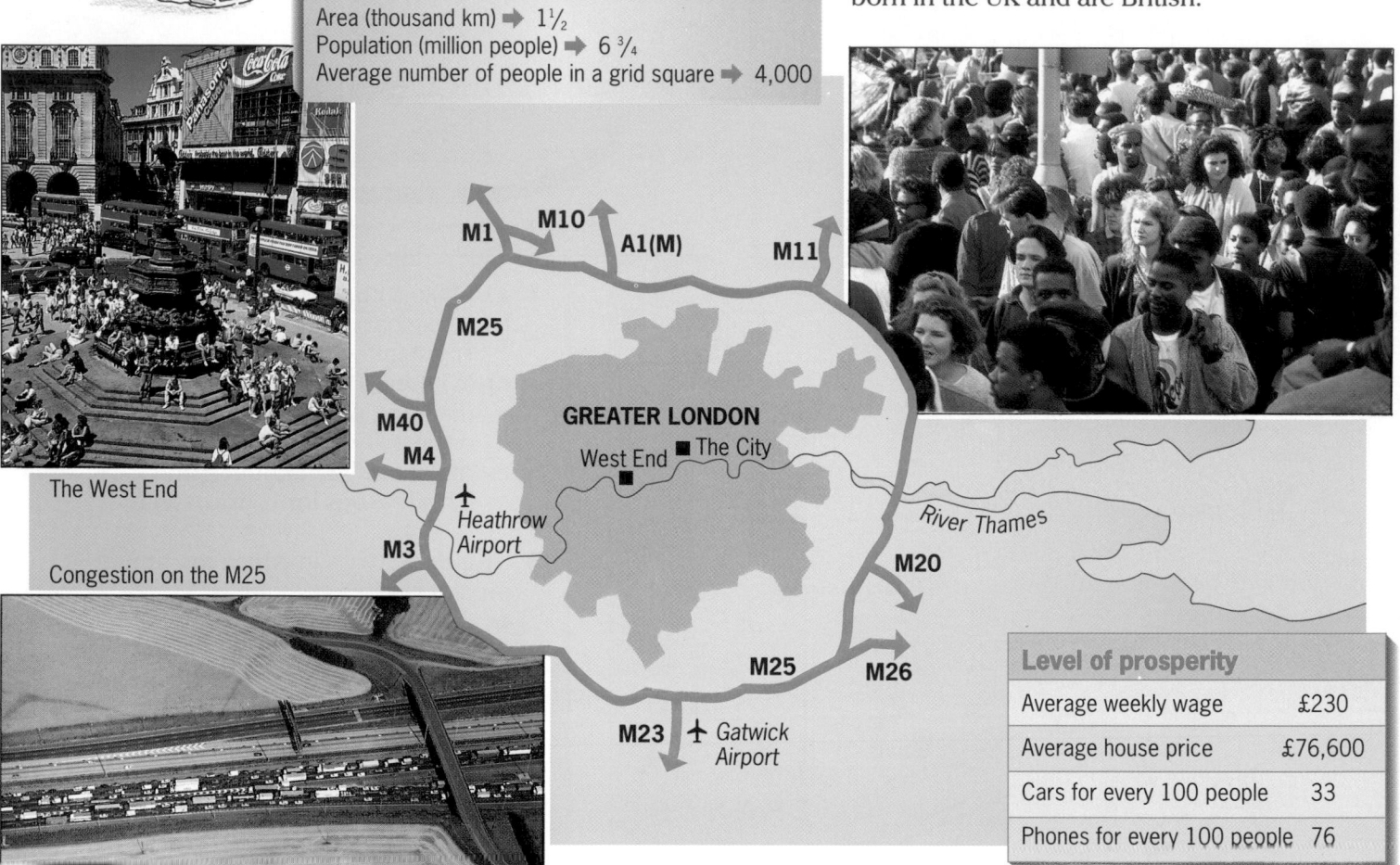

The West End

Congestion on the M25

M1   M10   A1(M)   M11

M25

M40

M4

GREATER LONDON

West End ■ The City

✈ Heathrow Airport

River Thames

M3

M20

M25   M26

M23 ✈ Gatwick Airport

Level of prosperity	
Average weekly wage	£230
Average house price	£76,600
Cars for every 100 people	33
Phones for every 100 people	76

Activities

1 In which river basin is Greater London?

2 Is this region lowlying or highland?

3 Is this region mainly urban or rural?

4 Name four motorways other than the M25.

5 Name two large airports.

6 Is your home region similar to Greater London or to Wales? Is it lowlying or highland? What is the largest town or city in your region? What are the main types of jobs?

Summary

Some regions are lowlying, are mainly urban and have many different cultures living in them. Greater London is an example.

What is your image of a region?

In this unit examples are given from two different regions. One of them may be the region you live in, or it may be similar to your region. They will give you an idea of how to study a region, what a region is like and what changes are happening there.

Wales is a region of great contrasts. There are large cities in the south and smaller towns around the coast, but most of Wales is **highland** and mountainous. Much of the land is **rural** and has not been built upon. Welsh people value their culture and history. Many are bi-lingual and speak both Welsh and English. Cardiff, the present capital, is as multicultural as any other UK city.

Area (thousand km) ➡ 20
Population (million people) ➡ 2 ¾
Average number of people in a grid square ➡ 150

Snowdonia National Park

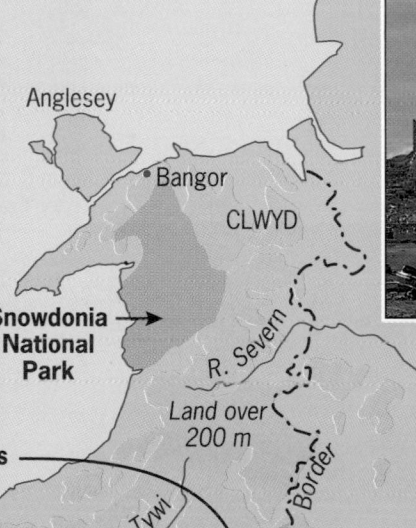

Anglesey
• Bangor
CLWYD
Snowdonia National Park →
R. Severn
Land over 200 m
Border
Brecon Beacons National Park
R. Tywi
Pembrokeshire National Park
Swansea •
Rhondda Valley
Newport •
Cardiff •
➡ **M4**

Conwy Castle, North Wales

Coalmining town

Level of prosperity

Average weekly wage	£170
Average house price	£49,450
Cars for every 100 people	30
Phones for every 100 people	58

Activities

1 Is this region lowlying or highland?
2 Is this region mainly urban or rural?
3 Name the main motorway.
4 Name **three** large cities.
5 Name **three** National Parks.

6 Is your home region similar to Greater London or to Wales? Is it lowlying or highland? What is the largest town or city in your region? What are the main types of jobs?

Summary

Some regions are highland, are mainly rural and have their own culture. Wales is an example.

What is the climate and landscape of the region?

Climate in London

Graph **A** shows that the summers are warm. This is because the sun heats places in the south of Britain more than those in the north. Winters are cold as there is no warm current of water to raise temperatures. This is explained on page 20.

Graph **B** shows that this region does not get much precipitation. This is because moist air comes from the Atlantic Ocean and gives heavy rain as it crosses the mountains in the west. This is explained on page 22. In summer there may be heavy **convectional** thunderstorms (see page 23).

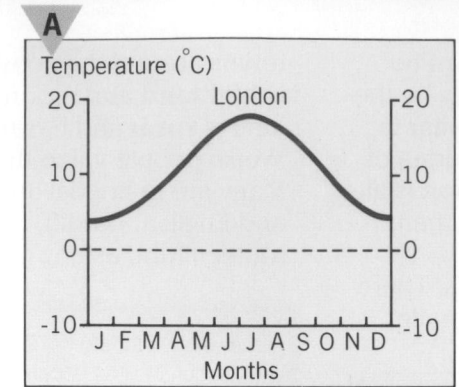

A

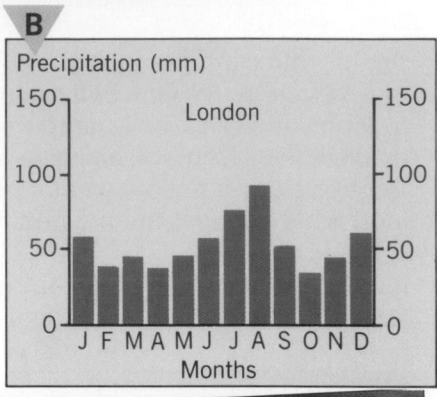

B

Climate hazards

In several recent summers this region has had a water shortage (see page 39). A long dry period of weather is called a **drought**. Sometimes, especially in autumn, the area gets thick **fogs** which make driving dangerous (photo **C**).

C

D

Landscape

The appearance of the landscape in this region is mainly due to human activity. At first trees were cleared for farming, but now the area is covered by houses, industry, roads and railways as in photo **D**. Apart from some large parks in central London there is very little open space until near the edge of the city.

Activity

Sketch **E** is of photo **D**. Draw this sketch and complete it by adding the following labels in the correct places:

main road
canal
railway
terraced houses
tall flats
wasteland
industry

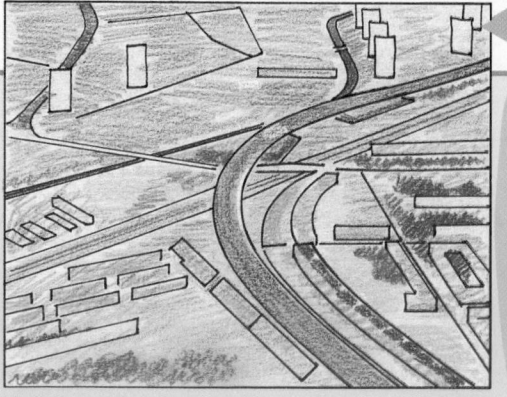

E

Summary

The Greater London region is in the south-east of Britain. It has warm summers and cold winters. It does not get very much rain and at times there can be a water shortage. The landscape is urban.

What is the climate and landscape of the region?

Climate in Wales

Graph **F** shows that because the sun heats places in the south of Britain more than those in the north, summers are warm. Winters on the coast are mild because of the North Atlantic Drift, a warm current of water which raises temperatures in the west of Britain (see page 20). Temperatures are much lower in the Welsh mountains. This is because temperatures fall by 1°C for every 100 metres in height (see page 20).

Graph **G** shows that this region gets a lot of precipitation. Moist air and warm and cold fronts all come from the Atlantic Ocean. These give **relief** and **frontal** rainfall as they cross the Welsh mountains. This is explained on pages 22 and 23.

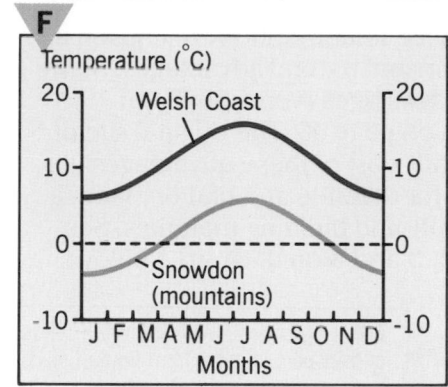

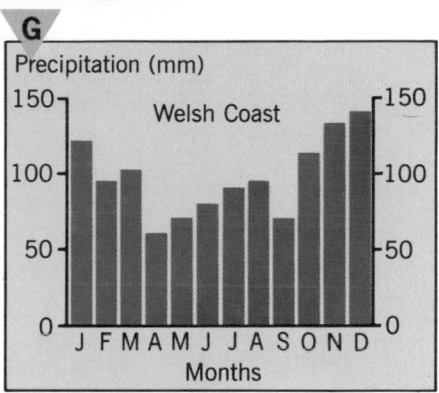

Climate hazards

The heavy rain gives a water surplus but can cause river **flooding** (see page 35). The hills can get heavy **snow** in winter as in photo **H**. The region gets many **gales**. These strong winds can cause damage to property as well as causing snow to drift and high waves to flood lowlying coastal areas.

Landscape

The boundary on three sides of Wales is the sea. Much of the coastline is attractive with cliffs and sandy bays. Inland there are mountains, river valleys and natural lakes (photo **I**). The highest land is moorland but deciduous trees lower down have either been removed for farming or replaced by coniferous trees. The built-up areas are mainly in the south of the region.

Activity

Sketch **J** is of photo **I**. Draw this sketch and complete it by adding, in the correct places, the following terms:

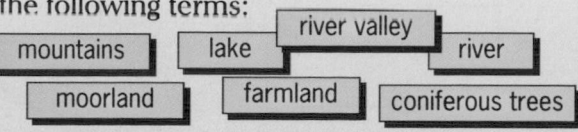

mountains		river valley	
lake		river
moorland	farmland	coniferous trees

Summary

Wales is a mainly hilly and mountainous region in the west of Britain. In this area the lowlying parts have warm summers and mild winters. The mountains are much colder. The heavy rain gives a water surplus. Apart from parts of South Wales, the landscape is rural.

How has the region developed?

Early **sites** for settlements were chosen if they had several natural advantages. Some of these advantages were shown on diagram **A** on page 46. The original site of London had most of these advantages. It was good for defence and had dry land, a water supply and building materials. See points **1, 2, 3** and **4** on diagram **A** below.

Even if a place had a good site there still had to be a good reason why a settlement had to have a **function** (pages 44–45). London had several early functions (see map **A**), including being a market town and a port. Since then it has developed new uses and now has administrative, transport and holiday functions.

A

Site factors

Later functions

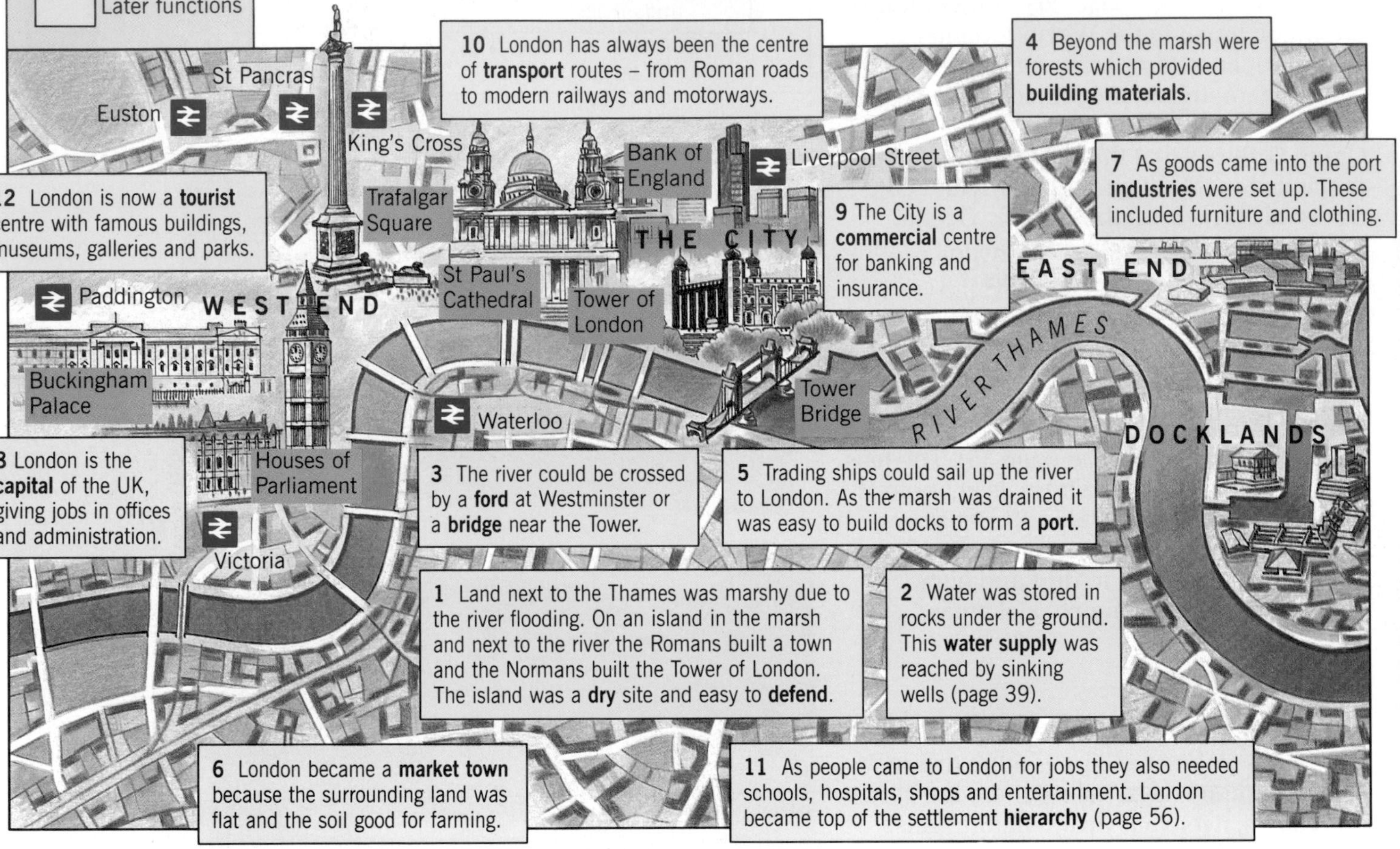

St Pancras
Euston
King's Cross

10 London has always been the centre of **transport** routes – from Roman roads to modern railways and motorways.

4 Beyond the marsh were forests which provided **building materials**.

12 London is now a **tourist** centre with famous buildings, museums, galleries and parks.

Trafalgar Square

Bank of England

Liverpool Street

7 As goods came into the port **industries** were set up. These included furniture and clothing.

9 The City is a **commercial** centre for banking and insurance.

Paddington
WEST END

St Paul's Cathedral
Tower of London

THE CITY

EAST END

Buckingham Palace

Houses of Parliament

8 London is the **capital** of the UK, giving jobs in offices and administration.

Tower Bridge

RIVER THAMES

DOCKLANDS

Waterloo

Victoria

3 The river could be crossed by a **ford** at Westminster or a **bridge** near the Tower.

5 Trading ships could sail up the river to London. As the marsh was drained it was easy to build docks to form a **port**.

1 Land next to the Thames was marshy due to the river flooding. On an island in the marsh and next to the river the Romans built a town and the Normans built the Tower of London. The island was a **dry** site and easy to **defend**.

2 Water was stored in rocks under the ground. This **water supply** was reached by sinking wells (page 39).

6 London became a **market town** because the surrounding land was flat and the soil good for farming.

11 As people came to London for jobs they also needed schools, hospitals, shops and entertainment. London became top of the settlement **hierarchy** (page 56).

Activities

1 Complete star diagram **B** by adding labels to show which factors led to the growth of London. Write only one or two words in each box.

2 What factors led to the development of your nearest town or city? Put your answers in the form of a table. One column should have the heading *Site factors*, and another column the heading *Later functions*.

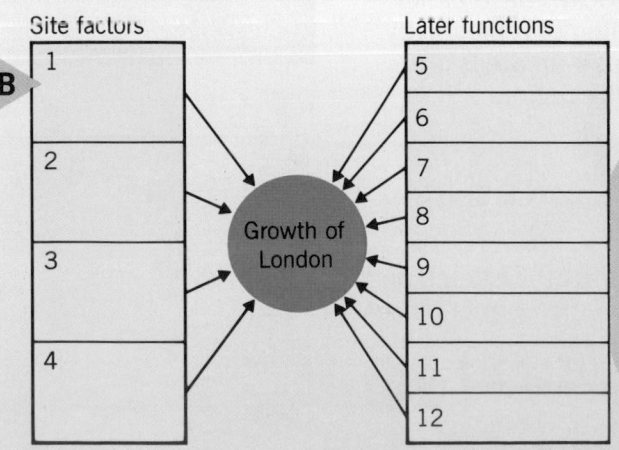

B

Site factors
1
2
3
4

Growth of London

Later functions
5
6
7
8
9
10
11
12

Summary

Big cities like London often have several natural advantages. As these cities find new functions they continue to develop.

How has the region developed?

The land was an important factor in the development of Wales. Upland Wales was suitable for sheep farming. Lowland Wales was ideal for dairy farming. In the north materials such as slate and copper were quarried. In the south coal and iron were mined. Farming, quarrying and mining have, until recently, employed large numbers of people.

C

Upland Wales
Sheep farming

- The land is too steep and hilly for crops
- Thin soils only give poor quality grass
- The weather is too wet, cold and windy for crops
- Transport to market towns is poor

Lowland Wales
Dairy farming

- The flat land suits dairy cows
- Deep soils give good quality grass
- Rain all year and mild winters help grass to grow
- Transport to market towns is good

Coal was found in the many river valleys of South Wales. There were often several coal mines in each valley. The famous Rhondda Valley once had 60. Each mine employed several hundred workers. Iron ore was also mined and this led to the growth of hundreds of small ironworks and, later, steelworks. Other factories were then opened to use the iron and steel. Large ports, like Cardiff, were needed to send the coal and iron and steel overseas. In the last century South Wales became one of the most industrialised regions in the world (see photo **D**).

Slate used to be quarried in large amounts in Snowdonia (see photo **E**). One particular quarry employed 2,000 people. It led to the growth of the small town of Blaenau Ffestiniog which had its own railway to take the slate to the coast. This slate was sent all over the world. Today both the quarry and the Ffestiniog narrow gauge railway are open as tourist attractions.

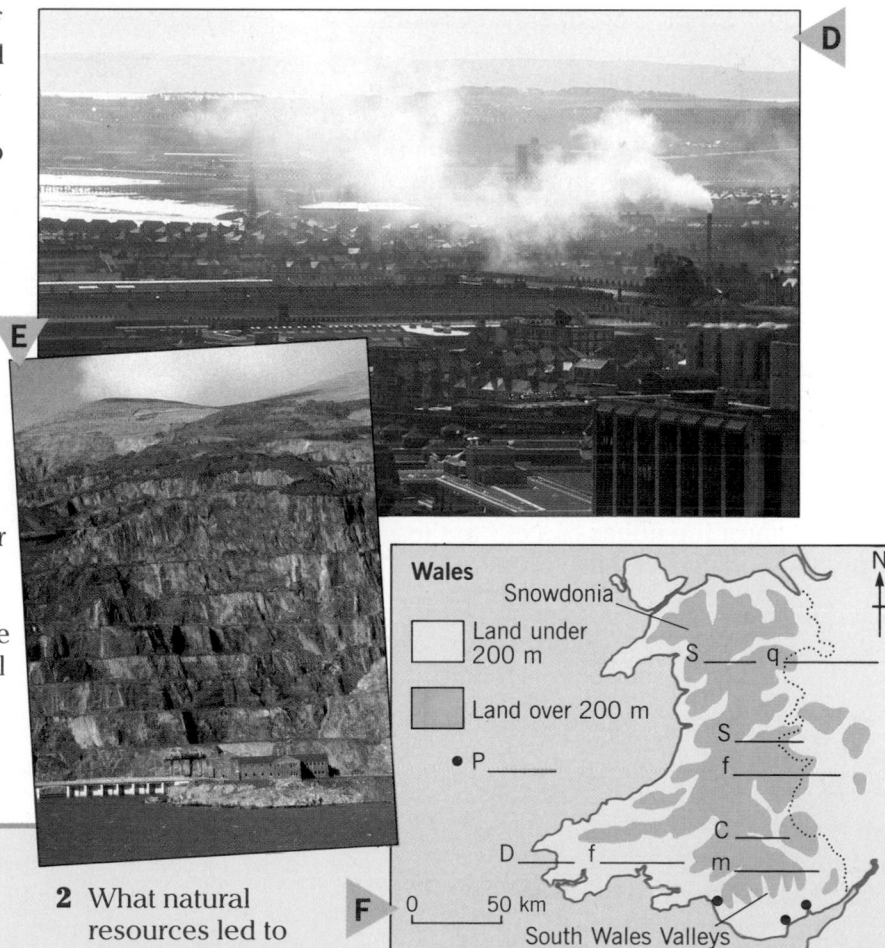

D

E

Wales

Snowdonia

☐ Land under 200 m

▨ Land over 200 m

• P_____

S_____ q_____

S_____ f_____

D_____ f_____ m_____

C_____ m_____

N

0   50 km

South Wales Valleys

F

Activities

1 On a larger copy of map **F**
   a) complete the key and
   b) put the following labels in the correct place:

   sheep farming   ports
   dairy farming
   slate quarrying   coal mines

2 What natural resources led to the development of your home region? Put your answers in the form of a table. You could head your columns *Farming, Quarrying and mining, Water supply, Forestry,* etc.

Summary

Some regions develop by using their natural resources for farming, quarrying and mining. Wales is an example.

What is the settlement pattern in a city?

It was in the nineteenth century that London, like other British cities, began to grow very quickly in size. Houses were packed closely together (**nucleated**) to save space as in **Zone B** on diagram **A**.

London also grew rapidly in the 1920s and 1930s due to improvements in transport. The London Underground was extended and more people owned their own cars. People could now live further from their place of work. A **linear** settlement pattern developed along new transport routes (**Zone C**).

In the 1960s London again grew outwards as more people became wealthy (**Zone D**). Other people had to be rehoused as nineteenth century slum housing was cleared. The **green belt** around London was meant to stop new building taking place (page 86).

What is the population distribution of a city?

A distribution map shows how people are spread out across an area. It shows places which are crowded and places which have plenty of space. Map **B** shows that places near to the centre of London are crowded. Places nearer the edges of a city are less crowded and people have more room.

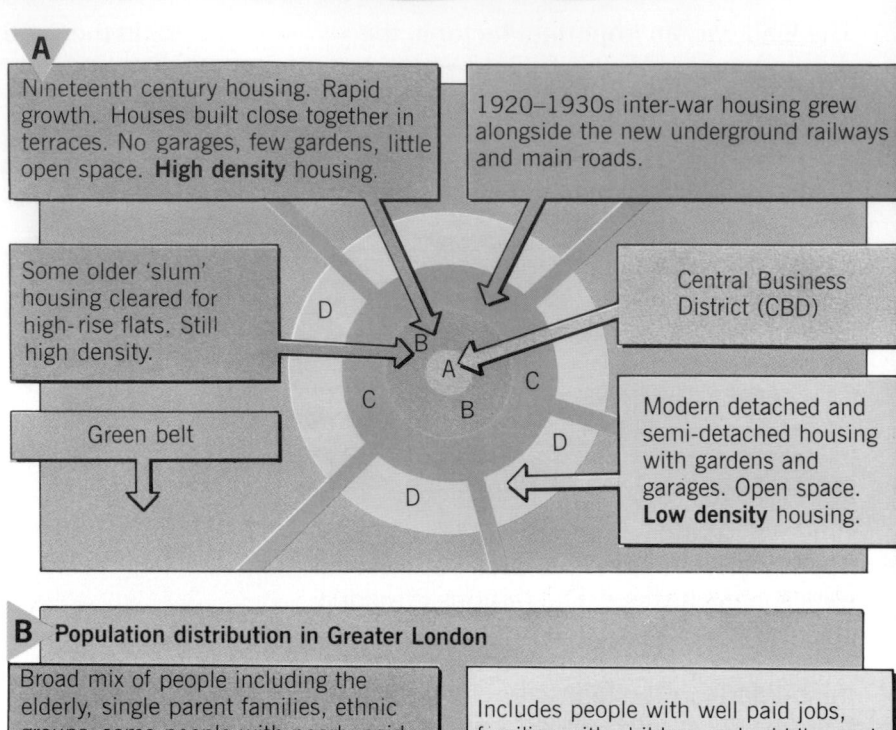

A

Nineteenth century housing. Rapid growth. Houses built close together in terraces. No garages, few gardens, little open space. **High density** housing.

1920–1930s inter-war housing grew alongside the new underground railways and main roads.

Some older 'slum' housing cleared for high-rise flats. Still high density.

Central Business District (CBD)

Green belt

Modern detached and semi-detached housing with gardens and garages. Open space. **Low density** housing.

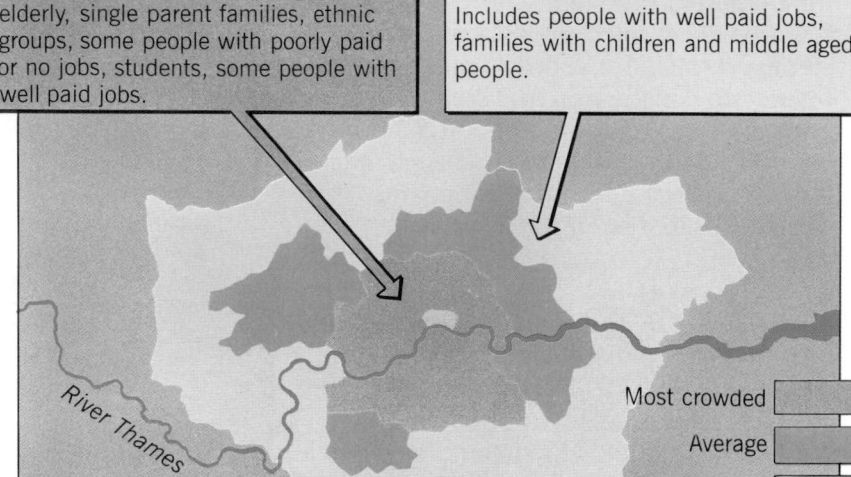

B Population distribution in Greater London

Broad mix of people including the elderly, single parent families, ethnic groups, some people with poorly paid or no jobs, students, some people with well paid jobs.

Includes people with well paid jobs, families with children and middle aged people.

River Thames

Most crowded

Average

Least crowded

Activities

1 Draw diagram **C**.
   a) Using diagram **A** from pages 52–53, name **Zones A, B, C** and **D**.
   b) Label one area with high density housing and one with low density housing.

   A B C D

   C

2 a) Describe the distribution of population in your nearest town or city, or in London, by completeing the following sentences.
   The most crowded area in _____ is _____.
   The least crowded area in _____ is _____.
   b) Give **two** reasons for each answer.

Summary

London has a settlement pattern similar to most big cities. It is nucleated with a linear pattern along main routes. The areas near the city are more crowded than those places near the edges.

What is the settlement pattern in a rural area?

Three main types of settlement pattern were described on page 47. Each type can be found in a different part of Wales.

Dispersed settlement is found in the sheep farming areas of upland Wales. As the grass here is not very good, a lot of land is needed for the sheep to feed upon. This means each farm has to be large and will probably be far away from the next farm (photo **D**).

Nucleated settlements are found in coastal areas where there are ports and industry. It was convenient to have everything close together – docks, industry, workers' houses, shops, schools and hospitals (photo **E**).

Linear settlements are found in river valleys in South Wales. These valleys are long and narrow. The only flat land is next to the river. When coal was found here the miners' houses had to be built in long lines on the lower slopes of the valley as in photo **F**.

What is the population distribution of a rural area?

A distribution map shows how people are spread across an area. It shows places that are crowded and places that have plenty of space. Map **G** shows that most people in Wales live near to the coast or in the valleys of South Wales. Few people live in the upland parts of Central Wales. This is because of differences in climate, the height of the land, transport and jobs in the two areas.

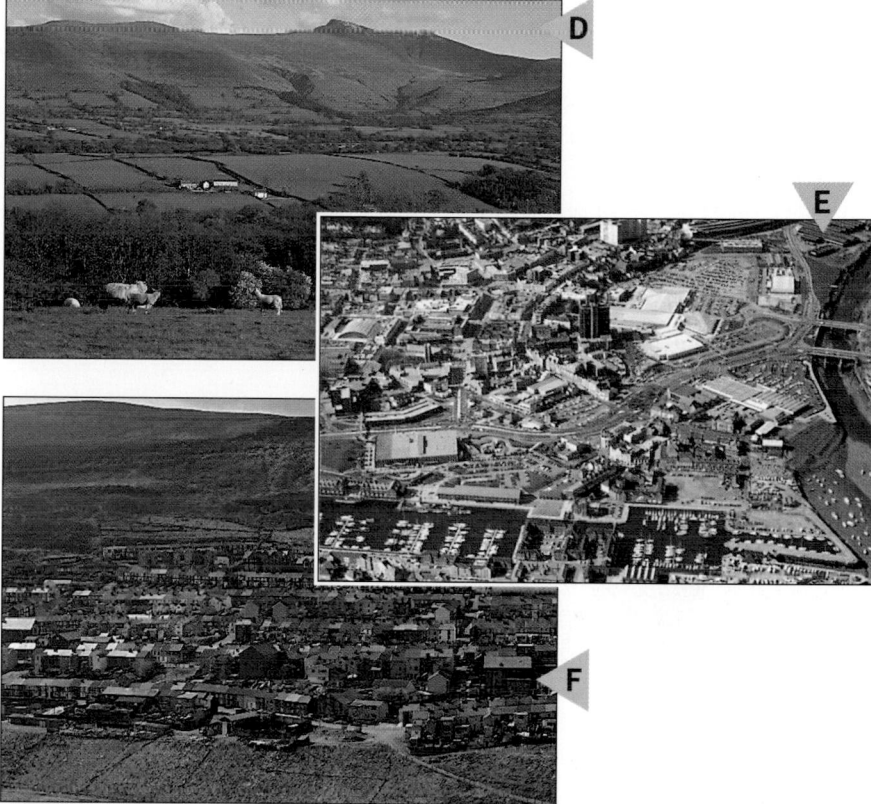

D

E

F

G

N

	Few people
	Average number
	Many people
· ·	Towns and cities

0   50 km

Summary

Dispersed, nucleated and linear settlement patterns are found in different parts of Wales. This is a settlement pattern often found in mainly rural areas. The population distribution of the region shows that more people live in the lower areas near to the south coast than in the central and northern upland areas.

Activities

1 Write one sentence to explain why settlements are:
  a) dispersed in Central Wales
  b) nucleated in the ports
  c) linear in the South Wales valleys.

2 Copy out table **H**. Complete it for your nearest rural area or by using the information on this page on Wales. Remember to include the title.

Why more people live in lowland than in upland rural areas H

	Upland Wales	Lowland Wales
Climate		
Height of land		
Farming type		
Jobs		
Transport		

Why are there so many roads and railways in a city?

The London region has the highest **density** road and rail **network** in the UK (see page 66). This high density is due to both physical and human factors.

Physical factors

- The relatively flat land was easy to build upon.
- Routes could be almost straight. They did not have to detour round hills (page 64).
- It was easy to dig tunnels under London for the underground railways.

Human factors

- Transport was needed to link the many settlements which grew here.
- As transport improved more people came to live here. This meant more and better routes.
- As London grew bigger, commuters had a longer distance to travel to work.

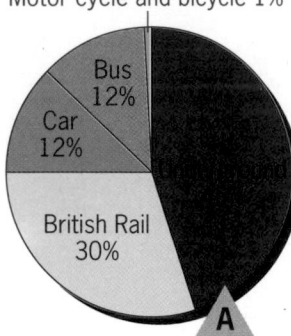

Motor cycle and bicycle 1%
Bus 12%
Car 12%
British Rail 30%

A

Commuters are people who live in one place but who work in a different place. Commuters who work in central London often have a long way to travel. Many live in **suburbs** on the edge of the city. Others live in towns beyond the green belt. Graph **A** shows how commuters travel to work. Over one million people commute into London every day. This causes the traffic problems described on page 70.

Transport links in an urban area

Diagram **B** shows how the M25 motorway makes a circle around London. People who drive on the M25 call it the 'Magic Roundabout'. It seems to be in the news programmes every day for, although it was built to help motorists, it has created many new problems.

Diagram **B** shows motorways leading out of London. They go in all directions. London has good road and rail links with the rest of England and Wales.

Diagram **B** also shows Heathrow and Gatwick airports. Some people commute to London by air from Manchester, Scotland and Northern Ireland. These two airports also link London with the rest of the world.

B

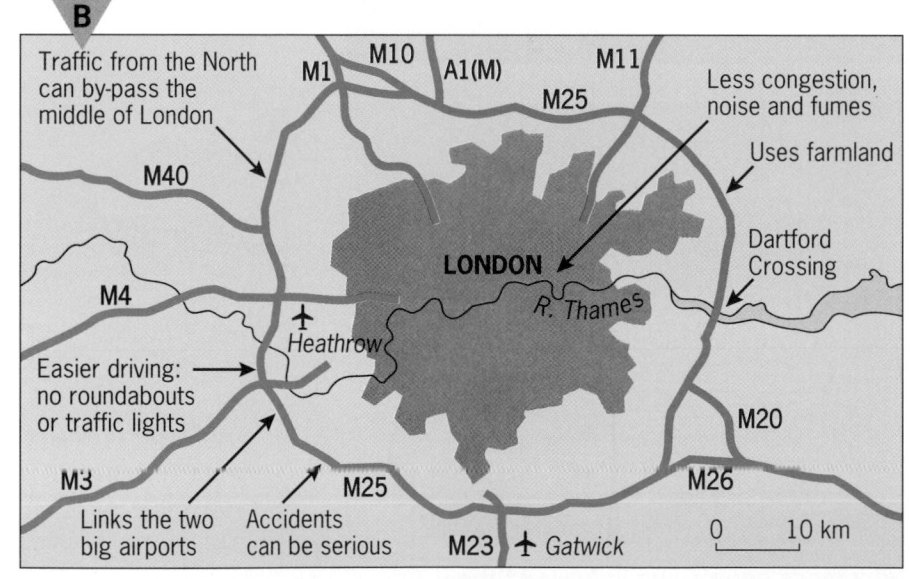

Traffic from the North can by-pass the middle of London
M1 M10 A1(M) M11
M25
Less congestion, noise and fumes
Uses farmland
M40
LONDON
Dartford Crossing
M4
R. Thames
Heathrow
Easier driving: no roundabouts or traffic lights
M20
M3
M25
M26
Links the two big airports
Accidents can be serious
M23 ✈ Gatwick
0   10 km

Summary

Areas with flat land and many settlements have high density traffic networks. Commuters may travel a long way to work.

Activities

1 What is a commuter?

2 Draw a bar graph to show the types of transport used by London commuters.

3 What is your nearest motorway?

4 Complete the table below to show the good and bad points of **either** your nearest motorway **or** the M25.

Good points	Bad points

5 Which motorway links the M25 with
a) Heathrow, b) Gatwick?

Why are there fewer main roads and railways in a rural area?

Apart from South Wales and part of North Wales, this region has one of the lowest **density** road and rail **networks** in the UK (see page 67). This low density is due to both physical and human factors.

Physical factors	Human factors
◆ The hilly land is difficult to build upon. ◆ The hills mean most routes had to have big detours (page 64).	◆ As many parts had few settlements there was less need for more and better routes. ◆ Many people had to travel only a short distance to work.

Transport links in a rural area

There are few roads and no railways between North and South Wales (map **C**). In most of the region the main routes are next to the coast. Inland routes have to follow the flatter land of river valleys. It is often hard to get from one river valley to the next because of the highland between them (photo **F**, page 83). The main transport link within Wales is the M4 motorway (diagram **D**). It was built to link the main towns, ports and industries of South Wales. At the same time it by-passed the centres of big cities. In North Wales the A55 is a major transport link.

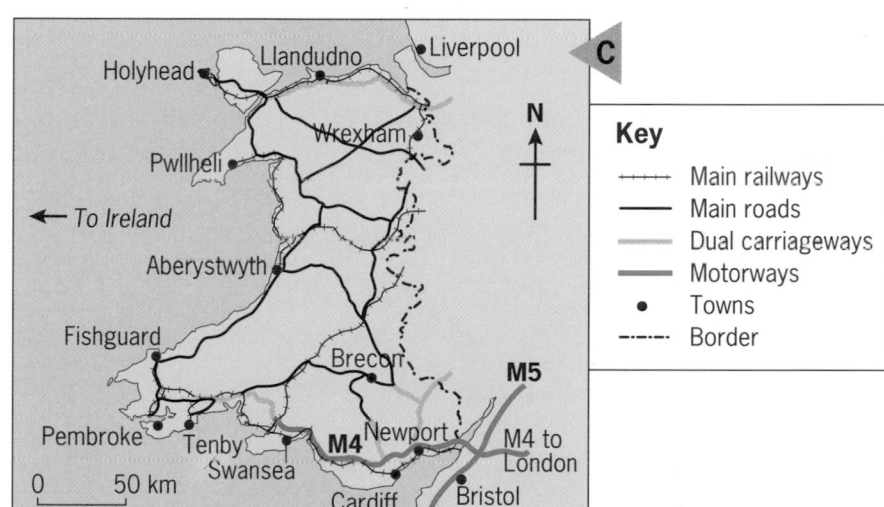

Key
- ┼┼┼┼ Main railways
- ——— Main roads
- ——— Dual carriageways
- ——— Motorways
- ● Towns
- —·—·— Border

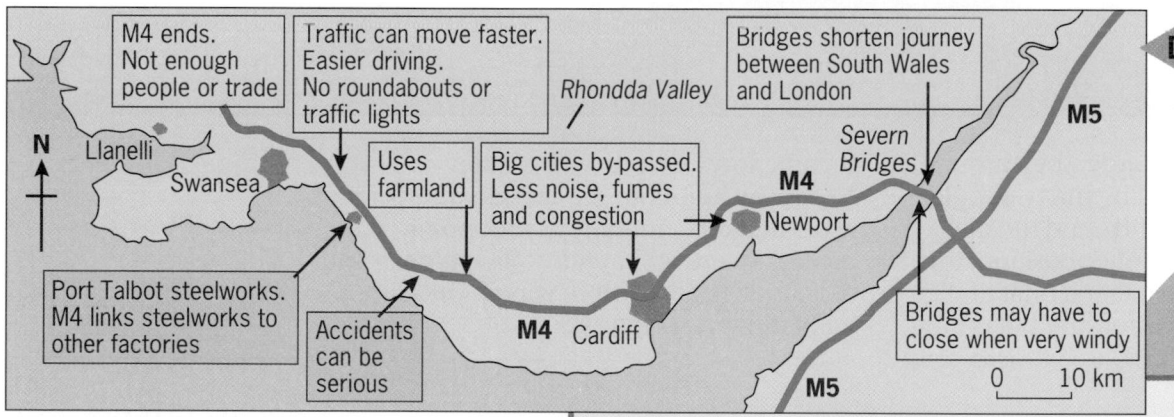

Map **C** shows that the M4 is also the main link with England. There are two main railways from England. These go to the ports of Holyhead and Fishguard. Ferries from these ports link Wales with the Republic of Ireland.

Good points	Bad points

Activities

1 Name **three** places in South Wales which are linked to each other by the M4.

2 What is your nearest motorway?

3 Complete the table on the left to show the good and bad points of **either** your nearest motorway **or** the M4.

Summary

Areas which are mainly highland and have few settlements tend to have low density traffic networks. In Wales, the density is highest in the south. People do not often travel far to work.

What pressures do we put on the countryside?

London's green belt

London has always attracted people to it. As more people arrived the city grew outwards, getting bigger and bigger in size. We have already seen that to try to stop London getting bigger a **green belt** was created around it (page 82). Green belts were later put around other large British cities. Green belts had two main functions.

1 To stop outward growth of cities by restricting the building of houses, factories and roads.

2 To leave the area around the city free for farming and for recreation.

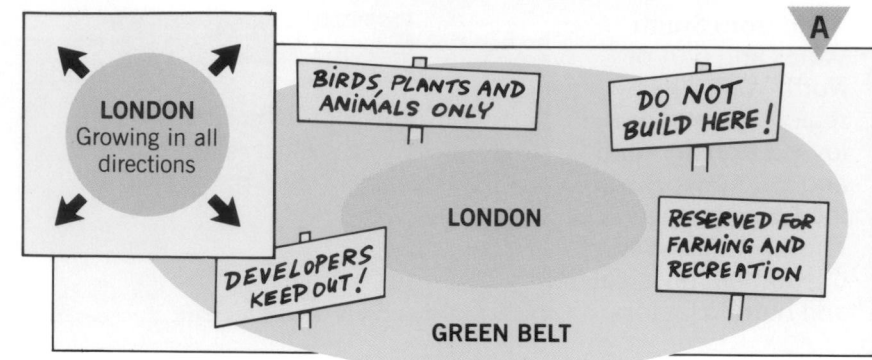

Present day pressures on green belts, especially in London, are enormous. Some of these pressures are shown in cartoon **B**.

One pressure put on the green belt around London was the demand by many people for a new motorway to surround the city. Although there was a lot of opposition, the M25 was eventually built. Once built and opened, it added to the pressure put on the green belt.

Drivers now need service stations. Motorway interchanges are ideal sites for hypermarkets, out-of-town shopping centres (page 58), hotels, office blocks and industrial estates. There is now pressure to build these near the M25.

Activities

1 a) What is a green belt?
   b) Give **four** reasons why people might want to build in the green belt.

2 Divide your class into small groups. Each group will speak for a group of people in the community. Some groups will want to protect the green belt, while others will want to develop it. Think of groups for yourselves. You might consider long distance lorry drivers, bird watchers, property developers, local residents and so on. Decide why the group you represent will be for or against development of the green belt.

Summary

Green belts were created to stop cities spreading into the countryside. There are many pressures put on green belts for their development.

What pressures do we put on the countryside?

Wales – Snowdonia

Pressures are put on the countryside in rural areas. Snowdonia is one of three **National Parks** in Wales (see map on page 77). National Parks are areas of natural scenic beauty where people can enjoy open-air recreation. Snowdonia has many attractive mountains, lakes and coasts. However, these attractions put many pressures upon the area. A major problem is 'How can visitors be attracted to Snowdonia without the environment being spoilt?' Some of the problems are shown in cartoon **C**.

Most visitors to Snowdonia go by car. This causes congestion on the narrow roads. When car parks are full, people park on grass verges. Walkers destroy vegetation and wear away footpaths. Wildlife is frightened away. Some tourists want picnic areas, toilets and camp sites. They often drop litter, leave field gates open and do not always have their dogs under control.

Elsewhere in Snowdonia tourists want:

● access to forests owned by the Forestry Commission

● access to reservoirs owned by Dwr Cymru Welsh Water

● to buy 'second homes' to use at weekends and during holidays.

Summary

Visitors put great pressure upon attractive, scenic areas. National Parks were created to encourage people to visit such places, while at the same time protecting the natural beauty and wildlife of an area.

Activities

1 What is a National Park?

2 Name the three National Parks in Wales. The map on page 77 will help you.

3 Divide your class into small groups. Each group will speak for a group of people using Snowdonia. Think of groups yourselves. You might consider the Forestry Commission, Dwr Cymru Welsh Water, local farmers, local shopkeepers and weekend visitors. Decide why the group you represent will be for or against encouraging more visitors to the area.

Why do people have different views on changes in their local region?

Any change will affect people and the environment. Some individuals and groups of people like change if it makes their lives easier and more pleasant. Others will not like change if it makes their lives harder and less pleasant. An example of a suggested change in the London region is the need for an extra airport runway, or a new terminal building.

Perhaps you have already flown in an aeroplane. Thirty years ago very few people had. People fly on business or to go on holiday. Many going on holiday have to fly from one of London's two main airports. Each year the number of people flying from Heathrow and Gatwick increases (see graph **A**). As more people fly, airports get very full, planes are delayed and the risk of mid-air crashes increases. There has been talk about improving London's airports for many years. Two suggestions are that Gatwick should have a second runway, or that Heathrow should have a fifth terminal.

A

Passengers at Heathrow and Gatwick

Millions: 150, 100, 50, 0

1976   1988   2000

B

How might people react to a second runway at Gatwick, or a fifth terminal at Heathrow?

Pilot

If there is an accident on the runway we cannot land. A second runway would be much safer.

Residents

More planes would mean more jobs and more money.

Passengers

Any additions could mean pulling down my house.

Airline official

Environmentalist

We already have lots of noise from planes. Roads are busy with people using the airport.

At present there are long waits and overcrowding at both airports. The new runway and terminal would allow more planes to land and take off.

Villager in Charlwood

Either change would be very harmful to wildlife and would increase pollution.

Most people agree that another runway or terminal is needed. However, nobody wants them to be near where they live. The problem is to try to improve the safety and convenience of air passengers, while at the same time protecting the environment and the quality of life of local residents.

Activities

1 Using diagram **B** make two lists. In the first, name the groups of people who think a second runway or a fifth terminal is needed. In the second, name those groups who are against the suggestions.

2 Write **two** letters to your local newspaper. Each letter should be about half a page in length.
   a) In letter 1 give the views of people who see advantages in having a second runway at Gatwick or a new terminal at Heathrow.
   b) In letter 2 give the views of peole who do not want the proposed scheme.

Summary

There are always people who want change in the local area and others who do not.

Why do people have different views on changes in their local region?

No place stays the same for ever. Places are always changing. Changes affect people and the environment. Some people like change while others are opposed to it. A recent example in Wales was when the last coal mine in the Rhondda Valley closed.

The two valleys which make up the Rhondda lie north-west of Cardiff (see map on page 77). In 1850 the valley was described as 'a green wilderness with the air smelling of wild flowers'. By 1900 the Rhondda was one of the major coal mining areas in the world. There were over 60 pits and several thousand miners. Each village had its own mine which was often the only source of work and money. Since 1930 the numbers of pits and miners have fallen in the Rhondda and in other Welsh valleys. The rapid fall in coal production is shown in graph **C**.

C Coal production in Wales

D How might people in the Rhondda have reacted to the closing of the last coalmine?

Miner: I am 45. I have been down the pit all my life. I am not trained to do any other job. I was offered a job down a pit in Yorkshire but I do not want to leave this area.

Girl school-leaver: Girls have always found it very hard to get jobs locally.

Young mother: They plan to turn the valley into a leisure park. This will be safer and cleaner for young children.

Boy school-leaver: To get a job I will either have to travel to Cardiff each day or move away from home.

Grandmother: I am glad the mine has closed. My husband was killed in an underground accident. My son has health problems due to breathing in coal dust.

Union leader: They should have built factories to make up for the loss of the pit. A leisure park is no use if people have no jobs.

Shopkeeper: With so few jobs in the valley people will have little to spend in my shop. People who work in Cardiff will also shop there.

British Coal official: It cost so much to get the coal out that the pit was losing money.

Activities

1 Using diagram **D** make **two** lists. In the first name the groups that were pleased that the mine closed. In the second name the groups who did not want the mine to close.

2 Write **two** letters to your local newspaper. Each letter should be about half a page in length.
   a) In letter 1 give the views of people in the area who saw advantages in the closing of the mine.
   b) In letter 2 give the views of people in the area who saw disadvantages in the closing of the mine.

Summary

There are always people who want change in the local area and others who do not.

Urban puzzles

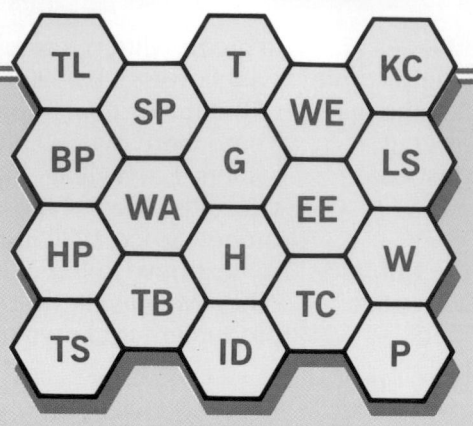

1 Make the *Blockbusters Gold Run* by solving the following clues to get a linking route across the puzzle. The letters in each shape are the start of words that are places in London. Start at the left hand side and make your way across the puzzle. When you solve a clue write down the answer and, if you have a copy of the puzzle, shade in the shape.

TL an old castle	**H** an airport
HP Big Ben is above this building	**EE** port and industry area
BP where the Queen lives	**WE** an area of shops and entertainment
TS Nelson's Column is found here	**TC** banking and commerce area
SP a cathedral	**KC** a railway station
TB a bridge which lifts up	**W** a railway station
WA a cathedral	**LS** a railway station
G an airport	**P** a railway station
ID part of London's Docklands	
T London's river	

2 The 12 missing words in the crossword refer to key geographical words used in the section on London. When finished the letters in the shaded boxes will make a title.

a) A settlement with buildings that are close together.

b) Where ships used to unload in London.

c) A settlement with buildings that are in a line.

d) Another name for the London tube.

e) People who travel a long way to work in London.

f) Type of rain which falls in summer.

g) A climatic hazard in summer.

h) An area around London where no new building is allowed.

i) A climatic hazard in autumn and winter.

j) This describes the relief of this region.

k) Gatwick and Heathrow are these.

l) This describes the landscape of most of this region.

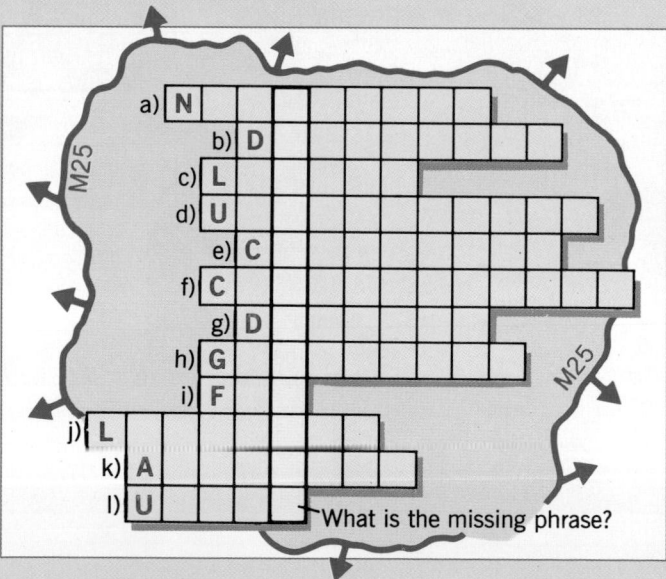

What is the missing phrase?

You should now be able to make a short summary of your home region. You can do this by using **key words** to complete this table.

Climate	Temperature	
	Rainfall	
Landscape	Physical	
	Human	
Settlement	Functions	
	Patterns	
Transport		
Environmental problems		

E X T R A

Rural puzzles

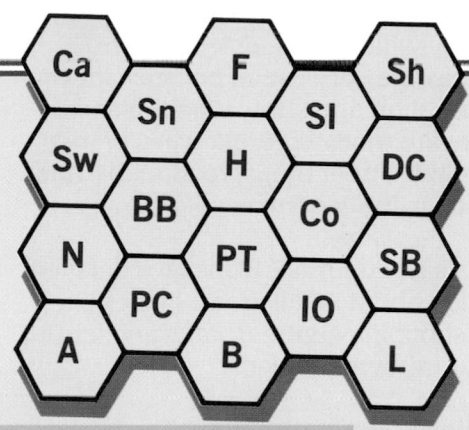

1 Make the *Blockbusters Gold Run* by solving the following clues to get a linking route across the puzzle. The letters in each shape are the start of words which are connected with Wales. Start at the left hand side and make your way across the puzzle. As before, when you solve a clue write down the answer and, if you have a copy of the puzzle, shade in the shape.

Ca capital city	**A** an island
N town on the south coast	**BB** National Park
Sn National Park	**F** ferry port
P National Park	**PT** steel-making town
H ferry port	**SI** quarried in North Wales
B town in North Wales	**IO** steel is made from this
Co mined in South Wales	**DC** farm animals in lowland areas
Sh farm animals in upland areas	**L** town on the north coast
SB M4 crosses this into England	
Sw large city	

2 The 11 missing words in the crossword refer to key geographical words used in the section on Wales. When finished the letters in the shaded boxes will make a title.

a) A climatic hazard in winter.
b) This was found in South Wales valleys.
c) A settlement with buildings that are close together.
d) A type of rainfall caused by mountains.
e) Settlement where buildings are spread out.
f) This describes the landscape of most of this region.
g) This is quarried in North Wales.
h) A climatic hazard.
i) A settlement where buildings are in a line.
j) Protected scenic areas which attract visitors.
k) A type of rainfall brought by depressions.

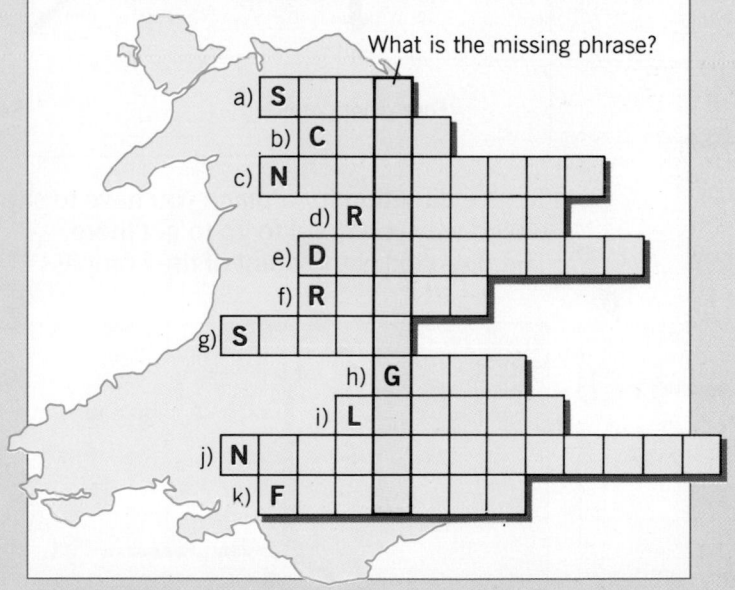

What is the missing phrase?

a) **S**
b) **C**
c) **N**
d) **R**
e) **D**
f) **R**
g) **S**
h) **G**
i) **L**
j) **N**
k) **F**

You should now be able to make a short summary of your home region. You can do this by using **key words** to complete this table.

Climate	Temperature	
	Rainfall	
Landscape	Physical	
	Human	
Settlement	Functions	
	Patterns	
Transport		
Environmental problems		

E X T R A

How can we show direction?

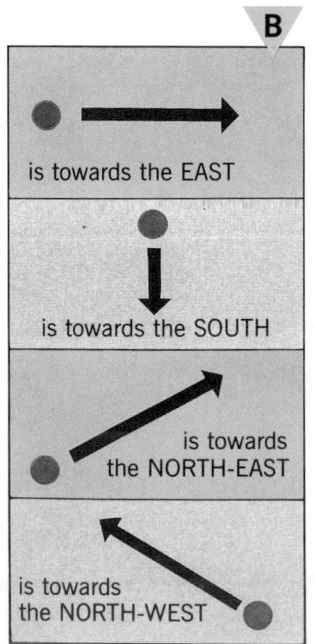

Maps show what things look like from above. They are very useful because they give information and show where places are. There are many different types of map. These include street maps, road maps, **atlas** maps and **Ordnance Survey** (OS) maps.

A **plan** is a type of map. Plans give detailed information about small areas. Places like schools, shopping centres, parks and leisure centres are shown on plans.

This section is about **direction**. The best way to show direction is to use the **points** of the compass. There are four main points. These are north, east, south and west. You can remember their order by saying 'Never Eat Shredded Wheat'.

Between these four main points there are four other points. These are north-east, south-east, south-west and north-west.

Most maps have a sign to show the **north** direction. If there is no sign the top edge of the map should be **north**.

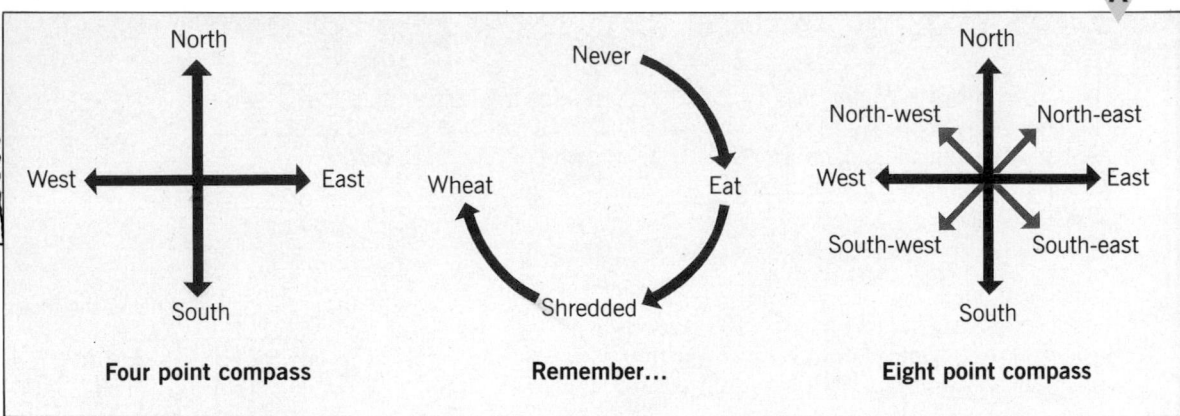

A

Four point compass   Remember...   Eight point compass

To give direction for a place you have to say which way you need to go to get there. The direction is the point of the compass *towards* which way you have to go. Diagrams **B, C** and **D** show you how to give a direction.

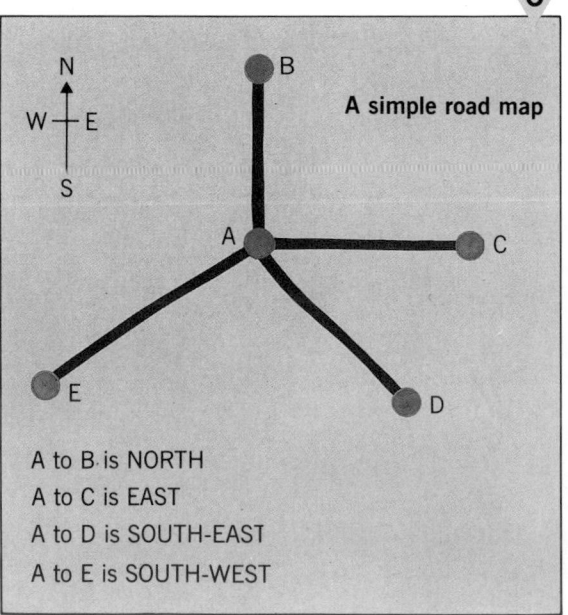

B

is towards the EAST

is towards the SOUTH

is towards the NORTH-EAST

is towards the NORTH-WEST

C

A simple road map

A to B is NORTH
A to C is EAST
A to D is SOUTH-EAST
A to E is SOUTH-WEST

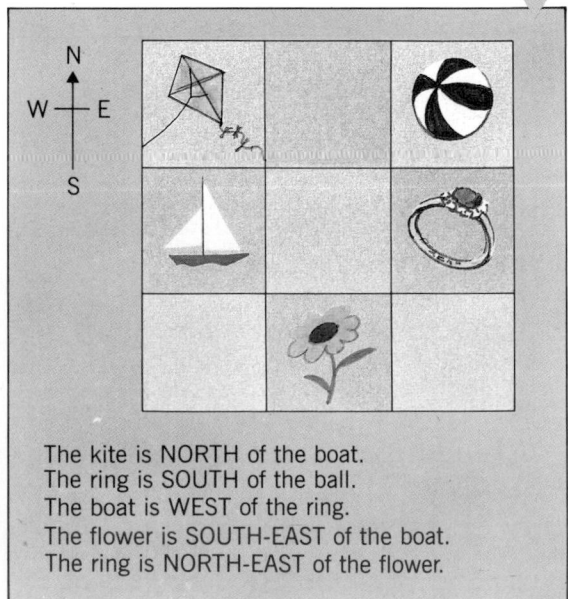

D

The kite is NORTH of the boat.
The ring is SOUTH of the ball.
The boat is WEST of the ring.
The flower is SOUTH-EAST of the boat.
The ring is NORTH-EAST of the flower.

Activities

1 Draw the compass in diagram **E** and label the unmarked points.

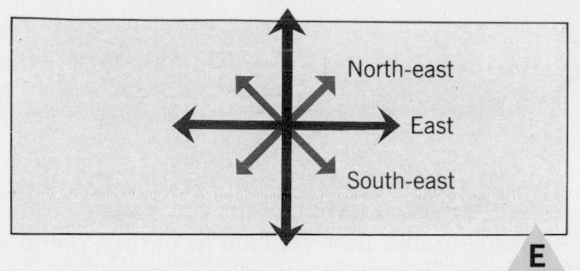

2 Copy these drawings and complete the sentences below them. The first one has been done for you.

 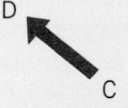  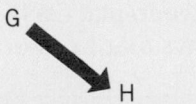 

B is north of **A**   **D** is . . . of **C**   **F** is . . . of **E**   **H** is . . . of **G**   **I** is . . . of **J**

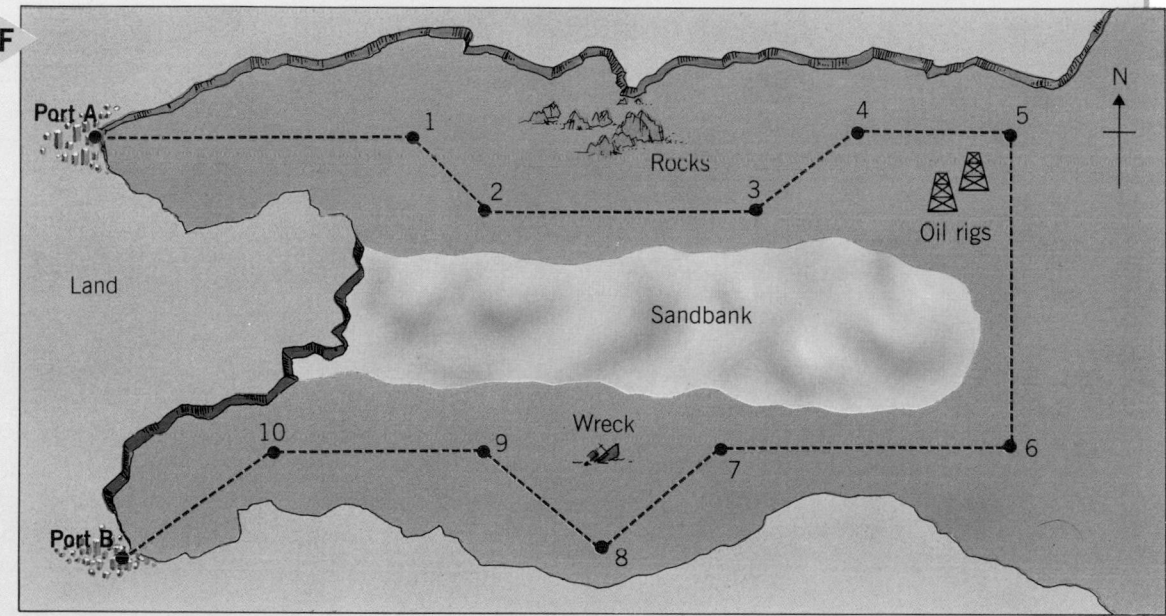

3 Study map **F** and give the following directions:
   a) from Port A to the rocks
   b) from the wreck to the oil rigs
   c) from the oil rigs to the rocks
   d) from the wreck to Port A
   e) from the rocks to the wreck.

4 a) A ship has landed its cargo at Port A. It must go to Port B to reload. The course the ship must follow is shown by the dotted line on the map. Give the Captain compass directions to follow between each numbered point. Start like this: *Leave Port A. Go east to point 1. Go south-east . . .*
   b) Imagine that the sandbank has been cleared to make ship movement easier. Work out the best course from Port B to Port A. Give compass directions to follow that course.

E X T R A

You will need to use the Ordnance Survey map of the Cambridge area for this question. It is on page 109.

Look at the villages near the bottom of the map. Give the following directions:
a) from Foxton to Whittlesford
b) from Foxton to Newton
c) from Great Shelford to Whittlesford
d) from Great Shelford to Haslingfield
e) from Haslingfield to Harston.

Summary

Maps are a good way of giving information and showing where places are. Direction can be described by using the points of the compass.

How can we measure distance?

A map can be used to find out how far one place is from another. Maps have to be drawn smaller than real life to fit on a piece of paper. How much smaller they are is shown by the **scale**. This shows you the **real** distance between places. In diagram **A** the scale line shows that 1 cm on the map is the same as 1 km on the ground. Every map should have a **scale line**.

Straight line distances are easy to work out. Diagram **A** shows how to measure the straight line, or shortest, distance between the church and the bridge.

A

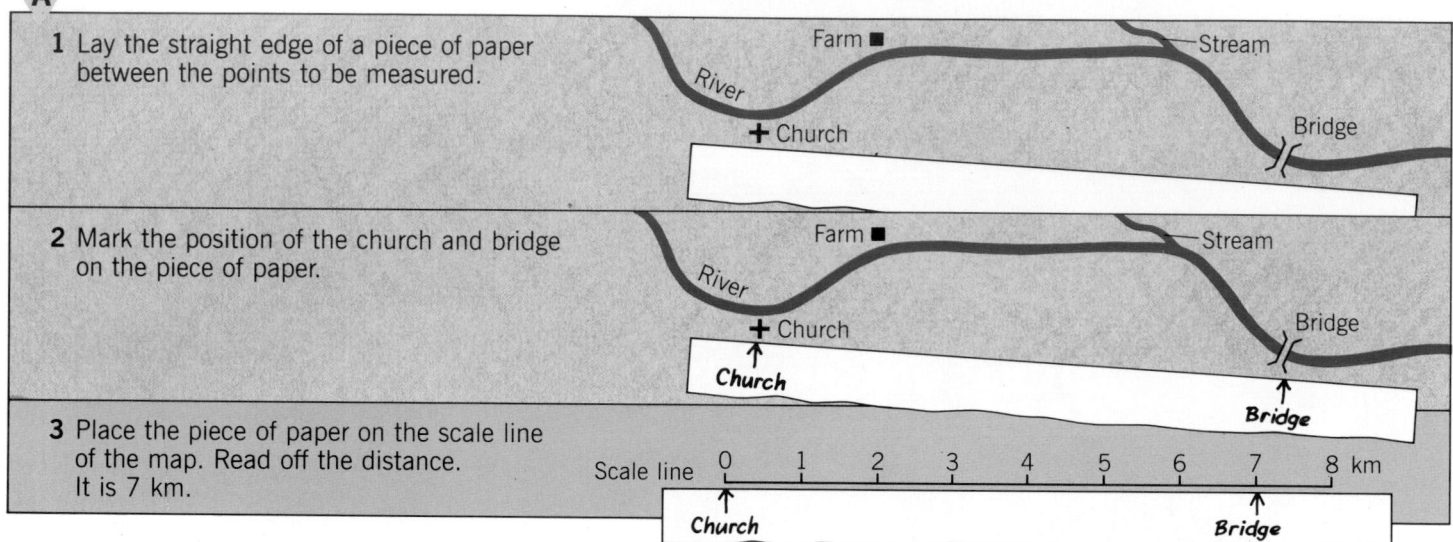

1 Lay the straight edge of a piece of paper between the points to be measured.

2 Mark the position of the church and bridge on the piece of paper.

3 Place the piece of paper on the scale line of the map. Read off the distance. It is 7 km.

The same method can be used to work out distances that are not straight lines. To measure these, divide the route into a number of sections and measure each one.

This can be done by using a piece of paper and turning it at each bend. Diagram **B** shows how to measure the distance from the church to the bridge, following the river.

B

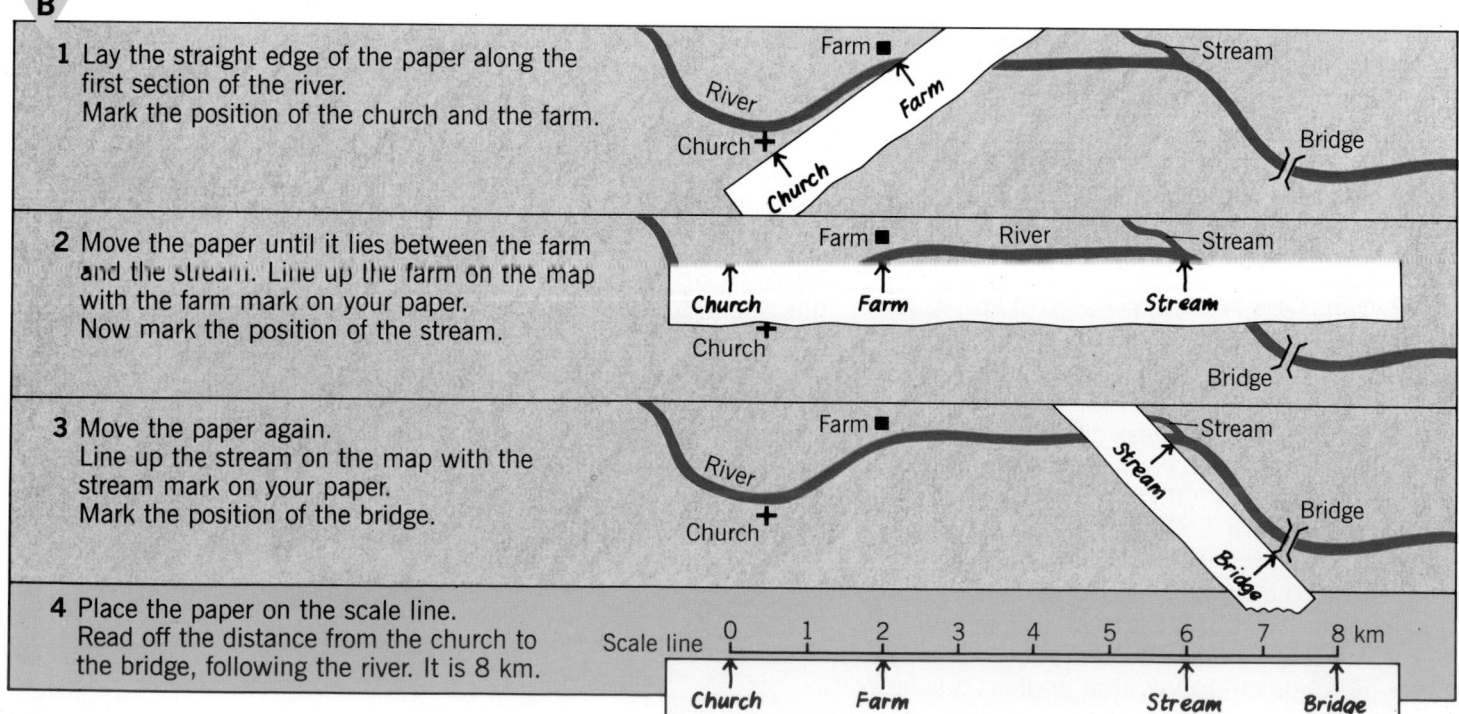

1 Lay the straight edge of the paper along the first section of the river. Mark the position of the church and the farm.

2 Move the paper until it lies between the farm and the stream. Line up the farm on the map with the farm mark on your paper. Now mark the position of the stream.

3 Move the paper again. Line up the stream on the map with the stream mark on your paper. Mark the position of the bridge.

4 Place the paper on the scale line. Read off the distance from the church to the bridge, following the river. It is 8 km.

Activities

1 Use the scale line from map **C** to give the lengths of these lines. Answer like this:
Line **a)** is ... metres (m) in length.

a) _____

b) _____

c) _____

d) _____

2 Use map **C** and the scale line to give the straight line distance between the places below. Choose your answers from the following:

| 40 m | 80 m | 100 m | 120 m |

a) Kate's house and the school.
b) Joanne's house and the post office.
c) Tim's house and the post office.
d) John's house and the garage.

3 a) Give the distance Joanne has to travel to school if she calls on Kate on the way.

b) Give the distance John has to travel to school if he calls at the shop and post office first.

4 What is the distance around the duck pond if you walk on the footpath? Give your answer in metres (m).

5 You have been given a map and instructions to help you find some hidden treasure. Follow the instructions to find out where it is.

Check the exact spot by sorting out the jumbled words in the treasure chest and choosing the correct answer.

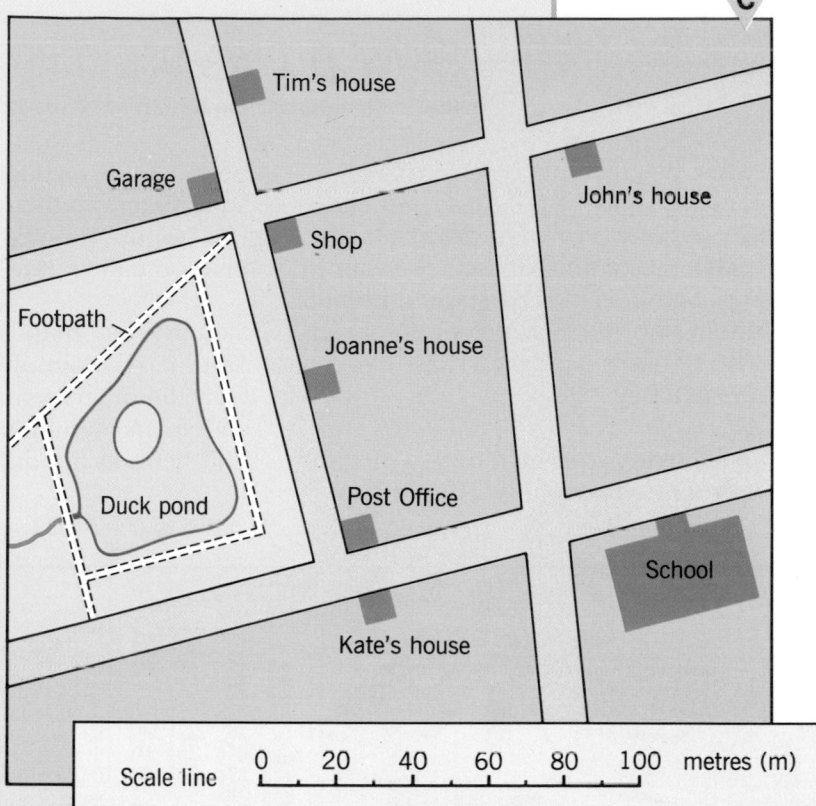

C

Tim's house

Garage

John's house

Shop

Footpath

Joanne's house

Duck pond

Post Office

School

Kate's house

Scale line 0 20 40 60 80 100 metres (m)

D

Find the treasure

N
NW   NE
W   E
SW   SE
S

Start here

Scale 0   1   2   3   4   5 km

Leave the wreck and go east for 2 km. Go north for 2 km, west for 1 km, then north-west for another 1 km. Now head north-east for 3 km and east for 2 km. Go south for 4 km and finally west for 1½ km.

NI EHT SLILH

REDUN ETH GIDBER
LWOBE HET GIB ERTE

Summary Distances on a map can be measured using the scale line. The scale line gives the real distance between places on the map.

95

How do we use map symbols?

A map must be clear and easy to read. There is always a lot to put on a map and it can easily become crowded. **Symbols** are used to save space and to make it easier to see things. Symbols may be small drawings, lines, letters, shortened words or coloured areas. The symbols used on a map are explained in a **key**.

If you are drawing your own map, you can make up your own symbols. They should be as simple as possible and look something like the feature they stand for. How would you show a post box, a library or a football ground?

Sketch **A** and map **B** show the same street. The map has simplified the street scene. Only the main features of the street are shown and symbols are used to save space. The symbols are explained in the key.

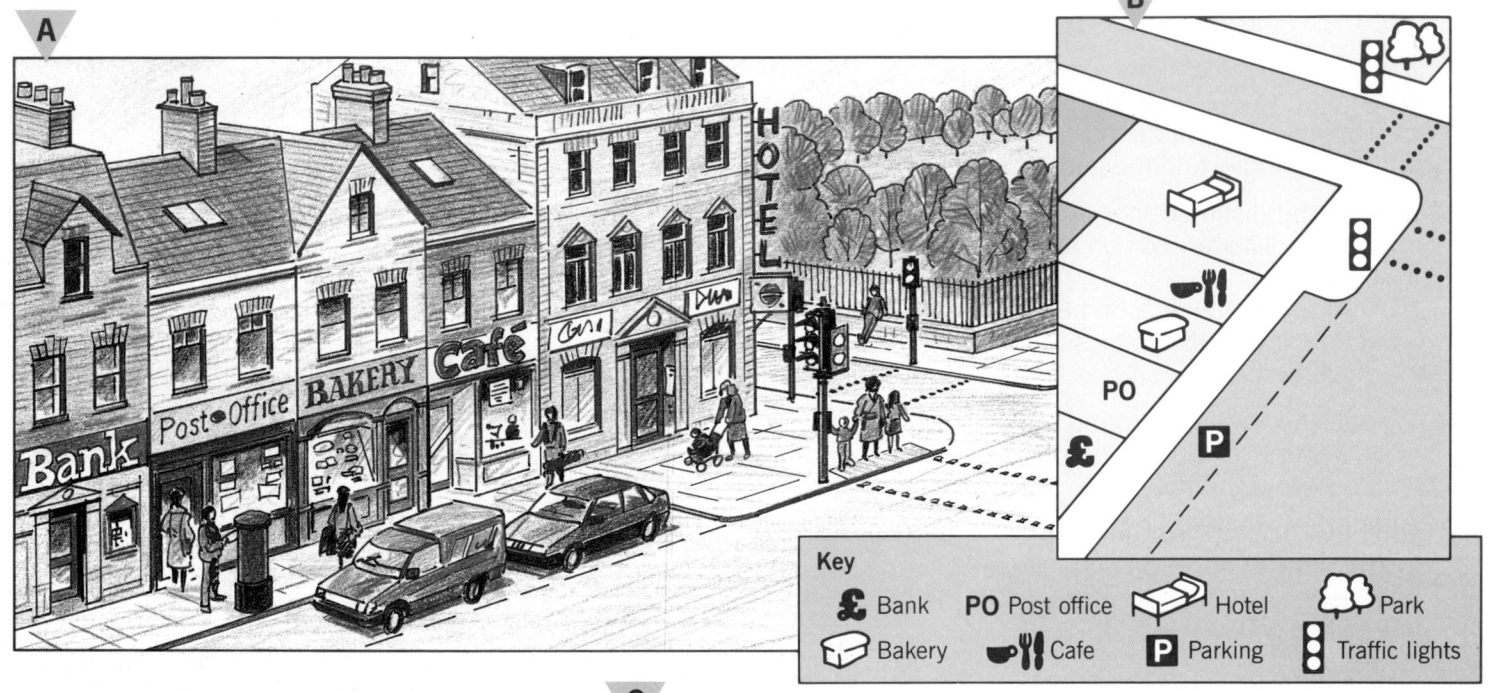

Key

£ Bank	PO Post office	Hotel	Park
Bakery	Cafe	P Parking	Traffic lights

The **Ordnance Survey** (OS) is responsible for mapping Britain. The OS produces very accurate maps that have a lot of information on them.

There is an Ordnance Survey map of the Cambridge area on page 109 of this book. The symbols used on that map are on page 108.

Look at the photos in **C**. They show some of the symbols used on Ordnance Survey maps. Which symbols could you work out without the answers being given?

Activities

1 Look at map **D**. It is part of the Ordnance Survey map of the Cambridge area from page 109. It has been enlarged to make it easier to read. The scale has changed so the 4 cm on the map equals 1 km on the ground.
   a) Make a copy of table **E** below.
   b) Draw the symbols from map **D** in the correct columns of your table.
   c) Say what each symbol shows. You will need to use the key on page 108. Some have been done for you.

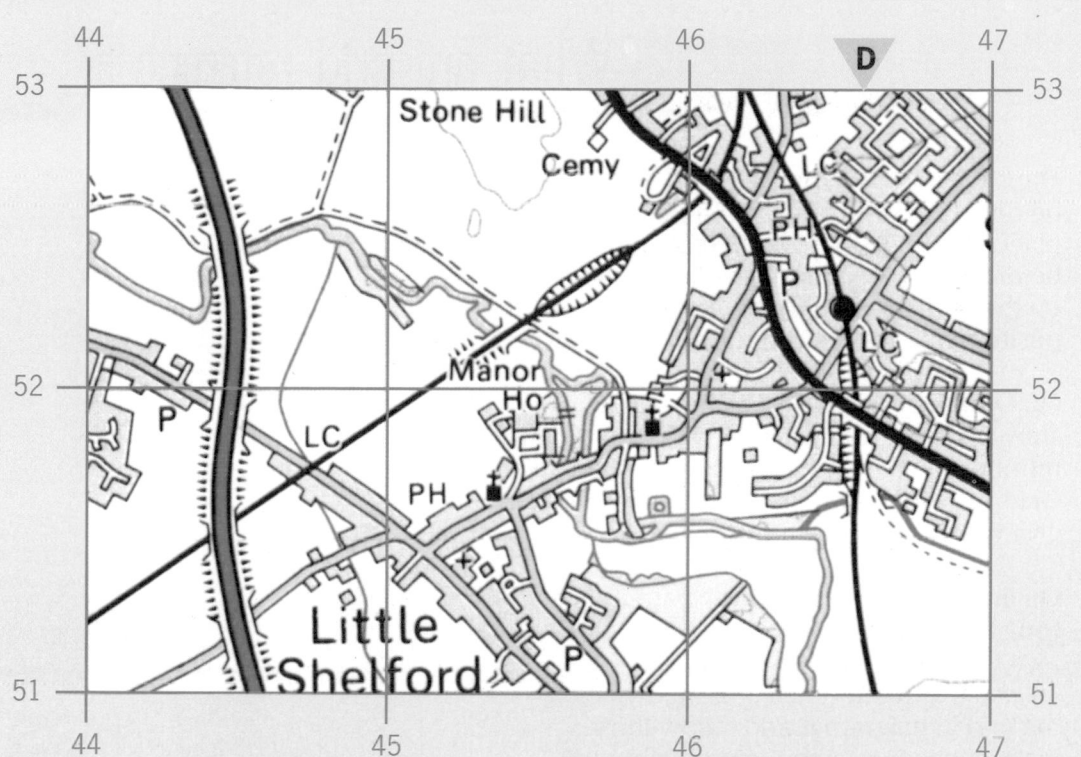

© Crown Copyright

E

Drawings	Lines	Abbreviations (letters/shortened words)	Coloured aeas
\\\\\\//// //||\\ = Embankment	⌒⌒ = Contour	Cemy = Cemetery	■ = Buildings

2 Make a larger copy of map **F**. It should be at least half a page in size. Using the Ordnance Survey symbols from page 108, draw on the map the following information.

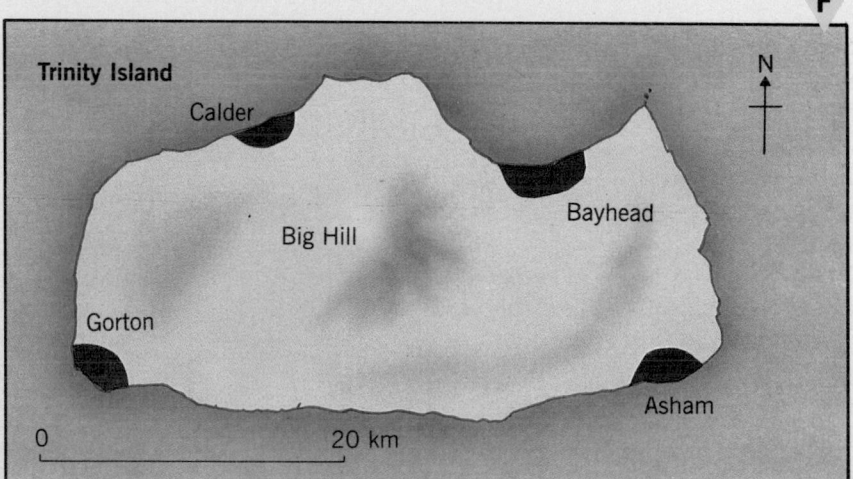

- There is a main road between Gorton and Bayhead, and a second class road between Bayhead and Asham. A minor road joins Asham and Gorton and goes on to Calder.

- A railway line runs from Asham to Gorton, to Calder and on to Bayhead. The station at Calder is closed but the others are open.

- Gorton has a church with a spire and a chapel. Bayhead has a church with a tower and a post office. Asham has a telephone box and a youth hostel.

- The spot height at Big Hill is 312 metres high. The land south of Big Hill is marshy.

- The River Bee rises to the north of Big Hill and flows into the sea at Calder. (Remember to use bridges.)

- There is a wood on the east coast.

3 Draw a map of an island of your own. Use at least **15** different symbols. Name your towns, villages and other main features. Give your map a title.

Summary

Symbols are simple drawings that show things on maps. All maps have a key to explain the symbols.

What are grid references?

Maps can be quite complicated and it may be difficult to find things on them. To make places easier to find, a grid of squares may be drawn on the map. If the lines making up the grid are numbered, the exact position of a square can be given.

On Ordnance Survey maps these lines are shown in blue and each has its own special number. The blue lines form **grid squares**. **Grid references** are the numbers which give the position of a grid square.

On these two pages you will learn about **four figure grid references**.

To *give* a grid reference is simple. Look at the grid in diagram **A** and follow these instructions to give the reference for the yellow square.

- Give the number of the line on the *left* of the yellow square – it is 04.
- Give the number of the line at the *bottom* of the yellow square – it is 12.
- Put the numbers together and you have a four figure grid reference. It is 0412.

In the same way, the Picnic Square has a reference of 0313 and the Church Square is 0512.

What will be the grid references for the Bridge Square and the Tent Square?

To *find* a grid reference is also easy. Look at the grid in diagram **B** and follow these instructions to find grid square 4237.

- Go along the top of the grid until you come to 42. That line will be on the *left* of your grid square.
- Go up the side of the grid until you come to 37. That line will be at the *bottom* of your square.
- Now follow those two lines until they meet. Your square will be above and to the right of that point. There is a house in it.

What is in squares 4136 and 4037?

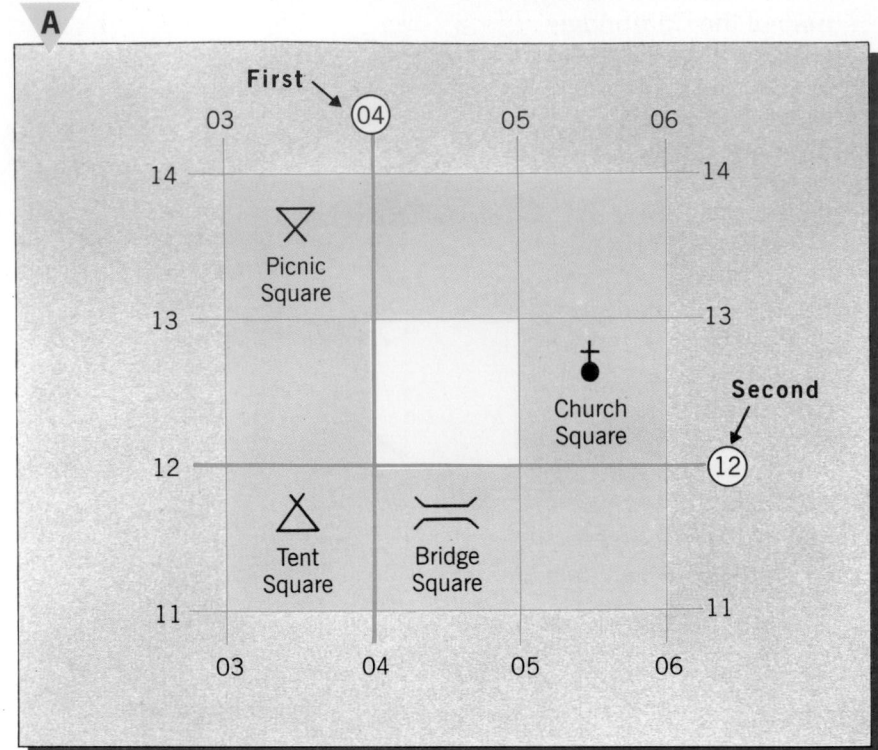

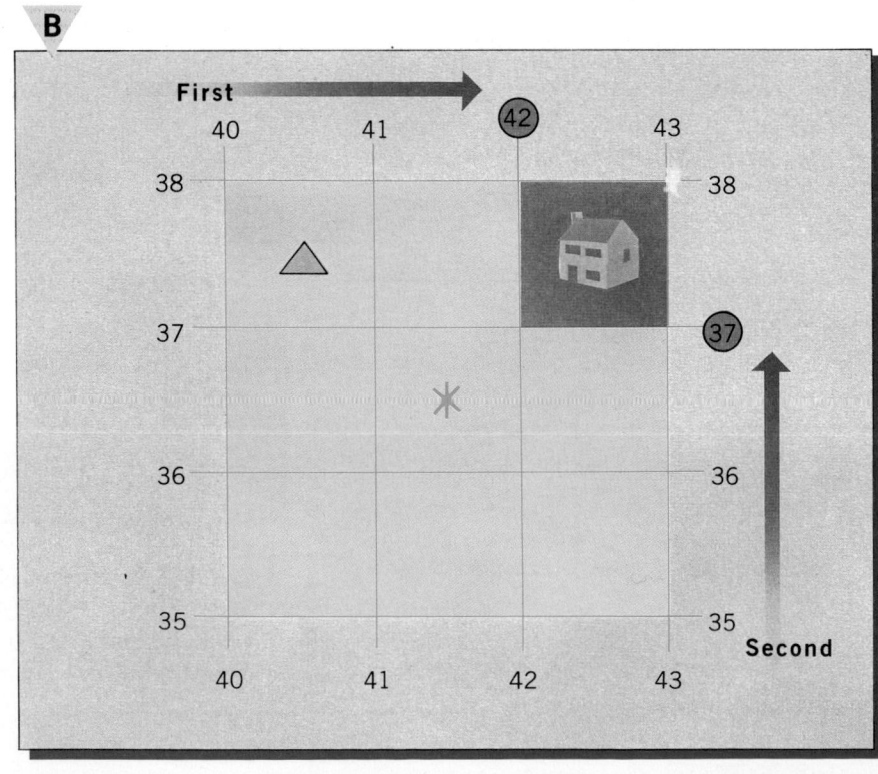

Activities

Look at map **C** of the British Isles. It shows some of the main towns, mountain areas and the three longest rivers. Use the map to answer the questions below.

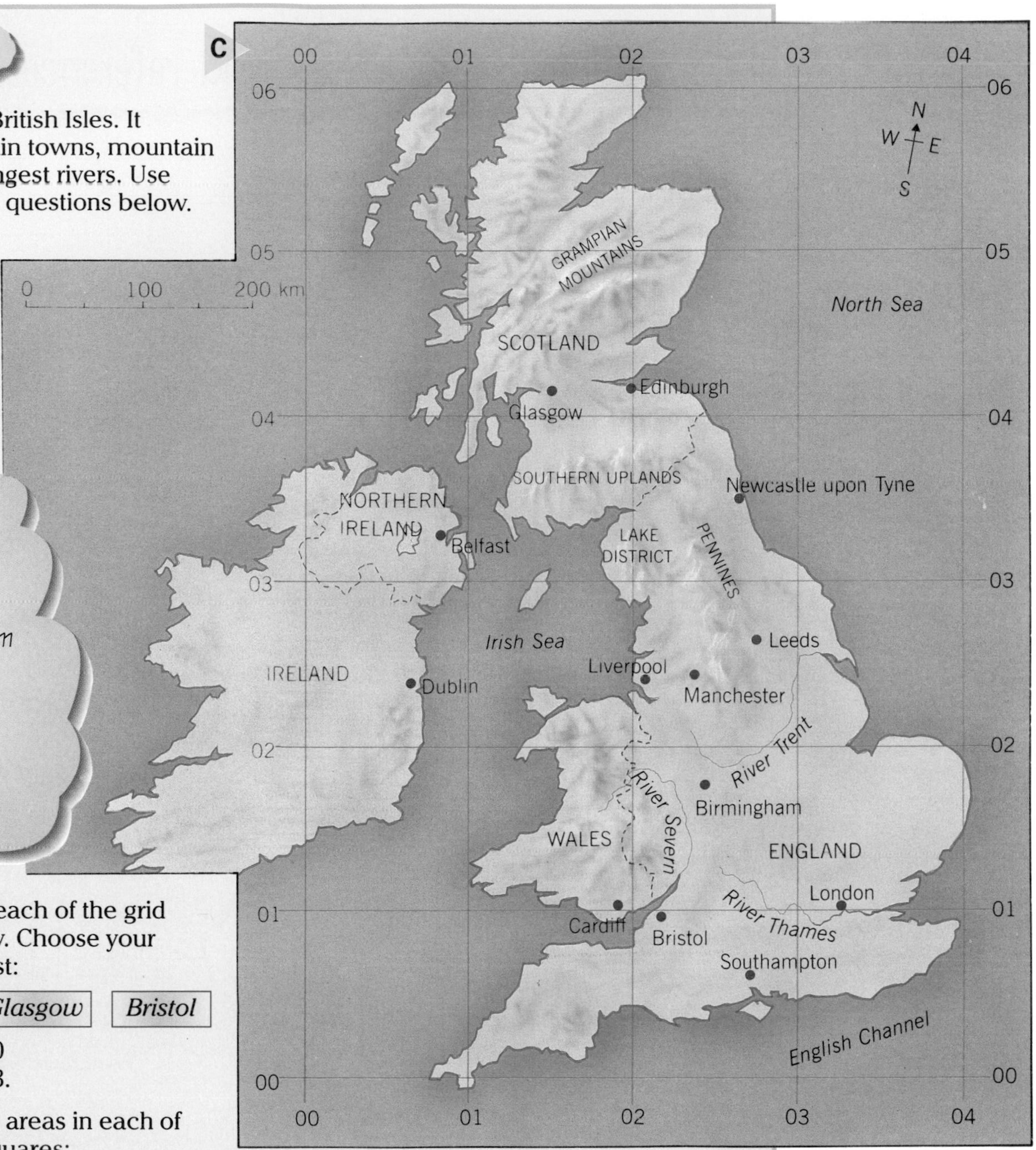

✔ **Remember**

✔ The line on the left comes first.
✔ The line at the bottom comes second.

It may help you to remember if you say '**Along** the corridor and **up** the stairs'.

1 Name the towns in each of the grid squares given below. Choose your answers from this list:

| Belfast | Manchester | Glasgow | Bristol |

a) 0202 **c)** 0200
b) 0104 **d)** 0003.

2 Name the mountain areas in each of the following grid squares:
a) 0104 **c)** 0202.
b) 0103

3 a) Which rivers flow through grid square 0201?
b) Which river reaches the sea in grid square 0201?

4 Give the grid references for these places:
a) Dublin
b) Newcastle upon Tyne
c) London
d) the Irish Sea.

5 Give the grid reference for the place where you live.

C

Map of the British Isles with grid squares. Labels include: GRAMPIAN MOUNTAINS, North Sea, SCOTLAND, Edinburgh, Glasgow, SOUTHERN UPLANDS, Newcastle upon Tyne, NORTHERN IRELAND, Belfast, LAKE DISTRICT, PENNINES, Irish Sea, IRELAND, Dublin, Liverpool, Leeds, Manchester, River Trent, River Severn, Birmingham, WALES, ENGLAND, London, Cardiff, Bristol, River Thames, Southampton, English Channel. Grid lines numbered 00–04 along the bottom and 00–06 up the sides. Scale: 0 100 200 km. Compass rose showing N, E, S, W.

E X T R A

Look at the Ordnance Survey map on page 109. Name the farms in each of the following grid squares (the symbol for farm is Fm).
a) 4149
b) 4156
c) 4456
d) 4650
e) 4257.

Summary

Grid references can be used to help describe the location of a place on a map.

How do we use six figure grid references?

Grid references are very useful in helping us to find places on maps. A four figure reference on an Ordnance Survey map equals an area on the ground of one square kilometre. This is quite a large area. To be more accurate we need to use a **six figure grid reference**. This pinpoints a place exactly to within 100 metres.

Look at the grid in diagram **A**. The six figure grid reference for the church is 045128. Follow these instructions and look at diagrams **B** and **C** to see how that reference is worked out.

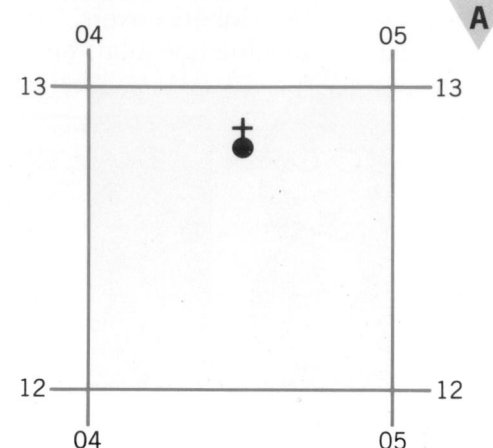

- Give the number of the line on the *left* of the yellow square – it is 04.

- In your head divide the square into tenths as shown in the grid in diagram **B**. Follow arrow **A** across the square. The church is about halfway across from the left. That puts it on the five-tenths line. Write down 5 after your number 04.

- You now have the first half of your six figure reference – it is 045.

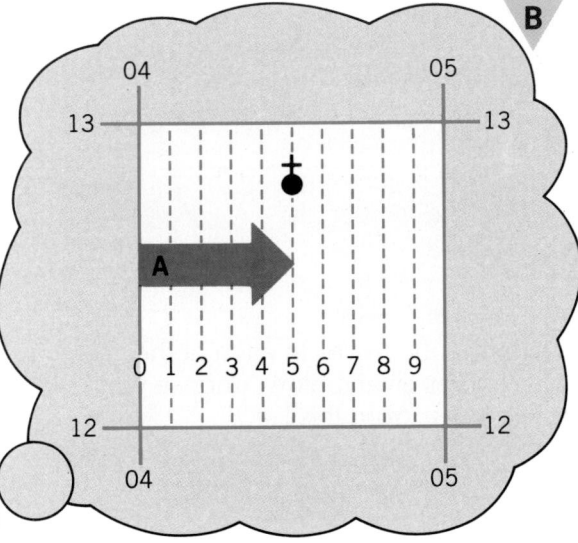

✔ Remember

- ✔ The numbers on the **left** come first.
- ✔ The numbers on the **bottom** come second.
- ✔ There must always be six figures.

- Now give the number of the line at the *bottom* of the yellow square – it is 12.

- In your head divide the square into tenths as shown in the grid in diagram **C**. Follow arrow **B**. The church is over halfway up from the bottom. That puts it on the eight-tenths line. Write down 8 after your number 12.

- You now have the second half of your six figure reference – it is 128.

- Put the two halves together and you have 045128.

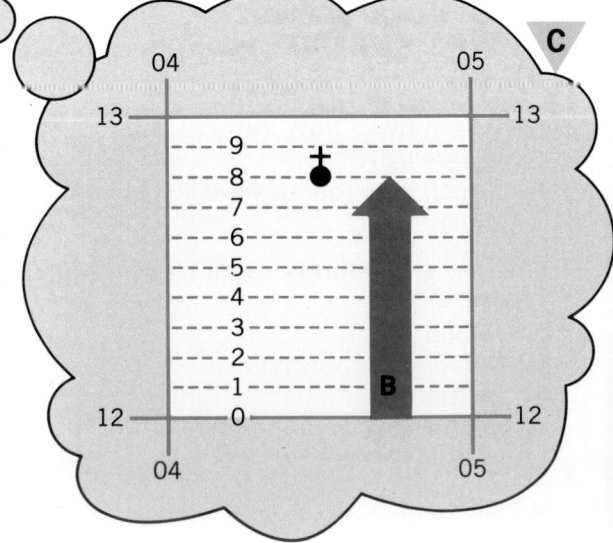

Activities

Look at map **D**. The 'tenths' lines have been added to help you with questions **1**, **2** and **3**. Check your references . . .

● The village of Eldon is in grid square 1623.
● The Mill is at reference 166256.
● Dingle Farm is at reference 170238.

1 Copy and complete the sentences below. Use the correct answer from the brackets.
  a) At 168245 there is a (church, post office, farm).
  b) At 165257 there is a (telephone, school, bridge).
  c) At 175233 there is a (farm, lake, level crossing).
  d) At 177244 there is a (station, wood, roundabout).

2 Give the six figure grid reference for each of the following:
  a) Eldon post office
  b) Causey railway station
  c) Padley school
  d) Burr Wood picnic site.

3 a) Follow these directions for a pleasant walk:

  Start at 170238. Walk down to 173237. Turn left and go to 177244. Go along the road to 171248. Follow the path to 178257. Turn left and finish your walk when the path reaches the road.

  b) Name the place where you finished your walk. Give its six figure grid reference.
  c) Where would you have stopped for lunch?
  d) How many churches did you pass on the way? Give their six figure grid references.

4 You will need to use the Ordnance Survey map of the Cambridge area for this question. It is on page 109.
  a) Make a copy of table **E**.
  b) Use the map to complete table **E**. The missing symbols, meanings and references are given in diagram **F**.

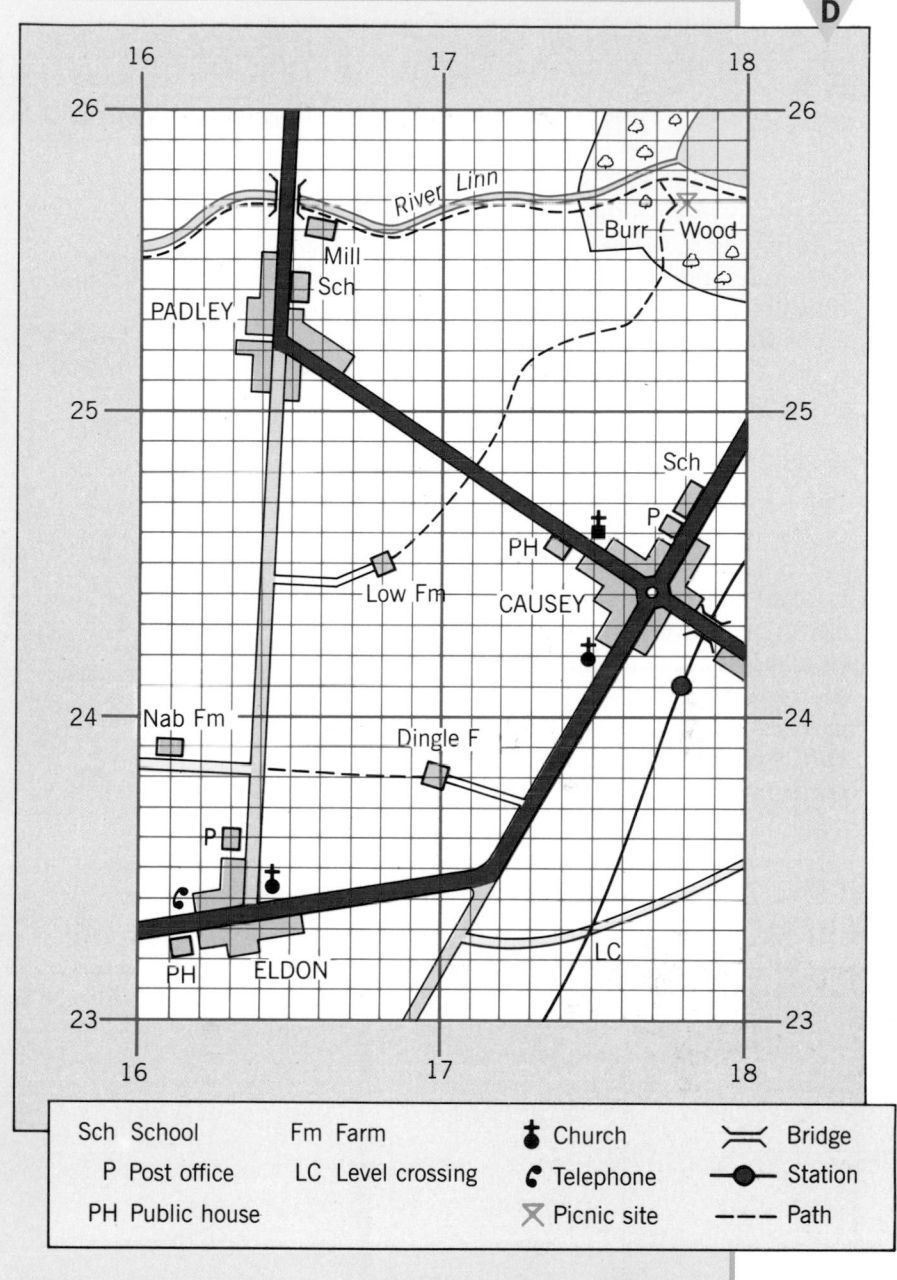

Sch	School	Fm	Farm	♣	Church	⋈	Bridge
P	Post office	LC	Level crossing	✆	Telephone	●—	Station
PH	Public house			✕	Picnic site	- - -	Path

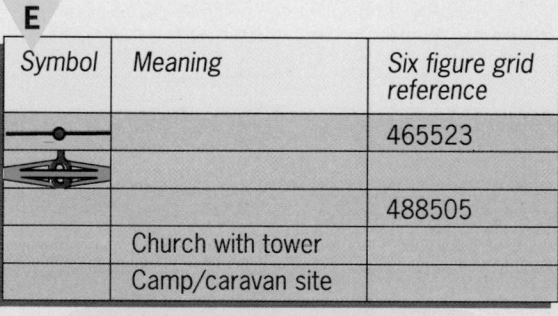

E

Symbol	Meaning	Six figure grid reference
●—		465523
⋏		
		488505
	Church with tower	
	Camp/caravan site	

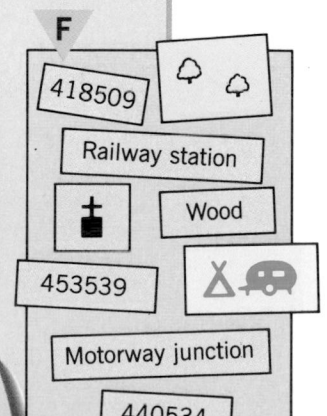

F

418509

Railway station

Wood

453539

Motorway junction

440534

Summary

Six figure grid references can be used to give the exact position of a place on a map.

How is height shown on a map?

The land around us is seldom flat. There are nearly always differences in height and differences in slope. Sometimes slopes may be gentle and at other times steep. There may be hills, mountains and valleys or areas that are quite level. The word **relief** is used by geographers to describe the shape of the land.

Map makers have to find ways of showing relief and height. How they do this is shown on the next four pages.

Look at sketch **A**. How can height on the island be shown on a flat piece of paper? Height is usually measured from sea level in metres. This can then be shown on a map in three different ways. These are by using **spot heights, layer colouring** and **contours**.

A

B

Spot heights

These give the exact height of a point on the map. They are shown as a black dot and each one has a number next to it. The number gives the height in metres. A **triangulation pillar** is also used to show height. These are drawn as a dot inside a blue triangle on the map.

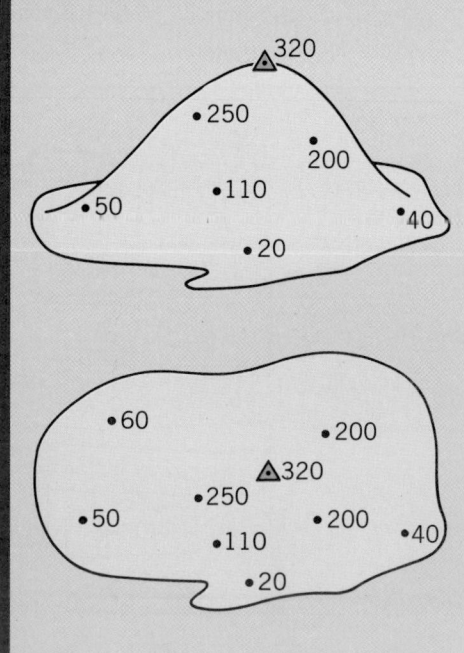

C

Layer colouring

This can also be called **layer shading**. Areas of different heights are shown by bands of different colours. Brown is usually used for high ground, and green for low ground. There always needs to be a key. Layer colouring is used in atlases to show height.

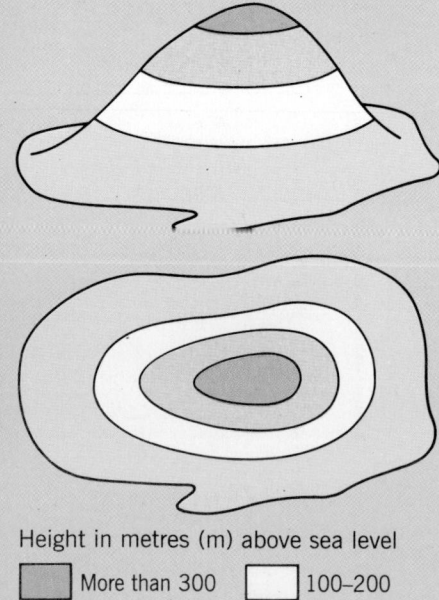

Height in metres (m) above sea level

▨ More than 300	☐ 100–200
☐ 200–300	☐ Less than 100

D

Contours

Contours are lines drawn on a map. They join places which have the same height. They are usually coloured brown. Most contours have their height marked on them but you may have to trace your finger along the line to find it. Sometimes you will have to go to the contour above or below to get the height. Heights are given in metres.

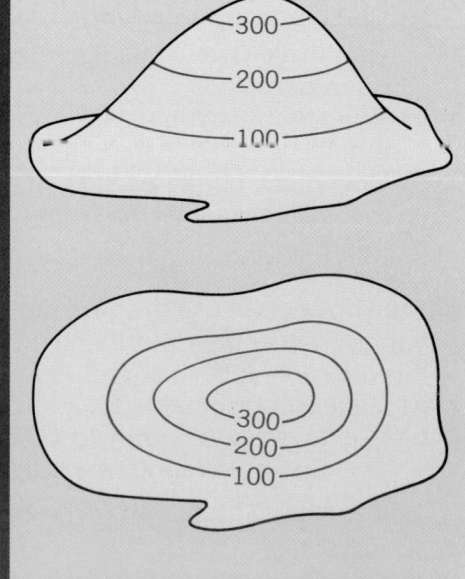

Activities

1 a) Copy out and complete crossword **E** using the clues below.
b) When you have finished, give the meaning of the downword in the orange squares.

Clues

1 Lines that join places of the same height.
2 Height at one place.
3 This can be gentle or steep.
4 Measured from sea level.
5 Colouring to show height.
6 A level area with no slope.

2 Look at map **F** of England and Wales. The map uses layer colouring to show height. The letters mark land at different heights.
a) Which letters mark lowland areas under 100 metres?
b) Which letters mark land between 100 and 300 metres?
c) Which letters mark land above 300 metres?

3 Use map **F** to answer these questions.
a) The highest mountain in England is Scafell Pike and the highest mountain in Wales is Snowdon. What colour are they shaded?
b) The Pennines are an area of high land in the centre of northern England. How high are they?
c) The Cotswolds and Chilterns are hills in the south of England. What height are they?
d) What height is the area where you live?

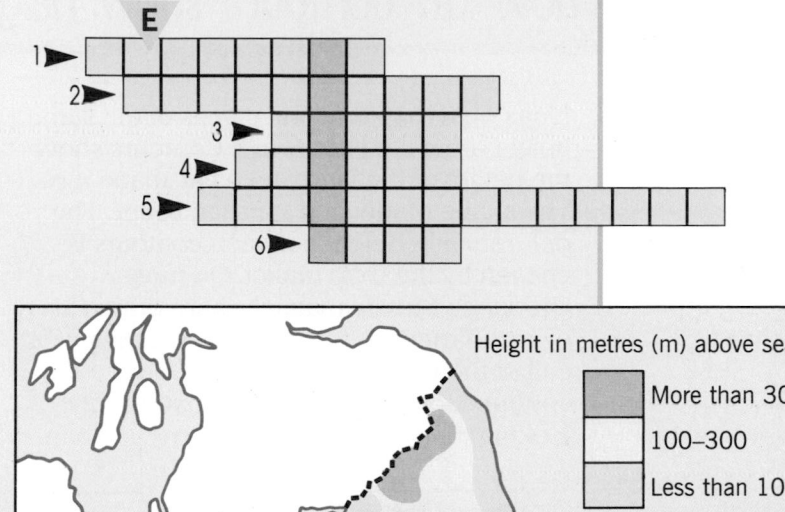

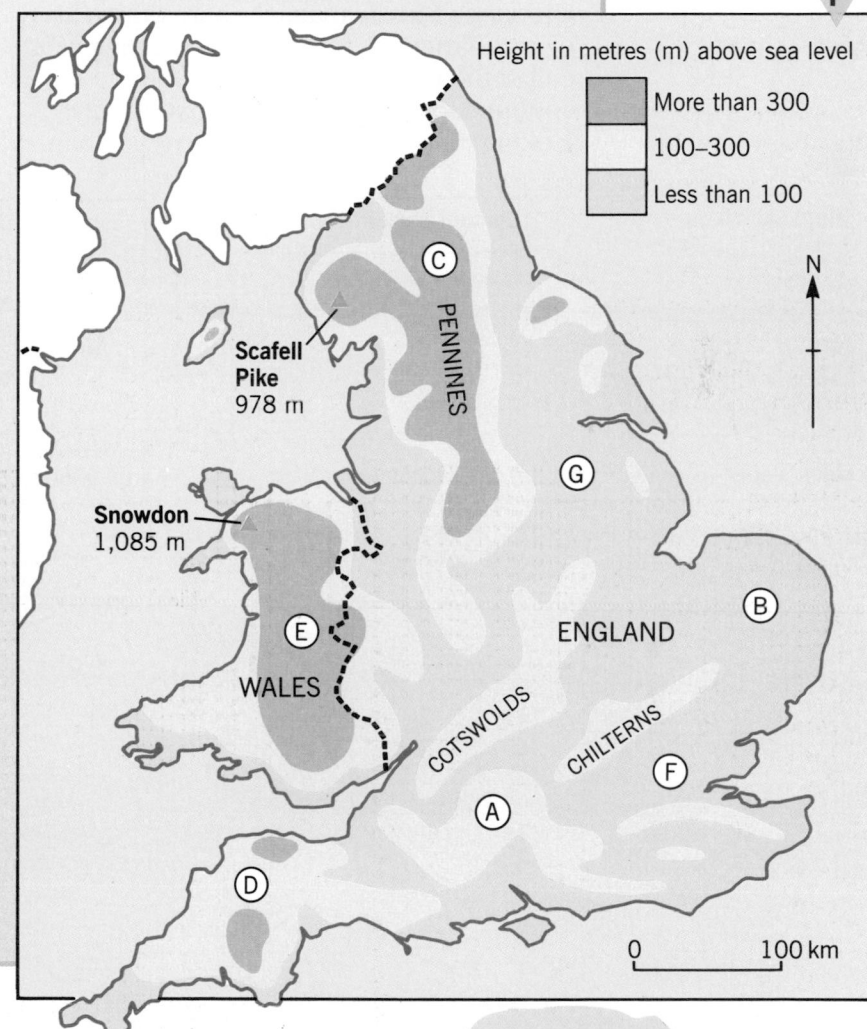

E X T R A S

Look at the Ordnance Survey map on page 109.

1 Give the heights above sea level of the following:
  a) the contours in grid squares 4852 and 4450
  b) the spot heights in grid squares 4151 and 4754
  c) the triangulation pillar in grid square 4051.

2 Look at Rowley's Hill in grid square 4249. Draw the pattern of contours and the triangulation pillar. Write in any heights that are given.

Summary

There are three main methods of showing height on maps. These are spot heights, layer colouring and contours.

How do contours show height and relief?

Lines on a map that join places of the same height are called **contours**. Contours show the height of the land and what shape it is. The shape of the land is called **relief**. The difference in height between contours is chosen by the map maker. On most Ordnance Survey maps they are drawn at every 10 metres. This difference in height is called the **contour interval**. Several contours together make up a pattern. By looking carefully at these patterns you can work out how steep the slopes are and what shape the land is.

Contour lines are drawn on maps by map makers; you cannot see them on the ground. In diagram **A** the contours have been drawn on the main sketch. You will see that they make up different patterns. An important thing to remember is that . . . *the closer the contour lines are together, the steeper the slope will be.*

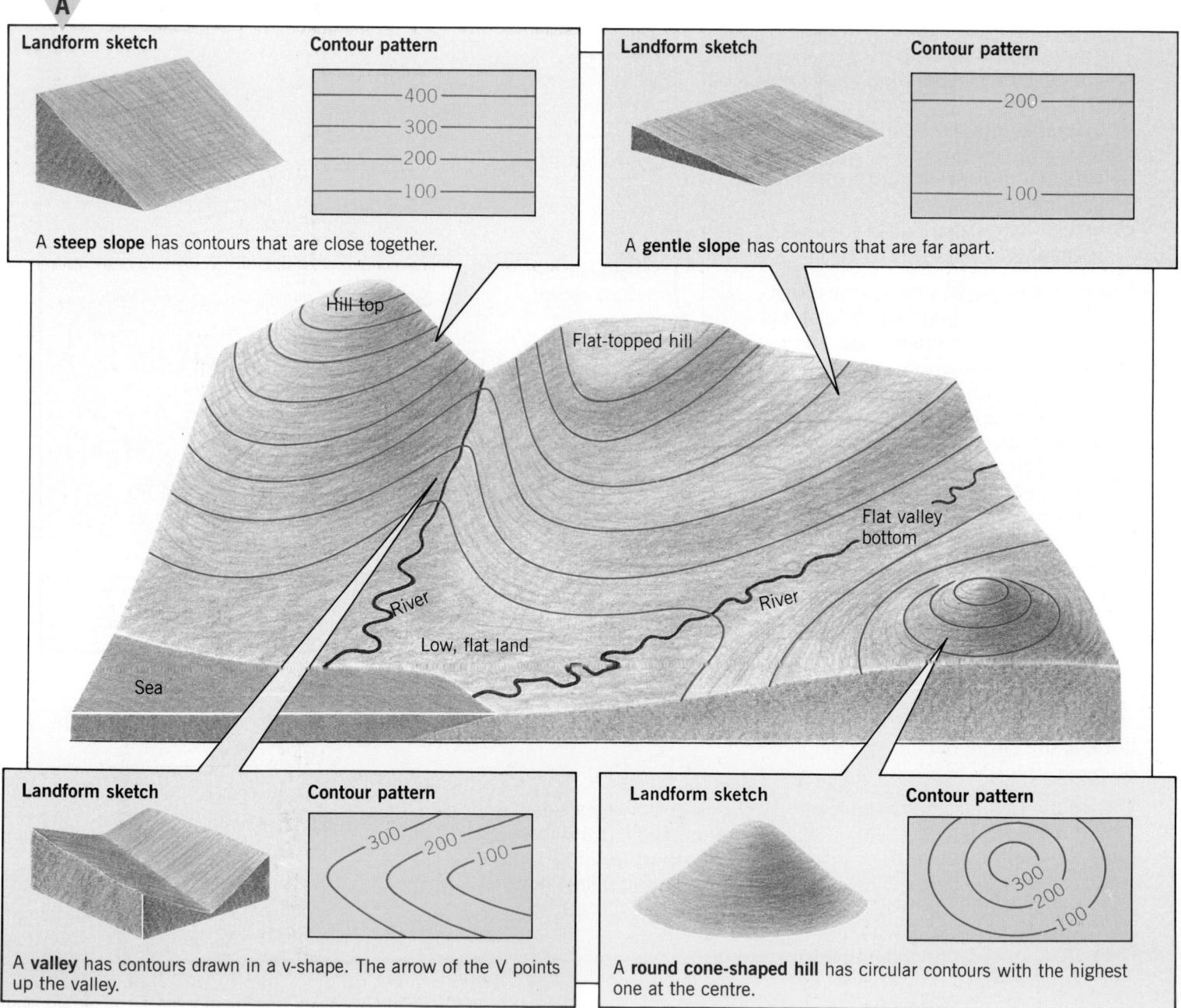

A

Landform sketch **Contour pattern**

A **steep slope** has contours that are close together.

Landform sketch **Contour pattern**

A **gentle slope** has contours that are far apart.

Hill top

Flat-topped hill

Flat valley bottom

River

River

Low, flat land

Sea

Landform sketch **Contour pattern**

A **valley** has contours drawn in a v-shape. The arrow of the V points up the valley.

Landform sketch **Contour pattern**

A **round cone-shaped hill** has circular contours with the highest one at the centre.

Activities

1 From map **B** give the heights of the following places. Choose your answers from those in the brackets.
   a) The highest point is (22, 48, 52, 40, 60) metres.
   b) Place **E** is (8, 42, 30, 20, 16) metres.
   c) Place **B** is (30, 20, 26, 46, 34) metres.
   d) Place **A** is (15, 10, 34, 6, 21) metres.
   e) Place **D** is (28, 10, 12, 22, 8) metres.

2 Look at map **B** and say if the following statements are TRUE or FALSE.
   a) **E** and **F** are at the same height.
   b) **D** is higher than **F**.
   c) **B** is higher than **E** but lower than **C**.
   d) **A** is the lowest place marked with a letter.
   e) **D** to **C** is steeper than **A** to **B**.

3 The photos in **C** show some landscape features.
   a) Draw a simple contour pattern for each of the photos.
   b) Write a description of the feature next to each of your drawings.

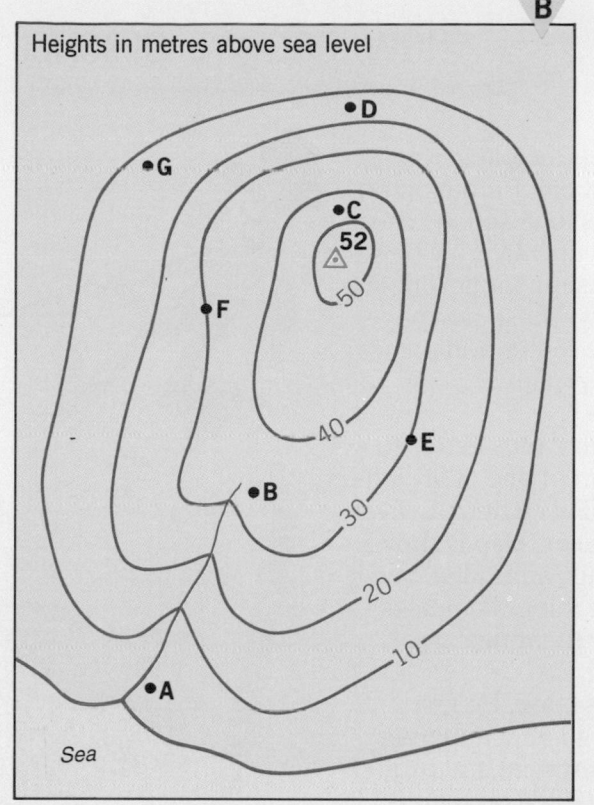

B
Heights in metres above sea level

Sea

C

Look at the six areas circled on map **D**. Match the letters to each of the following:
1 A gentle slope
2 A steep slope
3 A hill top
4 A flat valley floor
5 A valley with a stream
6 A valley without a stream.

D

Height in metres above sea level

Summary

Contour lines are a good way of showing height and relief on a map. Contours that are close together show steep slopes. Contours that are far apart show gentle slopes.

How can we describe routes?

Maps show what things look like from above. They have a lot of information on them. You can use this to describe where places are and work out what may be seen there. Maps are also useful for describing routes between places. These two pages show how to describe routes and places from Ordnance Survey maps.

Paul lives in Foxton. He writes letters to a friend called Chris. Part of one of his letters is shown in **A**. It describes where he lives and a walk he often takes. Map **B** shows the area, which is near Cambridge. See if you can recognise the things Paul talks about. Can you follow the route?

Paul's description was good. He first described the area in general and then mentioned both the **physical** and **human** features. These are labelled on map **B**. When describing a place or a route, there is no need to try to include everything, but you must be very accurate.

A

Rose Cottage
Foxton

Dear Chris,
I live in the small village of Foxton. It has a church, Post Office and Public House. The area around here is open countryside and mainly flat. I often take my dog for a walk across to Newton which is 2½ km away. We follow a path across fields until we reach a stream and some trees. Rowley's Hill is to the north. It is 50m high and gently sloping. We then follow the stream and trees until the path becomes a narrow road. The road passes a church and some gardens belonging to the Manor before it reaches Newton. My walk usually ends at the Post Office.

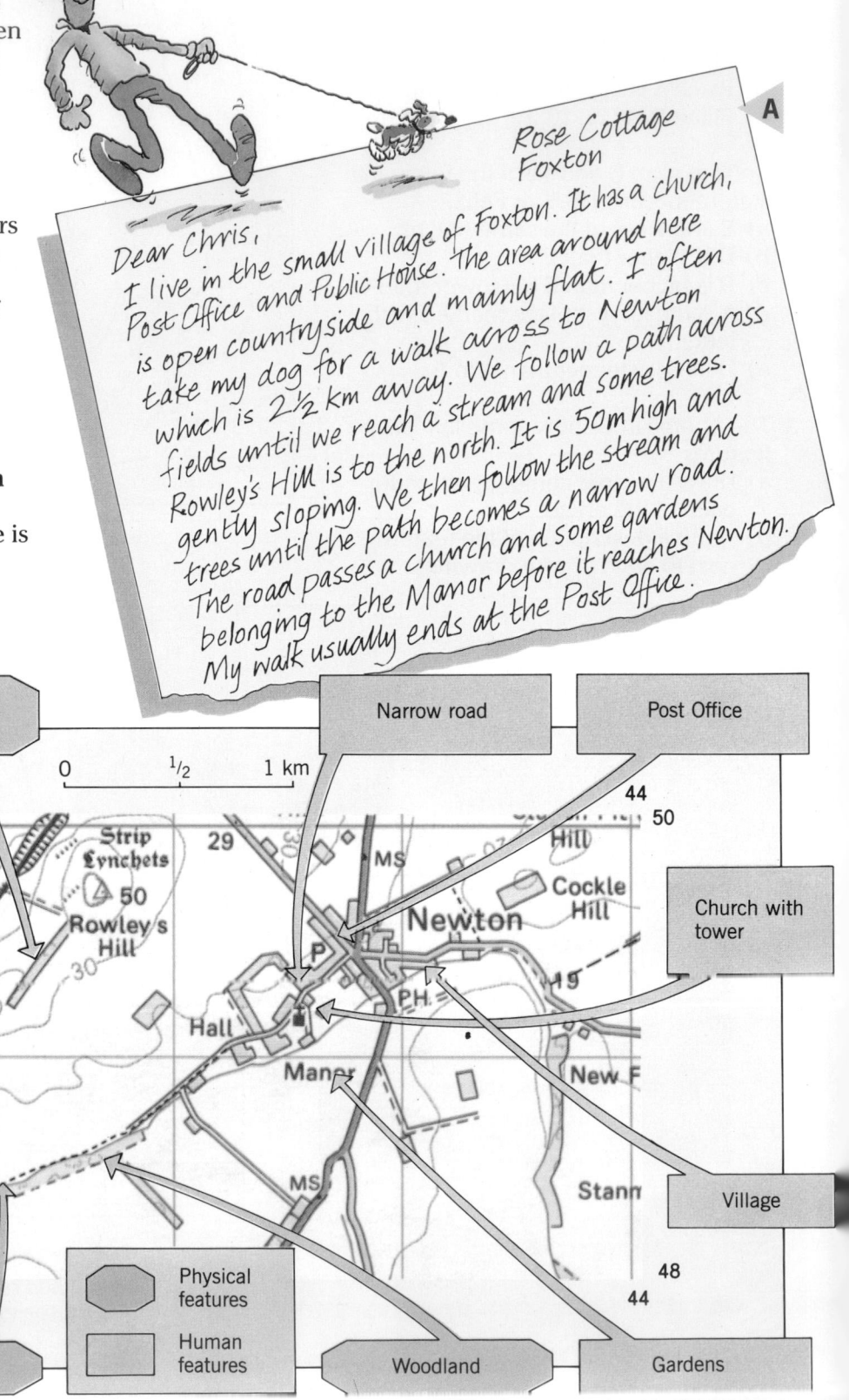

B

Few contours
Flat ground

Gently sloping hills

Narrow road

Post Office

Public House, Post Office and church

Church with tower

Village

Village

Physical features

Human features

Path

Stream

Woodland

Gardens

C

Activities

1 Look carefully at photo **C**.
  a) List **three** physical features and **three** human features on it.
  b) Write a brief description of the town.

2 Look at Newton on map **B**.
  a) List the physical features and human features in and around the village.
  b) Imagine that you own a cottage in the village that you want to rent out. Write a brief description of the village and surrounding area to advertise the cottage.

3 Map **D** shows part of the area covered by the OS map on page 109.
  a) Imagine that you have arrived by train at Great Shelford station and have to go to Hauxton post office. Some of the features that you will pass on your route are shown in diagram **E**. Write out features in the order you would pass them. Begin with the station.
  b) What is the distance from the station to the post office? Give your answer in kilometres.

D

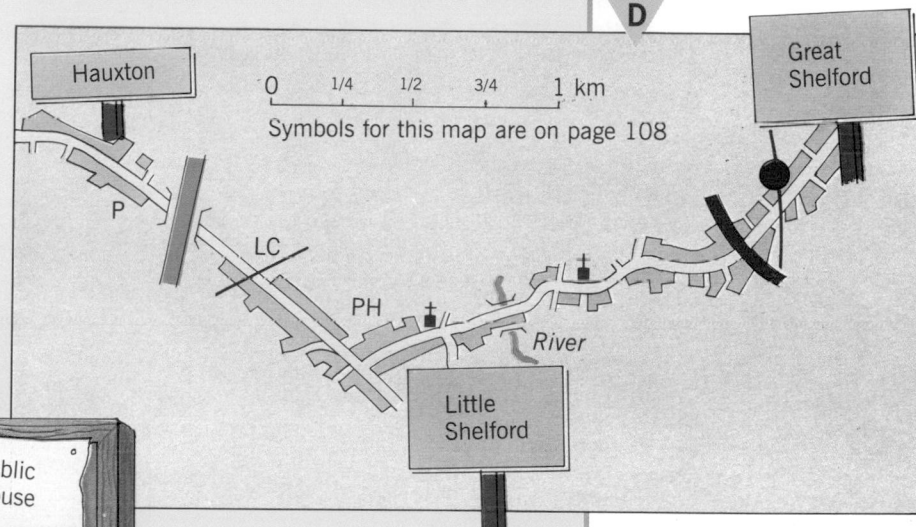

E

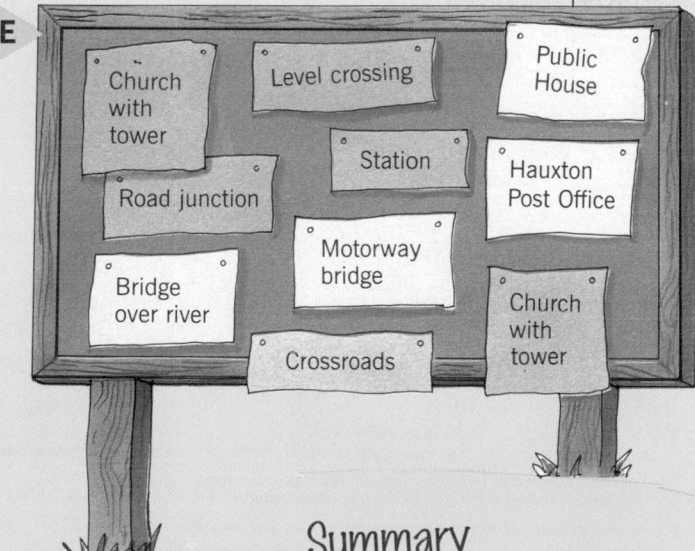

Summary

Maps can be used to describe routes and places. Accuracy is very important when describing things.

E X T R A S

Use the Ordnance Survey map on page 109 for these questions.

1 Follow this route:
    Start at Barton (4055).
    Go on the A603 to junction 12.
    Travel by motorway to junction 11.
    Follow the A10 (T) south-west for 2 km.
    Turn south-east down the B1368.
    Stop after 2.5 km. Where are you?

2 a) Describe the route you would follow by road from Haslingfield (4052) to Grantchester.
  b) Describe the village of Grantchester and the surrounding area. Mention both physical and human features.

KILOMETRE 1   0   1
STATUTE MILE 1   0   1

ROADS AND PATHS
Not necessarily rights of way

Service area M 11   Elevated
Junction number 12   En Viaduc überhöht   Motorway (dual carriageway)

Motorway under construction

Unfenced   Footbridge   Trunk road
A 11(T)
Dual carriageway   Main road
A 130
Main road under construction

Secondary road
B 1050
Narrow road with passing places
A 855   B 885
Bridge   Road generally more than 4 m wide

Road generally less than 4 m wide

Other road, drive or track

Path

Gradient : 1 in 5 and steeper
1 in 7 to 1 in 5

Gates   Road tunnel

Ferry P   Ferry V
Ferry (passenger)   Ferry (vehicle)

PUBLIC RIGHTS OF WAY
(Not applicable to Scotland)

....   Footpath
-- -- -- -- --   Bridleway
-- · -- · -- ·   Road used as a public path
-+-+-+-+-+-   Byway open to all traffic

Public rights of way indicated by these symbols have been
derived from Definitive Maps as amended by later enactments
or instruments held by Ordnance Survey on 1st May 1986
and are shown subject to the limitations imposed by the scale
of mapping. Later information may be obtained from the
appropriate County or London Borough Council

Extent of available information

**The representation on this map of any other road, track or
path is no evidence of the existence of a right of way**

Danger Area   MOD Ranges in the area. Danger! Observe warning notices

TOURIST INFORMATION

Information centre   ▲ Youth hostel
Parking   Selected places of tourist interest
Picnic site   Telephone, public/motoring organisation
Viewpoint   Golf course or links
Camp site   PC Public convenience (in rural areas)
Caravan site

RAILWAYS

Track multiple or single
Track narrow gauge
Bridges Footbridge
Tunnel
Viaduct
Freight line, siding or tramway
a   b   (a) principal
Station   (b) closed to passengers
LC   Level crossing
Embankment
Cutting

WATER FEATURES

Marsh or salting   Slopes   Cliff   High water mark
Towpath Lock   Flat rock   Low water mark
Aqueduct   Canal   Ford   Lighthouse (in use)
Weir   Normal tidal limit   Sand   Beacon
Lake   Bridge   Dunes   Lighthouse (disused)   Shingle
Footbridge   Mud
========= Canal (dry)

GENERAL FEATURES

Electricity transmission line
(with pylons spaced conventionally)   Quarry

> - -> - -> Pipe line
(arrow indicates direction of flow)   Spoil heap, refuse tip or dump

Buildings   Radio or TV mast

Public buildings (selected)   Church   with tower
or   with spire
Bus or coach station   Chapel   without tower or spire

Coniferous wood   ○ Chimney or tower

Non-coniferous wood   Glasshouse

Mixed wood   Graticule intersection at 5' intervals

Orchard   (H) Heliport

Park or ornamental grounds   △ Triangulation pillar

Windmill with or without sails

Windpump

BOUNDARIES

-- + -- + -- National   -- · -- · -- County, Region or Islands Area
-○ -○ -○ - London Borough   -+ -+ -+ - District

National Park or Forest Park

NT   National Trust   NT always open
NT opening restricted

FC   Forestry Commission   Pedestrians only -observe local signs

ABBREVIATIONS

P   Post office   CH   Clubhouse
PH   Public house   PC   Public convenience (in rural areas)
MS   Milestone   TH   Town Hall, Guildhall or equivalent
MP   Milepost   CG   Coastguard

ANTIQUITIES

VILLA   Roman   ⚔ Battlefield (with date)   + Position of antiquity which cannot be drawn to scale
Castle   Non-Roman   ☆ Tumulus

m   Ancient Monuments and Historic Buildings in the care of the Secretaries of State
for the Environment, for Scotland and for Wales and that are open to the public

The revision date of archaeological information varies over the sheet

HEIGHTS
Contours are at 10 metres vertical interval
— 50 —

·144   Heights are to the nearest metre above mean sea level

ROCK FEATURES
outcrop   cliff   scree

Heights shown close to a triangulation pillar refer to the station height at ground level and not
necessarily to the summit.

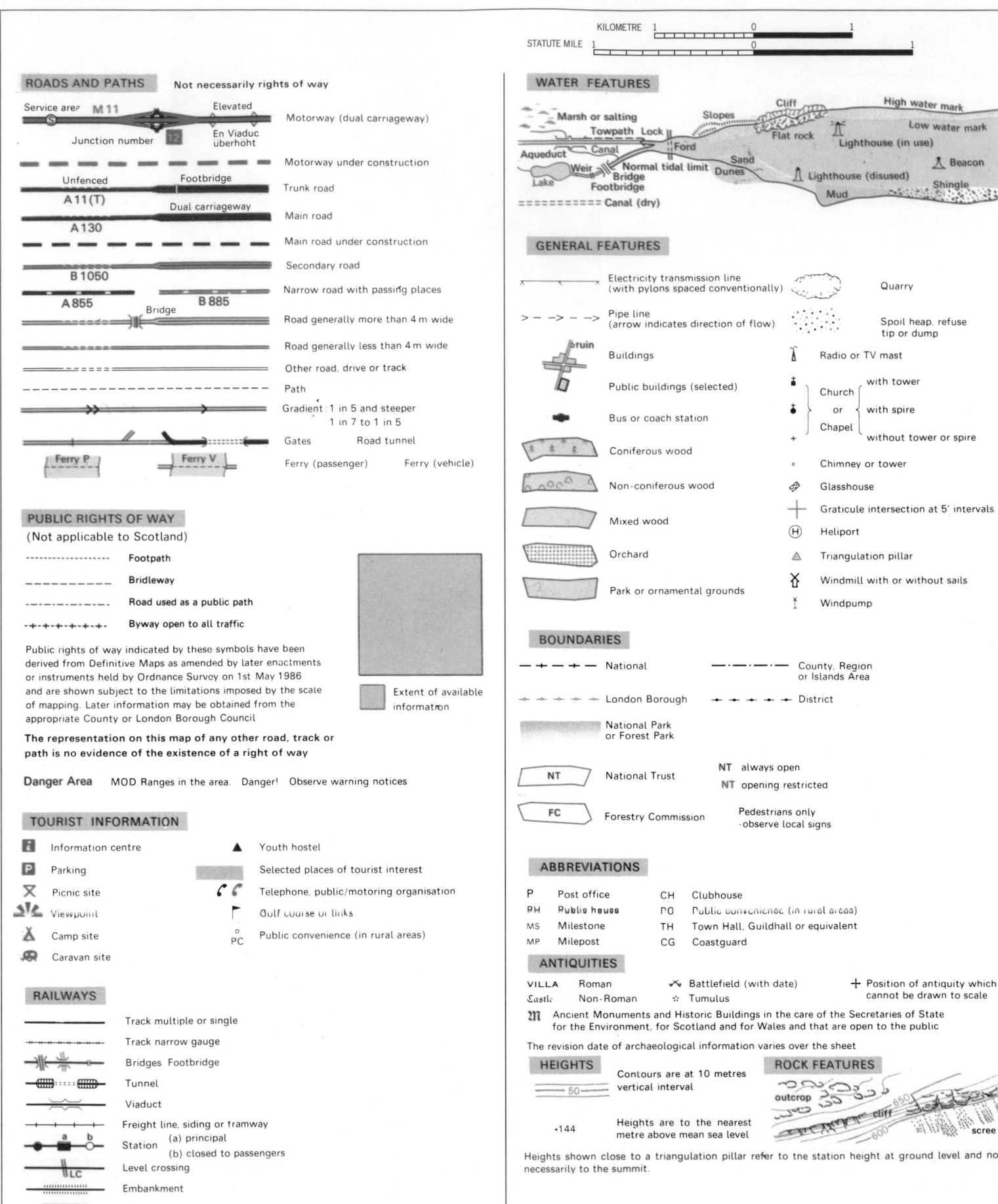

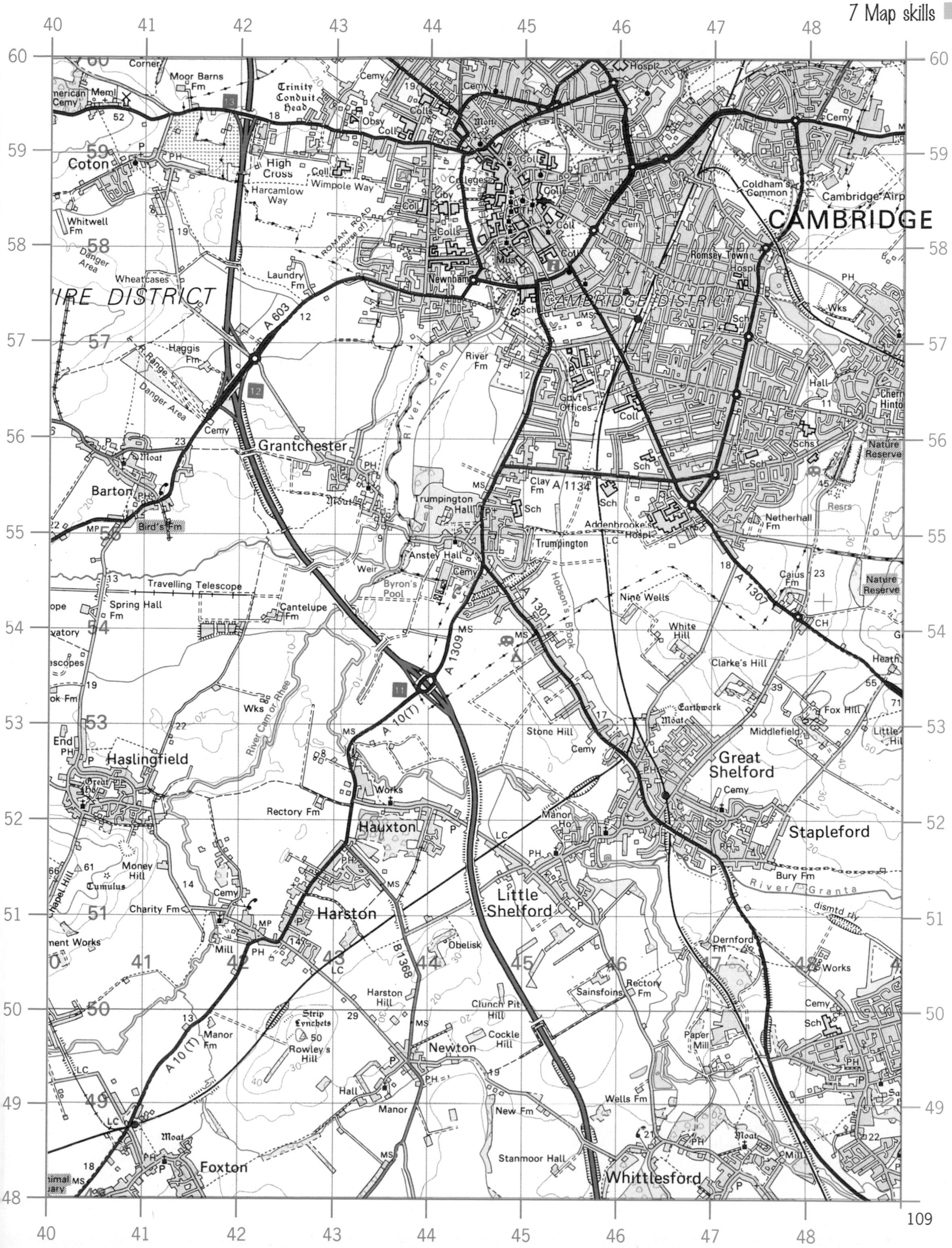

Corner
Moor Barns Fm
American Cemy
Mem
Trinity Conduit Head
Cemy
Obsy
Coll
Hospl
52
Coton
High Cross
Wimpole Way
Colls
Coll
Coll
Cemy
Coldham's Common
Cambridge Airp
CAMBRIDGE
Harcamlow Way
PH
Coll
Newnham
Romsey Town Hospl
Whitwell Fm
Danger Area
Wheatcases
Laundry Fm
A 603
CAMBRIDGE DISTRICT
Mus
Sch
MS
Wks
PH
Cherry Hinton
HIRE DISTRICT
Haggis Fm
Range
Danger Area
A 603
12
River Fm
River Cam
Govt Offices
Coll
Sch
Hall
11
Cemy
Grantchester
PH
Clay Fm A 1134
Sch
Nature Reserve
Barton
PH
Moat
Trumpington Hall
Sch
Addenbrooke's Hospl
Netherhall Fm
45
Resrs
MP
Bird's Fm
MS
Trumpington
LC
Caius Fm 23
Nature Reserve
Travelling Telescope
Weir
Anstey Hall
Byron's Pool
Hobson's Brook
Nine Wells
A 1307
CH
Spring Hall Fm
Cantelupe Fm
Cemy
White Hill
Clarke's Hill
Heath
Observatory
A 1309
MS
A 1301
55
Fox Hill 71
escopes
telescopes
19
A 1309
11
Earthwork Moat
Middlefield 39
Little Hill
ok Fm
Wks
A 10(T)
MS
Stone Hill
Cemy
Great Shelford
Haslingfield
End PH
P
Great Ho
22
Works
Manor Ho
PH
Stapleford
Money Hill
Rectory Fm
Hauxton
LC
Bury Fm
Chapel Hill 61
Cumulus
14
Cemy
MS
PH
River Granta
Charity Fm
Harston
Little Shelford
dismtd rly
Manor Fm
MP
PH
Obelisk
Dernford Fm
Works
Mill
Harston Hill
B 1368
LC
Sainsfoins
Rectory Fm
Cemy
ment Works
Strip Lynchets
Clunch Pit Hill
Sch
13
Rowley's Hill 50
Newton
Cockle Hill
Paper Mill
A 10(T)
LC
Hall
Manor
New Fm
Wells Fm
49
LC
Moat
Stanmoor Hall
Mill
Foxton
MS
Whittlesford
PH

Reproduced from the 1994 Ordnance Survey map of Cambridge by permission of the Controller of HMSO © Crown Copyright.

World Wide Leisure Corporation

174 Aspen Boulevard,
Denver,
Colorado 96543, USA

Tel./fax (303)569-8809

Dear Sir/Madam

I am the Personnel Manager for a large American company. We are planning to open four offices in Britain. These offices will be at Oban, Aviemore, Plymouth, and Cambridge. Each manager will bring the family with them, and they are likely to stay for three years.

Like many Americans, each family is keen on leisure and on doing things out of doors. Of course these activities in turn depend upon the weather and climate. Each family has different interests – as will be listed later in this letter. We are therefore allowing each of them to choose the office in the region where the weather and climate best suits their interests.

To help them do this we would appreciate your help. Please could you give us the weather and climate for the four places and suggest which you think is best suited to each of the families.

Yours sincerely

John F. Gates
Personnel Manager

This enquiry is concerned with weather and climate. Pages 20 and 21 of this book may be helpful to you as you work through the enquiry. Your task is to reply to a letter sent to you by a company in America. To do this you will need to look closely at Britain's weather and climate and answer the enquiry question given below.

There should be three main parts to your enquiry.

- The first part will be an introduction. Here you can explain what the enquiry is about.
- In the next part you will need to collect and present information about Britain's weather and climate. You can then use that information to answer the question set.
- Finally you will need a conclusion. Here you could write a letter to explain your findings.

What are the differences in weather and climate across Britain?

1 Introduction – what is the enquiry about?
You will need to use maps and writing here. Star diagrams or lists might also help.

a) First look carefully at the enquiry question above and say what you are going to try to find out.
- Give the meanings of **weather** and **climate**. Pages 16, 20 and the Glossary will help you.
- Describe how Britain's weather and climate can be roughly divided into four regions.
- Explain where these regions are, and then describe the different conditions in them.

b) Describe briefly what the letter has asked you to do. Show on a map where the four places are located. List the particular features of weather and climate that you will look at.

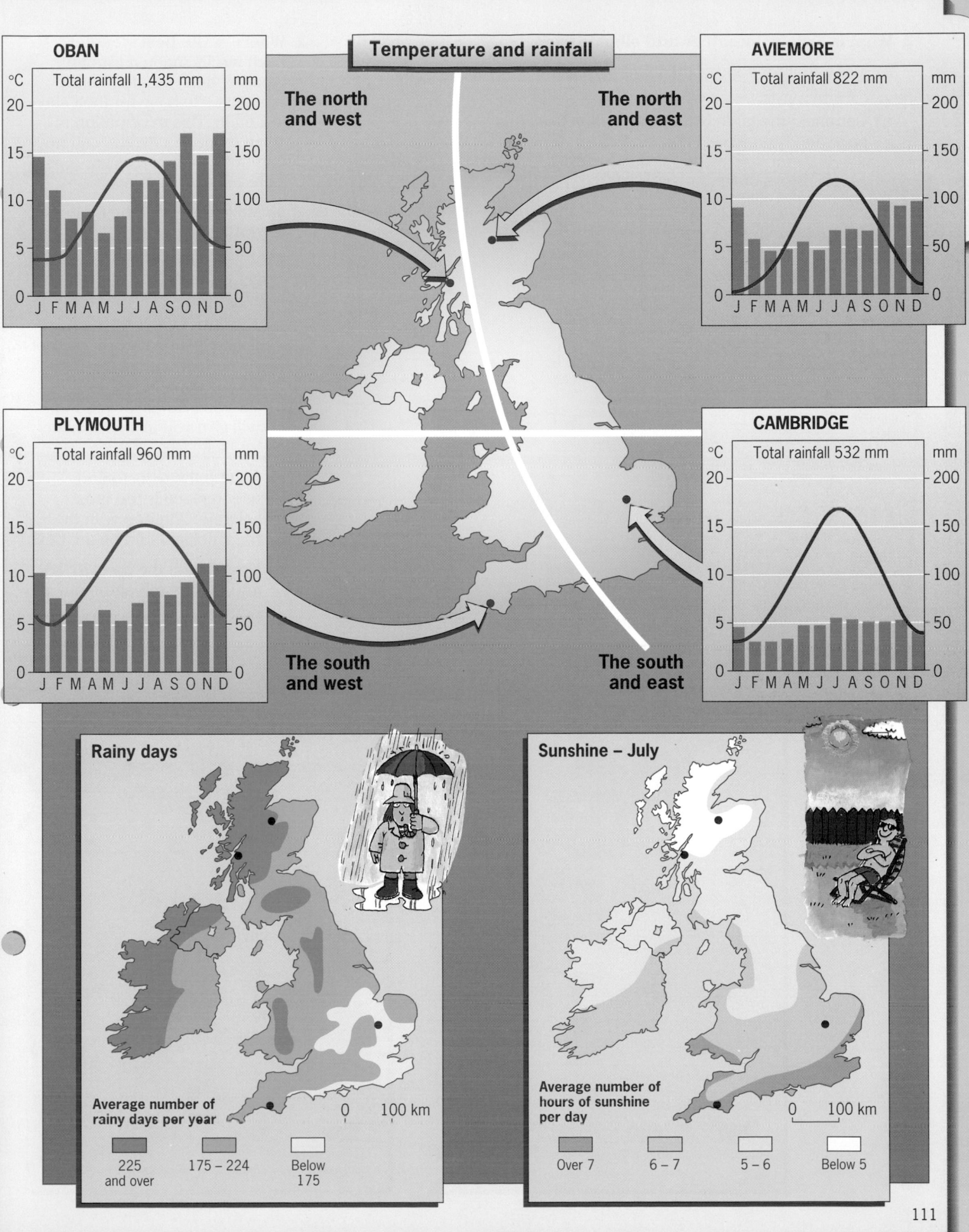

Temperature and rainfall

OBAN

°C   Total rainfall 1,435 mm   mm

The north
and west

The north
and east

AVIEMORE

°C   Total rainfall 822 mm   mm

PLYMOUTH

°C   Total rainfall 960 mm   mm

CAMBRIDGE

°C   Total rainfall 532 mm   mm

The south
and west

The south
and east

Rainy days

Average number of
rainy days per year

0   100 km

225
and over

175 – 224

Below
175

Sunshine – July

Average number of
hours of sunshine
per day

0   100 km

Over 7

6 – 7

5 – 6

Below 5

111

2 What is Britain's weather and climate like?

a) Make a larger copy of the table of Britain's weather.

b) Complete the table using information from this page and from page 111.

Britain's weather	Oban (north and west)	Aviemore (north and east)	Plymouth (south and west)	Cambridge (south and east)
January temperature (°C)				
July temperature (°C)				
January rainfall (mm)				
July rainfall (mm)				
Total rainfall (mm per year)				
Rainy days (number per year)				
July sunshine (hours per day)				
Snow lying (days per year)				
Average wind strength (description and km/h)				

3 Where is the best weather?

Each family made a list of the weather and climate that they would like to have for their stay in Britain. This information is given on page 113. You can now find out which places are most suited to each family.

a) Make a copy of the table for the Jackson family.

b) For each place in turn put:
  ✓ a tick if the weather is suitable
  ✗ a cross if it is unsuitable
  ? a question mark if it is not perfect but not too bad.
Your completed table showing Britain's weather will give you all the answers for this.

c) Add up the ticks to find which place is the most suitable. The one with the most ticks would be the best.

d) Now repeat the parts **a)**, **b)** and **c)** for each of the other three families.

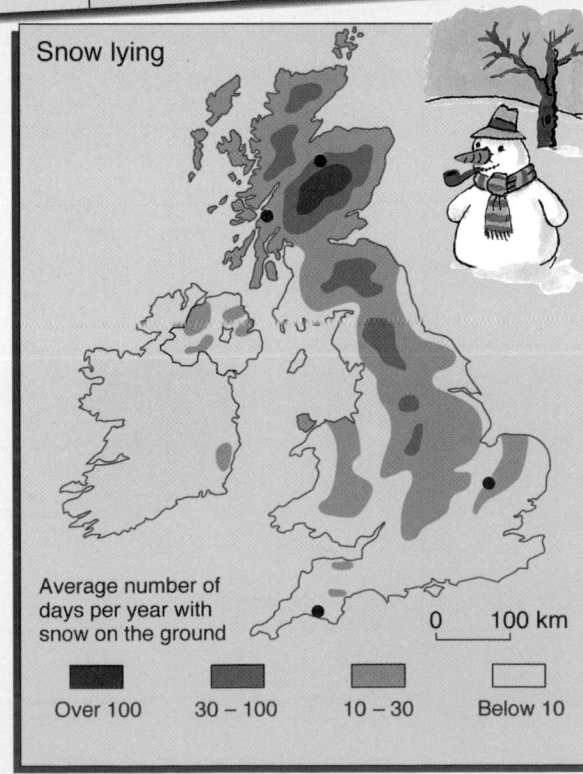

Snow lying

Average number of days per year with snow on the ground

0   100 km

Over 100 | 30 – 100 | 10 – 30 | Below 10

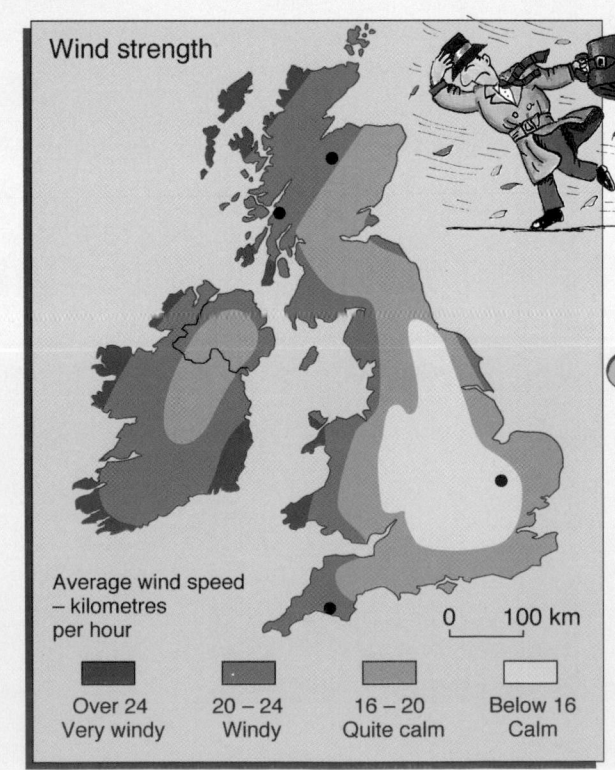

Wind strength

Average wind speed – kilometres per hour

0   100 km

Over 24 Very windy | 20 – 24 Windy | 16 – 20 Quite calm | Below 16 Calm

We are a cycling family so we don't like rain or wind. We prefer warm summers and cold winters.

The Jackson family	Oban (north and west)	Aviemore (north and east)	Plymouth (south and west)	Cambridge (south and east)
Cold winters (Jan. temp. below 3°C)				
Warm summers (July temp. 15–20°C)				
Dry (less than 175 rainy days)				
Quite sunny in summer (6–7 hrs per day)				
Very little wind (below 16 km/h)				
TOTAL				

We prefer it not to be cold or too snowy. We like to go fishing so rainy days can be good for us.

The Houston family	Oban (north and west)	Aviemore (north and east)	Plymouth (south and west)	Cambridge (south and east)
Mild winters (Jan. temp. 3–7°C)				
Mild summers (July temp. 10–14°C)				
Many rainy days (over 225 per year)				
A little snow (10–30 days per year)				
Windy (20–24 km/h)				
TOTAL				

We are keen walkers and skiers. Our favourite days are in winter when it is cold and snowy.

We enjoy barbecues and relaxing in the sun. We like warm sunny summers. Rain doesn't bother us but we really don't like the cold.

The Grant family	Oban (north and west)	Aviemore (north and east)	Plymouth (south and west)	Cambridge (south and east)
Cold winters (Jan. temp. below 3°C)				
Mild summers (July temp. 10–14°C)				
Quite dry (total rain 600–900 mm)				
Cloudy summers (under 5 hrs per day)				
Lots of snow (over 30 days per year)				
TOTAL				

The Stolberg family	Oban (north and west)	Aviemore (north and east)	Plymouth (south and west)	Cambridge (south and east)
Mild winters (Jan. temp. 3–7°C)				
Warm summers (July temp. 15–20°C)				
Quite wet (total rain 900–1,200 mm)				
Lots of summer sunshine (over 7 hrs per day)				
Windy (20–24 km/h)				
TOTAL				

4 Conclusion

Now you should look carefully at your work and answer the enquiry question. You could do this by replying to the letter from the World Wide Leisure Corporation. This could include writing and perhaps a labelled map.

a) Describe the weather and climate in each of the four regions of Britain. Your completed tables from this page will help you.

b) Say which place is best suited to each of the four families. Give reasons for your answer.

Dear Sir

The settlement enquiry

This enquiry is linked to the Settlement section on pages 44 to 61 of this book. You may need to refer to those pages, particularly when you are working on your conclusion. The Ordnance Survey (OS) key and map on pages 108 and 109 will also be useful.

Your task is to answer the enquiry question given below. To do this you will need to use information about four small settlements in the Cambridge area. You could work by yourself, with a partner or in a small group. Your finished enquiry could be in the form of a booklet or a display to be put on the classroom wall. You might be able to use a computer to word process your work and help with your graphs.

> **How does the size of a settlement affect the number of goods and services it provides?**

1 Introduction – what is the enquiry about?

a) Look carefully at the enquiry question and say what you are going to try to find out. Remember to mention that you will use settlements in the Cambridge area to do that. Explain what goods and services are. Pages 56, 57, 116 and the Glossary will help you.

b) Describe the area using maps, labelled sketches and writing.

Now how could I answer this?

First I shall need to explain what the enquiry is about.

Next I shall have to decide what information I need and where I could get it from.

Then I could collect the information and present it in an interesting and clear way.

Finally I could describe my findings and try to suggest reasons for them.

Description

Location of Cambridge

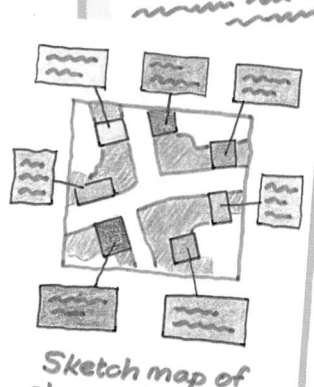

Sketch map of shops at Foxton

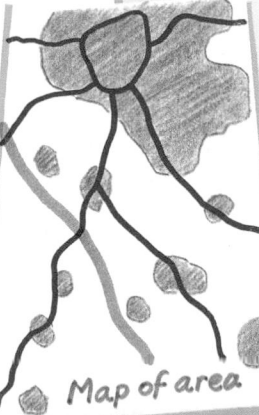

Map of area

The public house at the junction in Newton

Newton

Harston

Harston post office is on the busy A10 road

114

2 How large are the settlements?

a) By **population** – figures are given with the village plans on pages 116 and 117. Draw a bar graph to show your results. Arrange the bars in order of size with the largest on the left.

b) By **area** – measure this using the OS map on page 109.

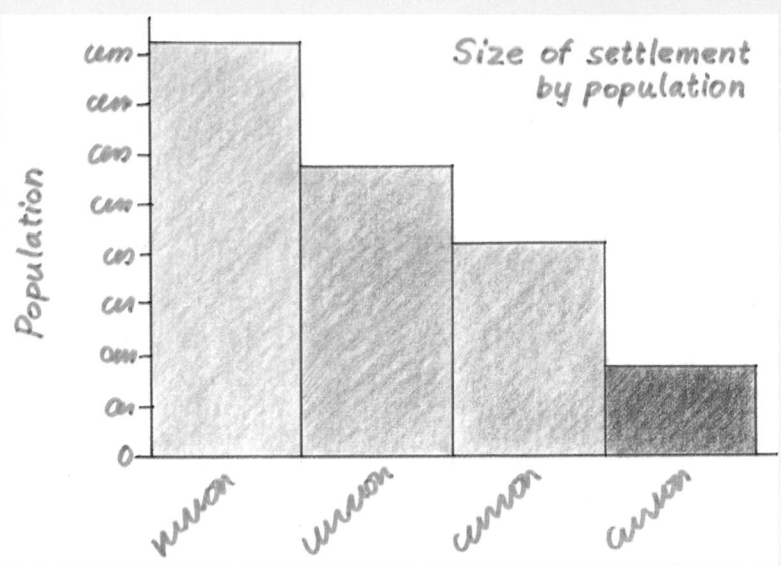

Size of settlement by population

Put a tracing paper grid over the map.	Count the squares covering each village.	Graph your results.

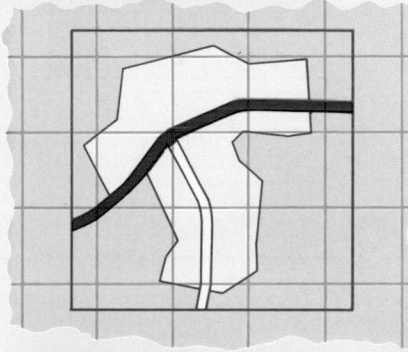

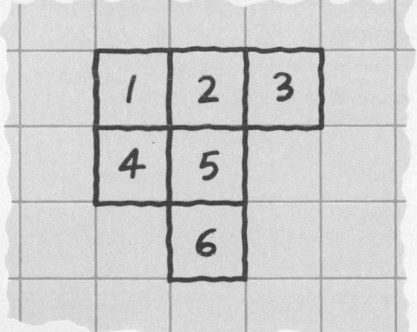

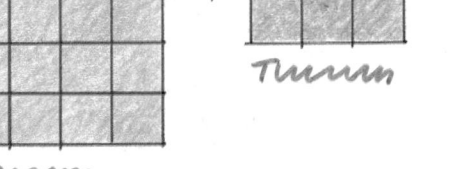

Size of settlement by area

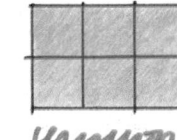

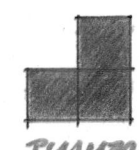

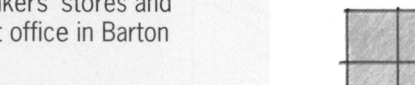

Barton

'Conkers' stores and post office in Barton

The post office in the village of Foxton

Foxton

3 How many goods and services are there?

Use the village plans and the OS map to find this out for each settlement.

- Count the number of **different** goods available, not just the total number of shops.
- If there is more than one of the same item in a village, give the **total** number. For example, two garages would count as two different items.

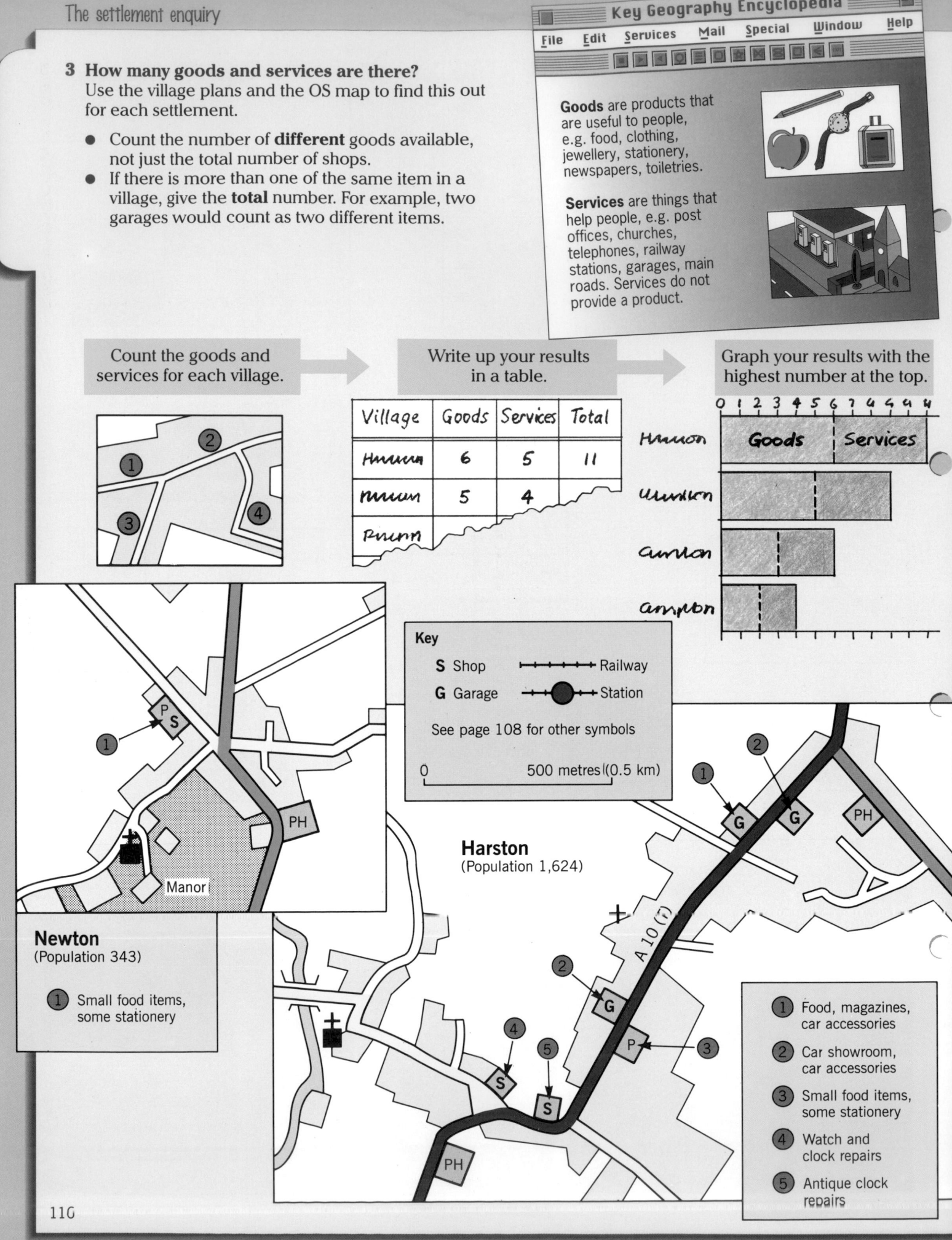

Key Geography Encyclopedia

File   Edit   Services   Mail   Special   Window   Help

Goods are products that are useful to people, e.g. food, clothing, jewellery, stationery, newspapers, toiletries.

Services are things that help people, e.g. post offices, churches, telephones, railway stations, garages, main roads. Services do not provide a product.

Count the goods and services for each village. → Write up your results in a table. → Graph your results with the highest number at the top.

Village	Goods	Services	Total
Harston	6	5	11
Newton	5	4	
Barton			

Key

S Shop

G Garage

Railway

Station

See page 108 for other symbols

0   500 metres (0.5 km)

Newton
(Population 343)

① Small food items, some stationery

Manor

Harston
(Population 1,624)

A 10 (T)

① Food, magazines, car accessories

② Car showroom, car accessories

③ Small food items, some stationery

④ Watch and clock repairs

⑤ Antique clock repairs

4 Conclusion

Now you must look carefully at your work and answer the enquiry question. Notice that it begins 'How . . .'. That means you will need to both describe your findings **and** try to explain them.

a) Make a summary of what you have found out. You could draw up a simple table and do some writing for this. Make sure that you keep to the question asked.

b) Suggest reasons for your findings.

Settlements in order ...	
... of size (largest first)	... of number of goods and services (most first)
1	1
2	2
3	3

Description
This enquiry has shown that ...

For example ...

Now this should be easy and straightforward.

Now are there any other reasons I can think of?

Goods and services are for people.

How will main roads affect the need for goods and services? I wonder why there are so many garages?

Surely the more people there are, the more goods and services there will be.

Not all people will be local, though. What about those who come from somewhere else?

So which settlements have the most people in them?

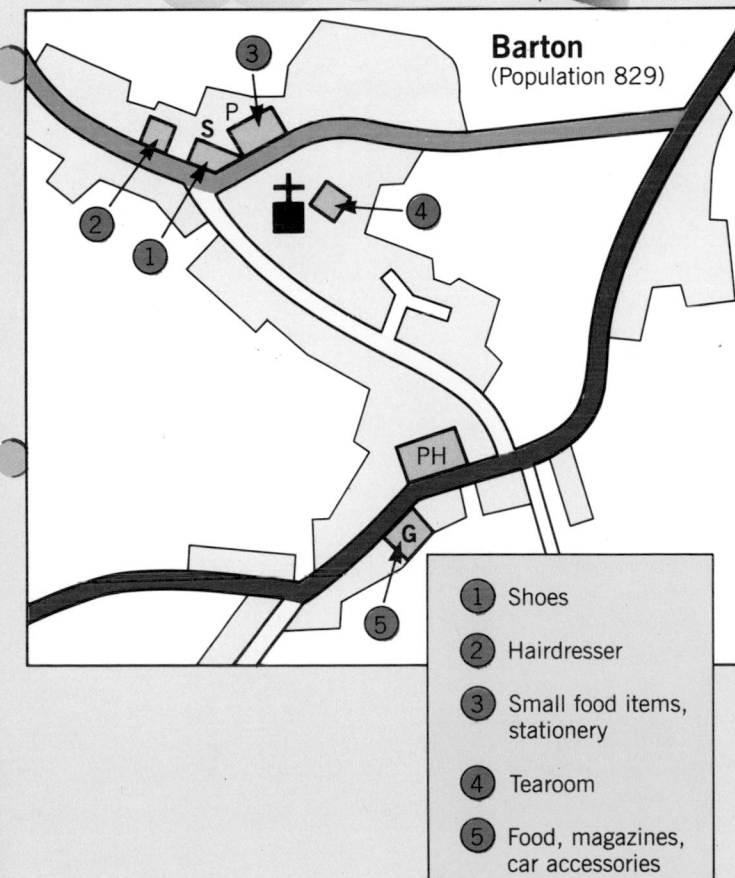

Barton
(Population 829)

1 Shoes

2 Hairdresser

3 Small food items, stationery

4 Tearoom

5 Food, magazines, car accessories

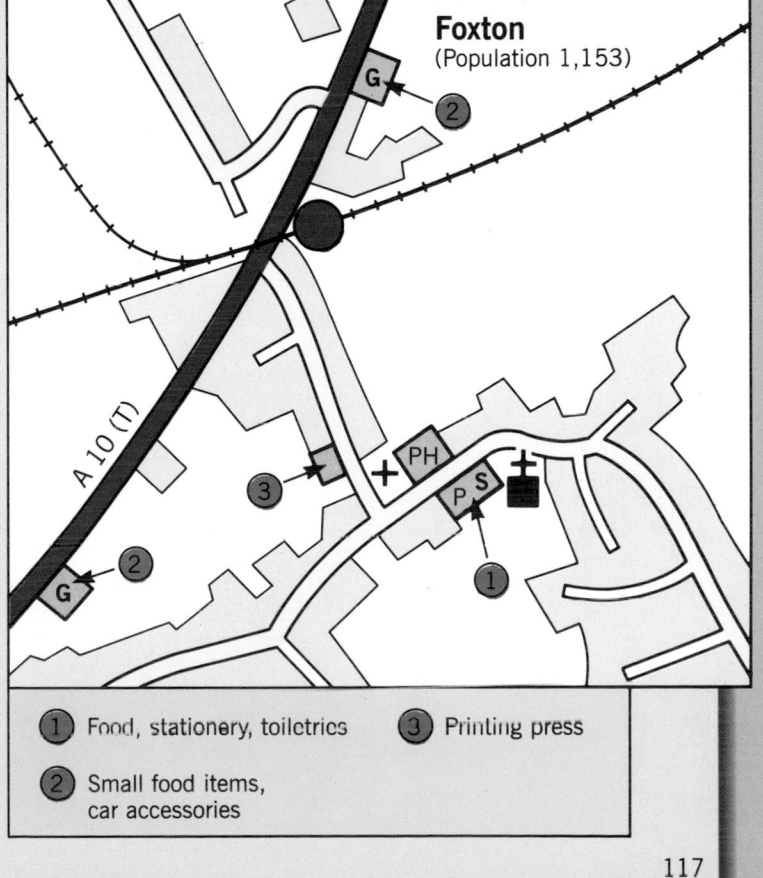

Foxton
(Population 1,153)

A 10 (T)

1 Food, stationery, toiletries

2 Small food items, car accessories

3 Printing press

Glossary

	Height	How high or low a place is. Measured in metres or feet above sea level. *102*
	Hierarchy	Putting settlements and shops into order based upon their size or the services they give to people. *56, 58*
	High and low order	These are goods sold in a shop. High order goods cost a lot but are not bought very often, e.g. furniture. Low order goods cost a lot but are bought more often, e.g. food. *58*
	Human geography	Where and how people live. *6, 7*
	Hypermarket	A very large self service shop usually found on the edge of a city. *58, 61*
I	**Industrial town**	Where people make things like steel, cars and textiles in factories. *44*
	Inner city	An area of factories and old houses next to the city centre. *52, 54*
	Irrigation	The artificial watering of the land in a dry climate. *40*
	Isobar	A line on a map joining places with the same atmospheric pressure. *26*
K	**Key**	A list of signs and symbols on a map or diagram with an explanation of what they mean. *96*
L	**Land use**	Describes how the land in towns or the countryside is used. It includes housing, industry and farming. *52, 82*
	Landforms	Natural features formed by rivers, the sea, ice and volcanoes. *4*
	Landscape	The scenery or appearance of an area. It includes both physical and human features. *78, 79, 106*
	Latitude	This says how far north or south a place is from the Equator. *12*
	Layer colouring	A method of showing height on a map by using colours. *102*
	Linear settlement	Buildings spread out in a line along a main road, a railway or a river. *47, 82, 83*
	Longitude	This says how far east or west a place is from the Greenwich Meridian. *12*
M	**Map**	A drawing which shows part of the earth's surface from directly above, on a reduced scale. *12, 92*
	Market town	The original function of the town was a place where people, mainly farmers, could buy and sell goods. *44*
	Meteorology	The study of weather. *16*
	Microclimate	The climate of a small area. *18*
	Migration	The movement of people from one place to another to live or to work. *6*
N	**National Parks**	Areas of scenic beauty which are protected so that people can enjoy open air recreation. *87*
	Network	A pattern of routes that are linked together. *66, 84, 85*
	Network density	The number of routes that are linked together in an area. *66,84 ,85*
	North Atlantic Drift	A warm ocean current that brings mild conditions to the west of Britain in winter. *20, 79*
	Nucleated settlement	Buildings which are grouped closely together. *47, 82, 83*
O	**Ordnance Survey**	The official government organisation responsible for producing maps in the UK. *92, 96, 106*
P	**Pattern**	How things like settlements and shops are spread out over an area of land. *47, 52, 82, 83, 104*
	Physical geography	Natural features and events on earth. It includes landforms and weather. *4*
	Place	An area on the earth's surface. It can vary in size from a desk in a classroom to a city or a continent. *10*
	Plan	A detailed map of a small area. *92*
	Points of the compass	A method of giving direction using north, south , east, west, etc. *92*
	Pollution	Noise, dirt and other harmful substances produced by people and machines which spoil an area. *9, 69, 70*
	Population	The people who live in an area. *6*
	Port	A place used by ships to load and unload people and goods. *45*
	Precipitation	Water in any form which falls to earth. It includes rain, snow, sleet and hail. *16, 22, 37*

	Pressure	Atmospheric pressure is the weight of air pressing down on the earth's surface. *24, 26*
	Public transport	Transport provided for the public and available to everyone, e.g. buses, trains, etc. *71*
Q	**Quality of life**	How content people are with their lives and the environment in which they live. *7, 48*
R	**Relief**	The shape of the land surface and its height above sea level. *102, 104*
	Relief rain	Rain caused by air being forced to rise over hills and mountains. *22, 79*
	Resort	A place where people go for holidays. *45*
	Resources	Things which are useful to people. They may be natural like coal and iron ore, and of value like money and skilled workers. *8*
	River basin	An area of land drained by a river and its tributaries. *30, 32*
	River channel	Where a river flows. It has a bed and two banks. *30*
	River mouth	The end of a river where it enters the sea or a lake. *30*
	River source	Where a river begins. *30*
	Rural	An area of land which is mainly countryside. *77*
S	**Scale**	The link between a distance on a map and its real distance on the ground. *94*
	Scale line	A short line on a map which shows how far real distances are. *94*
	Settlement	A place where people live. *7, 44, 56, 82*
	Shopping malls	Shopping areas which are under cover and protected from the weather. *58*
	Site	The actual place where a settlement first grew up. *46, 80*
	Six figure grid reference	A group of six figures used to give an exact position on a map. *100*
	Spot height	A point on a map with a number giving its height above sea level in metres. *102*
	Stores	Part of the water cycle where water is held in reserve in the sea, on land or in the air. *36*
	Suburbanised village	A village with many new buildings added to it. *50*
	Suburbs	A zone of housing around the edge of a city. *53*
	Surface water	Water which lies on top of, or flows over, the ground. *28, 37*
	Symbols	A simple drawing or sign used to give information and save space on a map. *17, 96*
T	**Temperature**	A measure of how warm or how cold it is. *16, 20*
	Transfers	Part of the water cycle when water or vapour moves between the sea, the land and the air. *36, 39*
	Transpiration	The process by which water from plants changes into water vapour. *37*
	Triangulation pillar	A concrete pillar used by surveyors to find the exact height and position of a place. *102*
	Tributary	A small river which flows into a bigger river. *30*
U	**Urban**	An area of land which is mainly covered in buildings. *6, 48, 76*
	Urban model	The pattern of land use in a town. *52*
	Urbanisation	The growing proportion of people living in urban areas. *34*
V	**Visibility**	The distance that can be seen. *17*
W	**Water cycle**	The never-ending movement of water between the sea, the land and the air. *28, 36*
	Water demand	Water needed by people for domestic, farming and industrial use. *38*
	Water supply	Water provided for people for domestic, farming and industrial use. *38*
	Watershed	The boundary between two river basins. *30*
	Weather	The day to day condition of the atmosphere. It includes temperature, rainfall and wind. *16*
	Weathering	Rock is broken up by nature to give soil. *5*